Yearbook Planning, Editing, and Production

N. S. PATTERSON

Yearbook Planning, Editing, and Production

THE IOWA STATE UNIVERSITY PRESS / AMES

For my wife, Velma, without whose encouragement and patience this book would not have come into being

N. S. PATTERSON founded and organized the National School Yearbook Association in 1950, and as director and supervising judge, he examined each of the many thousands of yearbooks sent to the critical service during the years prior to the transfer of ownership to Texas Tech University in 1973. In 1950 he also began publishing the magazine *Photolith* as a service to NSYA members and other advisers and staffs of yearbooks. He served as its editor until 1973, also writing numerous columns and articles for the publication. In between duties for NSYA and *Photolith*, he found time to speak widely at publications workshops and short courses, to write and revise the official NSYA *Judging Standards*, and to produce such occasional booklets as *Steps Toward Better Yearbook Layout* and *Prize Package*, the latter based on materials found in leading student yearbooks. He is a graduate of Baylor University, holds the M.A. from the University of Texas. He did graduate work at the University of Missouri and, on a fellowship, at Southern Methodist University. After teaching for nine years in public high schools, he was invited in 1940 to organize a program of journalism for the University of Houston. This was to become the second largest college journalism division in Texas by 1953. He also headed publications, including the college's first offset yearbook. As a faculty member of the University of Missouri School of Journalism, he headed the Missouri Interscholastic Press Association from 1955 to 1960, in 1956 organizing the school's first summer publications workshop. In 1975 Columbia Scholastic Press Association awarded him its Golden Crown certificate on the occasion of the association's 50th anniversary. Earlier, in 1970, National Scholastic Press Association gave him the Pioneer Award; and the National Council of College Publications Advisers presented its Distinguished Service plaque to him. In 1974 Journalism Education Association gave him its highest award, the Media Citation and medal. He is a member of Sigma Delta Chi and NCCPA.

© 1976 The Iowa State University Press
Ames, Iowa 50010. All rights reserved

Composed and printed by
The Iowa State University Press

First edition, 1976

Library of Congress Cataloging in Publication Data
Patterson, N   S   1911–
    Yearbook planning, editing, and production.
    1. School yearbooks. I. Title.
LB3621.P37   371.8'976   75–42009
ISBN 0–8138–1805–2

Contents

Preface

SINCE 1950 the yearbook industry has multiplied in volume many times over. There is improved equipment, some of it so magical the beholder hardly believes his eyes, and there are also new and better inks and papers. But just as impressive to me have been the educational contributions members of this unusual industry have offered. They have developed and provided helpful materials for staff workers, have sponsored and conducted useful clinics and workshops and contributed generously to others, and have trained and sent out many dedicated salespersons, often called counselors.

Educational aids have also flowed in increasing quantity from old and newer services, until the better yearbook of today stands as a model of excellence worthy of imitation anywhere—even, amazingly, by its much older brother, the school newspaper.

I salute the leaders of industry who have gone beyond the call of duty or the lure of profit; and I salute the associations—state, regional, and national—who have contributed much to the spread of knowledge through their literature, but even more through their sponsorship of meetings, conferences, workshops, and various courses.

And most of all, I salute the enterprising advisers and those young and energetic editors and staff members who have been willing to experiment, who have dared to try new things, yet have had the wisdom to stay within the bounds of good taste and the rules of journalism and art. I have taken the spirit of these modern pioneers to be my inspiration, and it is my purpose in this book to hold up for examination and imitation illustrations of the imagination and creativity found in a few typical modern yearbooks.

N. S. PATTERSON

Acknowledgments

THE AUTHOR gratefully acknowledges the help and counsel of H. Stephen (Steve) Carlson of Arizona State College for his careful reading of the manuscript; the equally careful reading by his daughter-in-law, Ginger; and the incisive editing of Mrs. Gertrude Burrell.

Special thanks are also due those yearbook publishing companies who sent sample yearbooks from which some recent illustrations were taken; to National Yearbook/Newspaper Association for books of recent years used in illustrating the text; to the advisers and staffs of those books from which excerpts were taken to show examples of superior planning and editing; and to the directors of National Scholastic Press and Columbia Scholastic Press associations for their comments on the present state of the yearbook.

Introduction

THE YEARBOOK is a unique medium. The newspaper and the magazine (the latter a fragile unit in the student publications program, where it exists at all) both owe their existence to the fact that there are well-established and commercially successful counterparts in the community and world outside school-college. These life-size models include the daily or weekly community newspaper, the area magazine, and the national magazine—general, special-subject, business, or literary. There are also the national and big city newspapers such as the *New York Times,* the *Christian Science Monitor,* the *Kansas City Star,* the *Wall Street Journal,* the *Dallas Times Herald,* and the *Houston Post.*

The student newspaper normally has its academic home in the journalism program, or perhaps the strong English department, and it may even receive cooperation from commercial or typing classes. It is a natural laboratory project and product of journalism instruction.

By contrast, the yearbook sprang solely from a felt need, the desire to memorialize and to record a full year in permanent form. Its originators sought to distill the essence of the year—originally in a most artificially literary style, and until many years later, with painfully immature essays and "poems," and with such misbegotten features as snapshots pages, which came like rank weeds and untrimmed grasses with the advent of good cameras and the engraving process.

As it evolved, this yearbook (often referred to as a "year book" or an "annual") had no commercial models, no professional practitioners, no formal class to support it, and no rules of planning and production established by and for professionals that might be adapted for the use of youthful learners. The wonder is that it survived at all.

One writer cites the beginning of the yearbook in 1845 as a senior memory book. It likely was full of essays and poetry (or rather, versification) and sentimental reflections on schooldays, on graduation, on prospects for the future, and on "life." As time went on, and as the engraving process appeared in the late 1880s to supplement improved cameras and camera techniques, pictures came in—portraits and posed individuals and groups, as well as snapshots.

In time a format evolved. Stiff formality of portraiture and group posing retained as "relief" those vestigial remnants of earlier days, artificial verse and prose, bad jokes, and senior features.

Various publications associations, which had generally been organized to support student newspaper journalism and perhaps to a limited degree student magazines, began to recognize the yearbook as a kindred medium and to give its staffs attention at their annual conferences and conventions. Soon the national services established sets of rules, produced modest guidebooks and scoresheets, and offered critiques, all based largely on what advisers and staffs of the larger college books had been able to evolve with the aid of enterprising printers and engravers.

By 1949, more than a hundred years after the prototype yearbook was printed, a guide and staff text was published by the late C. J. Medlin, a leading college adviser who had established a wide repute for his success at Kansas State University in directing staffs toward production of orderly, reference-style yearbooks. Models displayed in this first yearbook text contained a full complement of formal pictures of teachers, administrators, and students; and of formally posed clubs and equally formally posed athletic teams. Type was set by Linotype machines. Engravings, wherever possible blocked in very large groups of pictures, provided the art.

This first yearbook text suggested, at least through its illustrations, that all portraits and groups should be arranged in traditional, almost unvarying format, with clear labeling, a listing of the full names of all those shown, and with an absolute minimum of copy. The yearbook, this text indicated strongly, should be as correct and as decorous as a baccalaureate ceremony.

But then, starting slowly in the late 1930s, and burgeoning in the 1940s and 1950s, came the already old process of offset lithography or photolithography as a new method of printing yearbooks. The change was not always for the best, perhaps, but it was dramatic.

Little schools that could never have afforded a letterpress-engraved yearbook found that the new process was cheap enough to allow them to have their book for the first time. And the rediscovered offset process made it possible to use as many pictures as the staff could assemble, in whatever format, order, shape, or disorder they could devise, with no added costs for engravings (lithography, obviously, has no engravings, halftone picture negatives being transferred directly onto plates along with type and line art such as cartoons) and no costs for mortising. Offset also allowed for whatever type or handlettered writing one wished to intersperse among pieces of art, or even above art.

But freedom is always accompanied by problems. Since yearbooks had no established restraints or disciplines, no textbook-classroom rules for planning and production, high school staffs quickly learned to set up their own guidelines. A profusion of experiments developed, most of them monstrous. Although long essays about these unhappy outcomes of the offset process have been written, especially by the followers of old letterpress methods, I will confine my listing to only a few:

● Snapshots pages took on new dimensions of poor taste, as the number of separate pictures proliferated; the need to combine into single units vanished, and handwritten or typed "cutelines" or funny idents were stripped inside the pages at will; heads were cut out and impaled on stick drawings of bodies or around the outline of a football picture or drawing; or individual photos were trimmed and often de-featured to fit inside shapings of moons, stars, etc.

● Inappropriate or ugly backgrounds or new framings of crude hand art sprang up everywhere in response to the yearbook salesperson's urgings: "Why, offset can reproduce anything, even your grandfather's mustache!" Early editors of the Offset Age tried just about everything for special effects. They used busy wallpaper patterns as page backgrounds, superimposing pictures that almost failed to emerge into view. Or they used newspaper backgrounds from which pictures and type could not surface. Or they used good art and photography as backgrounds in which the story type was entirely lost. Or they used theme cartooning, done by enthusiastic but untrained or untalented staff artists, to frame all the pages of the book. Or they used doodad art fillers, insignia, designs, and cartoons provided by printers or by so-called art services, filling every bit of space that showed up in layouts after pictures and type had been mounted.

● Then there were those senior "last wills and testaments," tediously long and unfunny class histories, and never-changing class prophecies. These had sprung full-grown out of sterile imaginings of immature students 50 or so years ago, but somehow, they had a rebirth, with clumsy amateur art added, when offset came into use in the late 1930s. Even yet, they reappear here and there to adorn a book produced in a school still untouched by service literature or publications conferences.

But most of these experiments faded or passed. Editors and staffs began to listen to advice, to reexamine what they were doing, to see what offset lithography could achieve if properly used under discipline of sound art rules. Yearbook companies developed better techniques; gave better advice; discovered and used papers better suited to the process, along with improved inks and improved machinery; and provided better trained craftsmen.

Results began to show up in attractive, imaginative, story-telling yearbooks that reflected the age we live in, an age of photolithography, of functional design, of relative simplicity and honesty. (Oh, I am aware that *all* is not simple and honest in our age, but the trends are there!) By the 1940s, the yearbook, which had arisen out of an emotional urge and need to preserve a permanent record of the school year, an orphan project with no real or stable home in the high school or college, began to be adopted by English or journalism classes and to be studied seriously, either in short units or in full courses.

Content of this yearbook course was whatever the ingenious teacher could find from all sorts of references and remotely similar models. Admittedly, it was not a very consistent or a very solid discipline as compared, say, to math or history. Those who worked on the yearbook, in short, needed far more help than they were getting.

The Approach to Teaching
Yearbook Planning and Production

IT HAS LONG been my conviction that we should teach yearbook planning and production much as we do for the student newspaper. The idea of putting what started as a sort of orphan extracurricular activity into the course of study is hardly a new one. For more than 30 years, to my personal knowledge, the Houston public schools have included yearbook as part of the year's study in journalism classes. I introduced such a course at the University of Houston in the early 1950s, though it has likely been dropped in recent curricular reorganizations. We had no usable text and few reference materials, but the developing book offered ample lab projects.

While I know of no statistical study of yearbook instruction, I believe that there has been a great increase in recent years in the number of schools incorporating yearbook instruction into the curriculum, either separately or as part of a combined yearbook-newspaper course in journalism or English departments.

Charles R. O'Malley, director of the Columbia Scholastic Press Association, tells me in a letter of April 1975 that he knows of no actual classes in yearbook production but that the association's new *Yearbook Fundamentals* has been adopted as a textbook in several college and university journalism programs and in many high school journalism classes. He notes a 10 percent increase in yearbook and newspaper entries for 1974 critical service in CSPA. He adds the observation that schools are showing greater interest in the yearbook and that summer workshops are reporting greater attendance by yearbook staffs than by newspaper staffs.

One thing is certain: yearbook workshops, short courses, and clinics are drawing large numbers of enthusiastic yearbook staffs to college campuses and other centers for summer study and fall-spring conferences or sessions of state, regional, and national organizations.

Every staff has regular meetings under the guidance of an intelligent adviser chosen by school officials for interest and/or training in the field. Whether these meetings are part of a full, formalized course, with school or college credit, I submit this plan of study and laboratory activity. As a side thought, I offer it as the outline for a preparatory course for yearbook advisers, for in-school staff workshops, and for short courses for students in fall, spring, or summer.

The outline format is somewhat similar to that used for the highly successful and valuable text for student newspapers, *Scholastic Journalism,* by Earl English and Clarence Hach. I make no apology for the resemblance, and I sincerely hope that what I have written will be as helpful for student yearbook journalists and their teacher-advisers as the English-Hach book has been for young newspaper journalists and their adviser-teachers through the years.

My premise is that the class or staff has been formed and the teacher assigned, and that the work of producing a yearbook lies ahead. Thus I have assumed a situation in which you open to Chapter 1, poised for a beginning of the year, whether in late spring, in the summer preceding the actual start of the job, or during the first week of a hectic school term.

After this introduction you will find incidental or auxiliary material on the yearbook and on other matters of primary interest to the teacher or faculty adviser, who may of course pick up any or all of it and use it elsewhere in the plan of instruction, wherever it seems best to fit local needs. Maybe your entire staff serves in the drive to sell books and ads. Great! The chapters on these projects should be studied at the time they fit best into your program, not necessarily at the time indicated by their placement in the book.

My hope is that the text may provide skeletal material, or even bare bones plus a little flesh, useful to the adviser-teacher and the student staff in developing full discussions. Added sustenance for such discussions will be found in other sources or in the resources afforded by experience and imagination. The texts mentioned above may prove helpful. Access to past issues of *Photolith, Scholastic Editor/Graphics Communications,* and *School Press Review;* current subscriptions to selected magazines; and the bulletins and other materials provided by the critical services would be helpful. (See addresses of national services and magazines in "The Adviser and the Staff.")

In using this text-workbook you will find, following the outline itself, visual illustrations, mostly excerpted from recent yearbooks, which may give your staff fresh ideas or may at least stimulate their imaginations. In a third section of each chapter, I offer a selection of exercises and projects designed to round out student knowledge and perhaps to offer springboards for starting and even producing the various portions of the yearbook. Use those that seem applicable to your local situation.

The Adviser and the Staff

(NOTE: While this text is intended largely to help the already established staff and faculty adviser/journalism teacher or publications director plan and develop the yearbook, here are some suggestions addressed to the school administrator and the adviser, which may be of value at the appropriate time.)

THE ADVISER is important enough in the scheme of things that one respected pioneer in scholastic journalism has always followed a technique of very old writers of the language and capitalized the title.

I admire the spirit if not the journalistic preciseness of the practice, since to me, the adviser of publications, especially the yearbook adviser, ranks very high on the list of persons who deeply influence and direct youthful minds and supervises an educational project unparalleled in the school program. The administration rarely gives this important person enough credit for the job or allows adequate time in the schedule for the work that must be done.

My own recommendation to every school official is to reevaluate the position of yearbook-publications adviser, sponsor, or director; the time allowed for the work; the facilities assigned; the budgetary allowance; and even the faculty pay schedule.

Advisers of student publications and teachers of journalism should be carefully trained, and as carefully selected, for this important work. Although there are many fine teachers of English, social studies, business, art, and even mathematics all over the country who are now directing staffs of yearbooks and other school publications, with minimal or no formal journalism training, and often with considerable success, there are certain desiderata for teaching and advising in this field:

1. This teacher-adviser should have a college degree, with at least a minor if not a major in journalism;
2. Ideally (if not practically, at this time) he/she would have a speciality or cospeciality in the teaching of journalism and advising of student publications, preferably under cosponsorship of a school of journalism and a school of education; or alternately,
3. Having no formal instruction or training in the supervision of publications, the adviser should at the very first opportunity take a course in the field from some qualified teacher, under the aegis of a good journalism or education school.

(Many departments or schools of journalism offer summer courses, and some give these in evening sessions. The emphasis of most, unhappily for yearbook people, is on the student newspaper, with little or no time allotted to the yearbook. Yet even this course, as presented at the University of Missouri, for example, gives valuable background information and skills that may be transferred to yearbook planning: understanding and writing news headlines; understanding the value of timeliness; mastering journalistic style rules; mastering organization and content of news, feature, sports, and other stories; learning copyreading; learning and practicing proofreading; understanding the planning, assigning, selecting, trimming, and layout of pictures; learning newspaper makeup and its rules, which in many cases can be transferred to yearbook layout; surveying typography; and reviewing business management, including advertising, circulation or sales, bookkeeping, and promotion.)

The serious adviser who has had no college training beyond the publications survey course mentioned above may wish to add to his formal journalism training by taking night, weekend, or summer courses in newswriting, feature writing, editing, public relations, typography, and management. To these he may wish to add design and graphic arts courses from the art department; a course in basic printing techniques from the printing division; and at least a course in the basic fundamentals of photography from the photography section. Armed with knowledge and skills thus acquired, the publications teacher-adviser will add daily to his repertoire by the actual experience of directing students as they plan and produce materials for the yearbook.

☆　　☆　　☆

Now let's consider how the staff should be selected, trained, and motivated. College editors of student publications have frequently been elected by student vote, either by their staff peers or by the students at large. Results of this form of selection are at best mixed. Popularity as a quality is valuable only to a point. Obviously, being accepted as a "nice fellow" or a person who tries to get along with everybody can have its values in the assignment of work. Yet being agreeable provides no insights and helps not at all in knowing how to direct work, or even what work to direct.

In fact, the extreme extroversion that goes with great popularity (prime essential to being elected to any office) can be something of a handicap to an editor, who needs to be one who can spend long periods of time toiling over a desk or typewriter. Except on the rare and very large staff, where the editor acts more as executive editor or editorial director, or even student adviser or manager, the editor comes up from his own specialized work only often enough to give directions to those working with him, to delegate duties, to rally everyone to better efforts.

Of course, whether in high school or college, election of the editor by those in the journalism class or in the outgoing staff, from candidates who have satisfied certain preestablished requirements, would seem far better than election by the so-called student body. It might assure selection of one with the needed skills, experience, and basic intelligence, and at the same time allow students to have a leader capable of commanding staff support, that is, having leadership qualities.

Yet many teacher-advisers have argued the case *against election* and *for selection* of an editor as well as the business manager from those competent students, preferably seniors-to-be, who have proved their interest and ability by serving at least a year on the staff.

Adviser Richard E. Starr of Santa Rosa, California, spoke persuasively for selection. Writing in *Photolith* in May 1968, he discussed his own methods of handpicking not only the editor but other key staff members. Each spring, Mr. Starr looked for the most intelligent, hardest working students, asking those he chose to fill out application blanks. He said he gave strong consideration to intelligence and aptitude tests, scholastic record, personality, and working habits. He consulted counselors, teachers, even physical education instructors, before arriving at decisions. Then he appointed the editor-in-chief, the business manager, the advertising manager (at Santa Rosa he was called the advertising "editor"), and activities, sports, and special features editors.

While agreeing in general with the idea of selection rather than election, another Californian writing in a later issue of the same magazine (October 1968) cautioned against relying exclusively on intelligence as a quality of the editor. "It's not enough," said Laurence Christman, well-known adviser. In fact, he said that his own experiences told him that the "average student" will often do a better job as editor because of what Mr. Christman called a higher "interest quotient." He also pointed to the fact that honor students often scatter their efforts and energies widely, rather than concentrating, as the average student will frequently do, on the one project. A more recent writer, James Keyworth, of Wayne Memorial High, Wayne, Michigan, said almost the same thing in a 1972 article: "Choose workers as well as 'geniuses.'"

A mixed plan between selection and election presents a student board of publications or sometimes a mixed student-faculty board of publications. Martin Crutchfield of North Little Rock, Arkansas, told of his plan in the May 1973 *Photolith*. He and his outgoing editor named three candidates for editor from among the working staff, all members of the yearbook class. The student board of publications then selected the editor, who, with the advice of the adviser, named the layout editor, the photography editor, and the business manager.

For greatest effectiveness, a board of publications would have a membership fairly evenly divided between students and teachers. It is also to be hoped that all those on the board would be sympathetic with the purposes, and reasonably well informed about the workings, of the publications. Advisers, the publications director, and the editors all belong on the board, which generally serves to monitor publications in their observance of school policies and to elect editors.

As far back as 1961, Louise Tapp of High Point, South Carolina, outlined an interesting plan that used an "editorial board" in the role of the publications board mentioned above. Staff membership was open to sophomores, juniors, and seniors; candidates were required to file formal, written applications and get faculty recommendations; then this board made final selections. The board was composed of the adviser, the editor, the associate editor, the photography editor, and the business manager. Adviser Tapp carefully chose her fellow board members. Duties of all editors were outlined clearly at the first of the year. The editor, in consultation with the adviser, directed and assigned the staff in the work projects, planned the book, approved all copy, supervised the board, called all meetings.

Other staff members at High Point, selected by the editorial board, included editors in charge of administration and faculty, instruction (curriculum), athletics, activities (apparently events as well as clubs and organizations), student body (portraits and portraits pages), statistics (an unusual division, but one which could be valuable in achieving editorial accuracy), and advertising (presumably this editor helped the business staff produce ad copy and materials). Typists were assigned to editors in the preparation of material for the book.

Staff training has been handled with great ingenuity by many advisers and editors. At Evanston Township, Illinois, for instance, Adviser John Price devised a sort of duplicate yearbook in scrapbook format, which junior staff members compiled during the year while the staff as a whole was producing the regular yearbook. The juniors used duplicate prints of pictures, wrote their own copy, and planned new layouts. This young staff-in-training thus worked out ideas for use in the yearbook they would edit as seniors. Meanwhile, the adviser was able to discover talents and abilities that might not otherwise have been revealed and was therefore in a better position to select top staff members the next year.

One of the most intriguing plans of all was reported by former adviser Niki Economy of Wyandotte High School, Kansas City, Kansas (March 1966 *Photolith*). Called the "cub program," the plan required carefully selected junior apprentices (cubs) to serve after school for a year, doing such things as typing, compiling needed lists, filing, copywriting, alphabetizing, etc. Each cub was assigned one page in the yearbook for which she, or more rarely he, was fully responsible. After all the year's work was finished in the spring, cubs were required to attend a three-week course every day after school from 3:00 to 5:30. (It was during this course, said Miss Economy, that the new staff was selected.)

In a school of 2,300 students it was possible to be extremely selective. Grades (especially in English), teachers' recommendations, and availability of candidates to work after school on a regular basis were all considered. Only 15 apprentices were selected from an average of 75 applicants. And I should add also that at Wyandotte there was, at the time the article was written, a full senior course in publishing the yearbook.

In regular meetings through the summer, this new Wyandotte staff made significant preparation for the next year's work. They compiled the ladder mentioned in Chapter 2 of this text, decided on format and theme, discussed uses of color, even planned and carried through some money-raising projects. Anyone who can match the Wyandotte schedule and program is well on the way to success.

Another training-selection program was described by Nancy Ruth Patterson in an article of April 1973 in *Photolith*. This young adviser at Fleming High, Roanoke, Virginia, said that she issued a call via a bright young editor for students to "fill a very few vacancies in the yearbook staff."

Applications were screened for "passing averages, satisfactory citizenship, and records of reasonably regular school attendance," with no weighting for outstanding scholarship or for past successes of any kind.

Five afternoon sessions were set. At the first, the editor gave her ideas of the lasting value of the yearbook and her dreams of producing a fine yearbook to justify the faith of students willing to lay their money on the line for something yet to be planned. Three long sessions of instruction dealt with layout, copywriting, headlining, and captioning. On Friday, each applicant was assigned to develop a two-page layout based on his instructions and on materials given to each one.

Mr. Crutchfield of North Little Rock, to whom I referred earlier, believes in immersing the new editor in all the current materials he can find, scholastic magazines like *Photolith, Scholastic Editor,* and others; all the textbooks and reference books he can find; and all the exchange yearbooks he can get. He advises the editor to begin a notebook in which to assemble ideas and materials, and he urges developing a critical eye about photography, copy, and layout, and learning and applying stringent journalistic standards.

Then, Crutchfield reported, he dissociates himself as much as possible from the job, that is, he gives the editor as much leeway as he will exercise in planning and managing the staff and in keeping the work flowing. By such means, the adviser forces the editor to make decisions, based of course on preliminary training and guidance and supplementary reading materials that Crutchfield has been able to provide.

All of this is quite stimulating and inspiring. How far the adviser can go in relinquishing the wheel to the young "driver-trainee" depends on the personality and the ability of the adviser; on the character, intelligence, and trainability of the editor; on the quality of the supporting staff; and on local conditions. I have had editors who could take over and "drive" after a suitable training period, with nothing but an occasional word of encouragement or caution. I have had, and observed, others not quite so sure of hand, foot, and equilibrium, who nonetheless did a fine job, with proper guidance and support. And there have been still others!

Let me finally suggest that staff members should be given every reason during the year to feel pride in staff membership. I like the practice in some schools of awarding staff pins or buttons to be worn as symbols of staff membership. Organizations like Quill and Scroll provide these pins for newspaper members, and National School Yearbook/Newspaper Association, National Scholastic Press, and Columbia Scholastic all have staff awards to sell members and probably nonmembers. The addresses of these organizations are given below.

School assemblies at the time of book distribution have often been the occasion for special staff recognition. But the staff banquet, scheduled near the end of the school year, is my favorite method of giving due recognition to editors and other staff members who have served well. I used it with great success years ago at the University of Houston. Adviser Richard Celek of Ohio has reported on such a banquet. At Port Clinton, Mr. Celek persuaded the local Junior Chamber of Commerce to take over the banquet and make it memorable. After proper recognition had been given to staff members, a prominent citizen made the address. The story was given good display in the local newspaper. At Houston, local editors and other leaders were invited to speak, the board chairman and benefactors of the university and its journalism program were invited as special guests, and the college president and his wife were regular head-table guests at these banquets.

At Manhattan, Kansas, as recently as 1969, the staff borrowed the Ohio idea and asked local Jaycees to arrange things. One splendid embellishment originated by this sponsoring group is worth considering for your staff. The Jaycees purchased a large plaque on which there was room for 14 names of annual recipients of "Outstanding Yearbook Worker" awards. (Your plaque could have room for 5, 10, even 15 names.) What a beautiful way to close the staff year!

Here are a few end-of-year or first-of-year suggestions for the adviser and staff: Align yourselves and the publication with city, state, or regional organizations available to you. In Texas, this might be the Texas Interscholastic League Press Conference; in Missouri, it would be Missouri Interscholastic Press and/or a city-wide press group in Kansas City or St. Louis; etc. State, city, or regional groups hold fall and/or spring meetings and conferences. Plan to attend and to take key staff members, as the budget permits.

Also study the offerings of summer workshops or programs sponsored by colleges or groups you have confidence in, and plan to attend the one of your choice. It is important to take the incoming editor (or editor-in-chief) and as many top staff members as possible. (Be sure the speakers or teachers are really respected specialists in their fields. Advisers of award-winning books and judges in national critical services should have something to offer any staff and adviser. Your photographers can learn from photo teachers or professional photographers. Artists can help with layout and design. So can acknowledged typography experts.)

Examine possibilities for subscriptions to good publications magazines in the field. Also consider a critical service. This gives you the suggestions and expertise of leaders in the yearbook, usually successful yearbook advisers, and lets the new staff, especially, see how the book already published compares to standards established by a national organization, and how it compares with other yearbooks in high schools or colleges of like size and budget.

National associations and publications of special interest to yearbook advisers and staffs include these:

● National School Yearbook/Newspaper Association is located in Lubbock, Texas. Address the director at Box 4080, Texas Tech University 79409. *Photolith* is its official magazine, published eight times a year, starting in early fall. This service traditionally specialized in the yearbook, as did the magazine, but now tries to give equal attention to the two major student publications. It serves colleges and high schools alike.

● National Scholastic Press Association (NSPA) and the affiliated Associated Collegiate Press (ACP) sponsor *Scholastic Editor*. Address the association and magazine at 18 Journalism Building, University of Minnesota, Minneapolis 55455. The magazine is scattered in its interests but occasionally has excellent articles related to yearbook work. It too is published through the school year.

● Columbia Scholastic Press Association (CSPA), one of the older national services, gives aid to all student publications and sponsors a national magazine, *School Press Review*, which deals in news and associational promotion for the most part but carries occasional articles related to student publications, including the yearbook. The association also sponsors a little bulletin for advisers who belong to CSPAA (its advisers' association). The CSPA mailing address is Columbia University, Box 11, Central Mail Room, New York, N.Y. 10027.

● School journalism teachers and advisers of student publications will wish to affiliate with the Journalism Education Association, a division of the National Education Association which generally holds meetings concurrently with NSPA, mainly for convenience.

● In addition, college advisers will be interested in the National Council of College Publications Advisers, with executive offices at Indiana State University, Terre Haute 47809.

● While having no division or critical service for the yearbook, Quill and Scroll Society, with a magazine also named *Quill and Scroll*, serves student newspaper journalists very well, and now and then its publication offers articles of interest and value to yearbook journalists. Its location is at the School of Journalism, University of Iowa, Iowa City 52242.

Finally, let me suggest that editors and advisers read what Steve Carlson has to say about the philosophy of the modern yearbook staff and adviser.

As a yearbook adviser for many years, past president of the Journalism Education Association, prolific writer on yearbook problems, and judge of literally thousands of high school and college yearbooks over a period of 15 years, Mr. Carlson is one of the most knowledgeable yearbook authorities in the country.

In addition, Mr. Carlson succinctly and colorfully sums up my feelings and observations. Without in any sense disputing the importance of lively pictures, vigorous reporting-recording, and modern layout, Carlson shifts the point of view slightly to focus on what it is all about, namely, people.

> "We used to be told in college that we just *do* the yearbook!" She was a young, new breed adviser. "Now I have to find out *why!*"

It's a logical question. When this former adviser had his first job with a publication, back in 1953–54, I was given the yearbook. It was the thing to do. So we did it. There was no rationale. There was no philosophy. It was just a thing to do. A book with pictures of the students of Helmsburg, Indiana, High School. It was, looking back, awful, but we gave it our best shot. We tried. Our camera cost $4.95. Our pix were angled. Our copy was minimal.

Today, Ruth Slade, adviser at Oakland, California, High says, "Yearbooks are beginning to set a coherent, teachable, structured philosophy."

"We are on the threshold," Mrs. Slade continues, "of a discipline more explicit than any I was able to discern in the seven years I have been with yearbooks."

This discipline is being *used* by the best books today. When I was in Bay City, Michigan, at T. L. Handy High, it was "Headline #4" plus art type for cover and dividers. In '72, in Griffith, Indiana's *Reflector,* the headline schedule included 18-point News Gothic, 36-point Gothic condensed, 18-point optima, paste-up headline types, 24-point News Gothic, and Airport condensed. This is a structured, controlled, logical book.

—But back to basic philosophy. A book used to be a picture book; it used to be a "memory book"; it used to be the senior's book.

I would argue that a book is to be read by more than seniors, more than just students.

A book is to be read by relatives and friends. It is to be more than a picture book. The best yearbook, today, is a probing, sensitive look at life in school and in the community at a point in time: *this day, this year.*

Thus, there are certain things that a book must do. In events, school life, or some such section, a book must examine the home, community, and extracurricular lives of its students, and the issues that those students face. These must all be faced honestly, in words and pictures. Campus has opened up. In *many* schools, the community *is* the campus, from tide-pool trips to work-experience programs; from Future Farmers projects to the health careers classes helping in the wards.

Further, a staff must decide whether it's going to be a *people* book or an *events* book. Some books study the events and issues of the year. Others study the *effects* of these actions and events on *persons.* I would argue that the second approach makes a yearbook a more *personal* thing, fleshes it out. I would argue that this approach, too, demands better-written copy, possibly with a better use of quotations, and better use of action pictures—*well-planned* action pictures.

And finally, the book must report on the academic lives of its students, not just show the teachers. Teachers are but the facilitators of learning, and the learning that takes place in a school is its *raison d'etre.*

—These, then, are the multiple tasks of the yearbook and its staff. All the rest is in support of these duties.

—H. Stephen Carlson

Yearbook Planning,
Editing, and
Production

1.
Theme
or
Linking
Idea

I. The traditional word for the idea that ties a book together is *theme*. The word is still with us, though its meaning has changed radically in recent years. *Motif* is another word used occasionally to indicate the same thing.

A. Students once considered it clever to pick a theme word out of the air, somewhat as a rock group selects a name. It was not unusual for a school sitting on the prairies to boast a yearbook with a nautical theme like "Ships." Other well-worn ideas that seemed almost never to fit the books they were meant to adorn included "Footsteps," "Roads," "Pathways," "Trails," "Doors," "Clocks," "Time," "All the World's a Stage," and an endless list of popular song titles, mostly compositions that, like school songs, are better when their words are not written down or even clearly enunciated.

B. While most editors, staffs, and advisers of today have become convinced that such thematic hooks are doubtful ones for a yearbook, and that even relatively logical ideas may distract the reader from the purpose at hand, there remains a real need for a method of unifying the book—an idea, a device, or a technique. The search goes on.

II. One method of linkage is the design or special pattern, something thought to represent the school, its students, its teachers and administration, or its total personality. The symbolism says "modern," "dynamic," "exciting," "progressive," or "streamlined," much as the school mascot (in a less sophisticated way) symbolizes qualities attributed to athletic teams.

A. Such design or pattern not only means something to the staff and the artist but it must come through to the reader without undue prompting.

B. It must be used with restraint, and it should not take up excessive space. Frequent repetition of a design, pattern, or idea, like a finger in the ribs, or the Duchess' chin on Alice's shoulder, tends to irritate rather than amuse or intrigue the reader. (See added comments below on placement of thematic devices.)

C. It must be done artistically. Crude, amateurish patterns or drawings have no legitimate place in the modern yearbook.

    1. Use a professional artist for a few pieces of needed spot art. Producing a yearbook requires employment of the skills, even the artistry, of typographers, pressmen, and all those who must put the pictorial and word content together into a pattern that pleases the reader on the finished pages. Schools do not hesitate to pay professional photographers to shoot portraits, groups, and even action pictures as needed for their books.

    2. Staff members can employ and develop their skills, their talents, and their artistic instincts in planning the book, in gathering and writing and editing copy and headlines, in planning pictures, and in designing pages and divisions.

    3. Some purists have insisted that using art from outside violates the whole concept of a student-produced book. While I do not agree, you must of course follow your own conscience in the matter.

    4. If you do use student art, by all means avoid that which the sober judgment of unbiased observers recognizes as poor art and which detracts from the quality of the book.

    5. Unless unusual talent is at hand, why use student art at all? Good photography is hard to beat. The goal, after all, is to enhance the yearbook's beauty and to add vividness to the report of the year.

D. In general, avoid cartooning altogether. By its nature, cartooning is best for the newspaper or the news magazine.

    1. Its message or its goal is transient, not suited for the lasting medium, the yearbook.

    2. Further, the cartoon, like a stand-up comic, takes center stage, and thus distracts the reader's attention from the story you are telling, lessening the total effect.

    3. If you feel obligated to encourage young artists, find other uses for proffered cartoons. Use them for posters promoting the yearbook, for instance. Or introduce the young artist to the newspaper editor, or to the magazine editor, even at the risk of the friendship of your fellow editors!

    4. What about cartoons for "spot art" —to fill holes? No, especially not to fill holes. The holes inside indicate a flaw in planning. And especially avoid those monstrous doodads that printers and so-called art services make available, such bits as footballs, basketballs, baseballs, musical notes, stars, and moons.

    5. Some artists and printers have suggested the use of background screening in various patterns. These may be dots, lines, cross checks, or zigzags, and they are printed lightly behind pictures with the purpose of achieving special emphasis, catching the eye, or just adding beauty. After observing results of such combinations through the years, I would recommend either avoiding all such backgrounds, or at most using them sparingly and cautiously, because they often lessen the effect of good photographs, obscure details, and weaken contrast.

III. A slight modification of the purely symbolic link is the word or phrase that is itself given a pattern or design. The staff of a recent issue of the Paris (Texas) *Owl* chose the word "Vibrations" as its theme of the book. Special showcard lettering of professional quality spelled out the theme word, which always appeared with vibrating lines around it, like the heat waves rising from a radiator.

IV. Designs, patterns, combined words and patterns—all these beautify and link some of the best books of modern times. A few of these are worth mentioning here, and some of them will be illustrated on the pages immediately following.

A. A recent *Anchor* yearbook, at Mary Carroll High, Corpus Christi, Texas, uses a thematic block in opening and division pages, with varying but similar phrases asserting in one way or another that we will have a bright future if all of us, old and young, black, brown, and white, will deliberately seek to dissolve old walls of misunderstanding and prejudice.

1. The visible linkage device is established firmly on all division spreads in three vertical portraits, two to the left, one to the right, each with stippled background, and all laid on a solid black page background. The pattern is one that must be handled with great care.

2. An overlaid white patch, 2¼ × 4¼ inches, contains the division title and a small bit of philosophical copy. This rectangle is lined up at the base with the bottoms of the pictures.

B. Done by professionals, the design for all divisions of pages of a modern *Hack* (Centenary College for Women, Hackettstown, New Jersey) offers variations of a checkerboard theme. Spyros Horemis of Dover Publications, Inc., is given credit. In another case I observed recently, a thematic design taken from Hallmark cards is credited to the company and used with special permission. (See May 1972 *Photolith* for illustrations and review by J. W. Click.)

C. Combining art and an idea, a recent Catalina High School *Torch*, Tucson, Arizona, uses a theme that figuratively represents a "Perpetual Windmill," a "windmill of the mind" obviously based in part on a popular song. (See later cautions about popular song titles.) The windmill pattern has jagged edges and points and inserted cartoon art suggestive of life inside and outside school, as it impresses students. Somehow a nightmare effect is created. (Note: Where student art is used, be sure to credit the student. Where an idea is borrowed from a copyrighted song or from any other source, get the permission of its author or publisher, and *give due credit.*)

1. Four-color art spreads from the full left page over halfway into the second page of the theme-setting spread. The thematic passage is in unjustified type on the right of the art.

2. The passage begins, "Distorted, twisted, illusive windmills of the

mind attempt to comprehend. . . ." It lists some of the puzzling and violent bits of the day's news, speaking of the symbolic "windmill etching circles in space," like the "perpetual windmill" of life itself.

3. The cover of this book carries a standard windmill design, and all division pages have small windmill patterns in white over black background. Accompanying theme copy refers tersely to the pattern, and ample photographic art, taking major space on divider spreads, completes, yet dilutes and makes palatable, the theme idea.

D. Giving their book a thematic name, "Odyssey," staff members of a recent *Student Prince,* Princeton High, Cincinnati, Ohio, set a trend that may find increasing acceptance. The idea itself follows that of the automakers in giving every size and type of car its own special name—"Gremlin," "Pinto," "Impala," etc.

1. The total theme is really "Odyssey— a Search for Understanding." Flyleaf copy explains:

Swept by boisterous, ill-fated winds, delayed by adventures on land as he struggled ten years to reach home in Ithaca, Odysseus—Greek hero of the Trojan War—has come in the past 2500 years to signify man's search for identity, for meaning in life. And so, amid a world swept by conflicting ideas, his travels stand today as a symbol for students at Princeton High School in their personal . . . Quest for Understanding

(This final phrase actually carries over into, and serves as a thematic title on, the theme-setting title page itself, page 3.)

2. A block of words above the theme phrase includes "America," "Life," "Happiness," "Youth," "Love," "Nature," "Honor," "School," "Why," etc.

3. On successive theme pages, editors build the idea of an odyssey or a search for understanding of the many things that make up life, school life in particular. And they do it with subtlety and delicacy.

4. The block used on the opening theme page is repeated on all division spreads. A headline restates

the theme and introduces the division title. (Ex.: "Wide Experiences in Life Beyond the Classroom Become Available to Students by ACTIVITIES.")

V. But even more than art designs and patterns, *ideas* are being employed to set the pace, direct the course, or link the elements of the story in many of the best modern yearbooks, large and small. Photographic art, more often than any other, serves to illustrate the thematic idea. Happily, good photography is usually available when student art talent is lacking.

A. The 1972 *Milestone,* Eastern Kentucky University, Richmond, had access to photographers of rare artistic ability, and the editors made full use of their opportunities in focalizing on "The Year of the Building Boom" in splendid photographs, often fourcolor. Some of it was of highest artistic quality, equal or superior to most available drawings or paintings.

B. Another early 1970s book, that of Holy Cross High, New Orleans, Louisiana, centered attention on the school, which, the editors stated, is "an institution bound by tradition in an age when traditions are called meaningless." The book pictures (in photographs again) a blending of old and new. The theme was "The Real Story," and editors dedicated themselves, in a thematic prologue, to tell the "complete truth about ourselves in the hope that our story will instill in others a yearning for the truth everywhere."

C. I have hinted at another theme earlier. The editors of a recent *Quiverian,* Wyandotte High School, Kansas City, Kansas, got permission from Hallmark, the well-known card company, to use the idea "Life is what you are alive to." Opening pages, division spreads, and closing adapted the idea in rare poetic style, which must have pleased the officials of the company, as it certainly did readers of the yearbook. (See also *Photolith,* February 1973.)

D. While, as I stated in an earlier paragraph, highways, roads, pathways, footsteps, time, hands, and all that ilk

of theme ideas have been outdated perhaps since they were first used by wellintentioned but misguided editors, the *Lancer Legend* of a recent year took the highway on which the school is located and made of it a most effective thematic idea or linking device. The scenic nature of the highway made the job all the more pleasant and successful. If you do use a local setting for a theme, do as the *Lancer Legend* editors did and keep it all low key. Do not overstretch the analogy, and do get the most effective and pictorial photography possible.

E. The use of games in the analogy has resulted in some fine theme ideas in recent years. (I could have included these illustrations in the listing immediately above, since art is used to develop the ideas, but the ideas predominate.)

   1. "The Name Game" was the idea effectively used by the Griffith (Indiana) *Reflector* in a recent year, as reviewed by Steve Carlson in the September 1972 *Photolith.* The common habit of mistaking superficials for substance and thus mislabeling things is treated skillfully by the editors.

   2. "The Money Game" was the linking idea for a recent Western Hills annual, Cincinnati, Ohio. It is surprising how much in school life depends on availability of needed money.

F. Environment—specifically, the sun and its light—illuminated and tied together the 1972 *Legend,* Brookfield, Wisconsin. (The book is reviewed in the October 1972 *Photolith.*) Editors felt and expressed the thought that the primal force giving power to all life on earth has a special meaning at Brookfield, and they demonstrated the belief with fine art, with subheadings for divisions, and with copy.

G. Optimism, desire to live creatively, awareness of the world outside school walls, the urge to help others, the desire to take part in making the world a better place—all these find expression in modern themes.

   1. "Reach Out," urges the theme idea of the 1972 *Nanterrian,* Genevieve High School, Panorama City, California.

2. "Reaching Out" is the similar theme of the recent *Reflection,* Blackford High, Hartford City, Indiana.

3. "Yes," affirmed editors of a Franklin *Almanack,* Livonia, Michigan, in a book filled with the affirmation that life can be rich, challenging, and satisfying if we but face it with hope and energy. (See review in March 1971 *Photolith.*)

H. With imagination and yet simplicity, editors of the 1972 Paris (Texas) *Owl* sought to portray what was significant in the year in this city, using the idea "Relevance Was . . ."

I. Puns are dangerous devices, but as a one-time idea for their own special school (and maybe for any other university school), the 1972 editors of *U-Highlights,* Chicago University High, made effective use of the idea, "The YOU in U-High."

J. School consolidation spawned a brilliant theme at Dalzell, South Carolina: "1 + 1 = 1."

K. Individuality and the importance of its development gave one *Quiverian,* Wyandotte, Kansas City, Kansas, the splendid theme idea, "You Are You and I Am I."

L. Renewal and looking upward after a time of confusion gave the editor of the 1972 *Colonial Echo,* William and Mary College, Williamsburg, Virginia, an idea for a book theme: "Awakening." (See J. W. Click's review, *Photolith,* December 1972–January 1973.)

M. Changing times gave the Arlington (Indianapolis) 1971 *Accolade* a theme idea, "The Quiet Revolution." (The revolution was one of changing *ideas,* not of marching, protesting, or fighting.)

N. And what is more appropriate for a yearbook than "Flashback," theme of the 1972 book of Bishop Feehan High, Attleboro, Massachusetts?

O. Complete the phrase once, or for each section of the book, and you will have a theme idea, like that of the 1971 *Eaglet,* Somerset, Pennsylvania: "A Time for . . ."

P. Or consider how the school (or college) stands in relation to other parts of the society, or to the whole world, and you may wish to emulate the theme, "A World Within a World," as used effectively by editors of the 1972 *Amici,* Western Guilford High, Greensboro, North Carolina.

Q. A motto, neither stretched too much nor yet quoted and then abandoned, can serve well to link a book. Such was the theme device, brilliantly justified, in the 1972 *Elkonian,* Centerville, Ohio: "Those not busy being born are busy dying."

R. Those who bought the 1971 *Prize Package* booklet from National School Yearbook Association will remember the reference to an idea taken from Augusta Military's *Recall:* "There are many different ways of looking at things." Showing the varied facets of school life from a number of angles can provide a rewarding linkage plan for a book.

S. Let me cite other words and phrases that have been used effectively in books of recent years: "A Part Yet Apart" (focus on the individual); "Alive"; "Encounter" (the many interrelationships of school life); "Directions"; "Now"; "Challenge"; "Awareness"; "My World and Me!" (To name books in which I first saw each of the above would take undue space and excessive time.)

VI. I must caution that some of the above ideas, by the time they reach your attention, may well have been "done to death" by excessive usage, just as, unhappily, semiclassic songs like "Trees" and "Old Man River" and most top-of-the-list modern pop songs such as the inspired but now worn-out "We've Only Just Begun" have been or will soon be destroyed by overexposure. I recommend for immediate retirement the marvelous idea from scriptural sources, "To everything there is a season," with all the variations that have been applied by scores, perhaps hundreds, of editors since someone first discovered how beautifully it could tie a book together.

VII. If the idea is the thing, how does one go about looking for it, after exhausting all known reference books and magazines, exchange books, displays at conferences, etc.? Why not try brainstorming?

A. The staff sits in a circle around the editor, one by one offering suggestions. Most of the suggestions are without merit, like crude clay moldings, but now and then one has enough life and promise to earn consideration. It deserves your effort to make it live and breathe!

B. Consider your trial idea from all angles. Take the nostalgic pop song, for instance, and modify its title a bit: "These Were the Days."
   1. Would this sentence really fit your year and its days as they unfold before you?
   2. If your school is a quiet one, one without excitement, one that follows tradition and one in which your own school years are or were very much like those of 20 years or even 50 years ago, forget the thought.
   3. How about "The Quiet Years"? Someone fondly says, "We're just plain vanilla." (One school yearbook staff successfully followed a theme called "the salad years," and another used an actual ice cream motif. Maybe you should consider "Plain Vanilla" as a motif.)

C. Don't be too easily pleased by the way words ring or sound. They might make a beautiful song title or even book title and a terrible theme idea.

D. In considering a suggestion, think about the opening and closing passages and art, and try it out with every separate division of the book. Ask yourselves how the idea would fit each, what art would be used, what words would subtly suggest the linking idea without boring or oppressing the reader with an inappropriate metaphor.

E. Examine your motif for unintended double meanings, hints at things best forgotten.

F. Avoid the overwrought, the trite, the overly emotional or sentimental, the cute phrase.
   1. Like most song titles (see above) a far-fetched statement of what sounds impressive and true today may be thoroughly distasteful later on, especially after you have exposed it to use over and over through the months of yearbook planning. Simplicity and honesty

are good qualities to demand in a theme.
   2. The cautions here are especially applicable to the gaudy writings of a Rod McKuen and the verses of most modern pop singers (as well as those of yesterday's Tin Pan Alley writers, who were perhaps more rhythmical but no more inspired, as a rule).

G. A slight, fresh, and unusual twist of language may be the determining characteristic you seek in a theme idea. Look over the suggestions above and see if they suggest anything to you. Study your favorite aphorisms and slogans. Study Emerson and Thoreau and Oscar Wilde for this element.

H. Hold for ripening the idea you select, and reexamine it after a few days. Ben Franklin said that "guests, like fish, stink after three days." If your idea begins to emit a rancid aroma after being stored a few days, better discard it and look further.

VIII. When should you begin looking for the linkage idea?

A. Why not open the quest soon after the new editor is selected, in the spring, or at least as soon as the nucleus of the staff has been selected and is ready to start?

B. If you have made a tentative selection, you can then apply it and develop it into rough form at a summer workshop or short course. Whether a school project, or a city-wide or state or regional program, this is one of the most important parts of the year's program of action.

C. If the summer has been wasted without any attention to plans for the book or to the selection of the theme, this is obviously one of the very first things you will tackle in the new school year. Get about it with all the energy you can muster.

IX. Where does the theme idea or design go in a yearbook?

A. Obviously, again, you must make it part of the opening. Most editors carry it on a thematic opening spread or in an opening section. A page or even a spread may come before the title page (though it need not do so). A longer thematic introduction, as seen frequently in larger high school or college books, should follow the title, though a few editors have unfortunately postponed the title page until after the introductory section.

B. As already hinted above, the theme should "flavor" division spreads. Copy, design, and illustrative photography may combine to introduce the section and yet emphasize (as an example) that this was "A Year of New Beginnings," that (perhaps) these were the "Days of Creativity," or that yours is a "School That Encourages Individual Growth" (a rather bulky idea that needs a bit of trimming by proper exercise and diet). The challenge is in tying an idea into each division without strain, monotony, or intrusiveness: "It was a Year of Creativity—in ACADEMICS," etc. A picture that shows students working on an art project (art classes) or designing a rough cover for the yearbook (journalism) might serve to illustrate the point. Your selected design will complete the idea. Another brainstorming session may help in developing each division spread. (But see Chapter 7 on division spreads.)

C. Inside the book, there is real danger in attempting to keep the reader aware of the theme while yet telling him the story clearly and without interruption. A theme may come to be like the fabled taskmaster of an old first reader, who greeted a malingering student everywhere the unfortunate boy fled. In general, I would recommend against trying to insert the theme into stories: "It was a year of creativity" (or "These were days of growth") ". . . in the Erisophian Literary Society, which added four new members to its rolls. . . ." Whatever seems contrived or forced will offend the reader.

D. The closing should of course round out the story, and it should be consistent with the announced theme idea. Thus a modest and unstrained use of the motif may help unify without seeming artificial. I will not attempt to illustrate this, since to do so would perhaps distract you from the proper flow of your own creativity. But, of course, "Creativity" as a theme comes to fruition in the created object—a completed school year, a finished record. "Days of growth" leads to days when what is growing comes to a climax or high point in its life span, such as the close of school and the beginning of a new period. (The fruiting of a plant or a tree may be a bit too trite a metaphor here, but the subtle members of the staff will think of something, I feel sure, that will round out your fine linking idea and close your story.)

Pictorial Examples

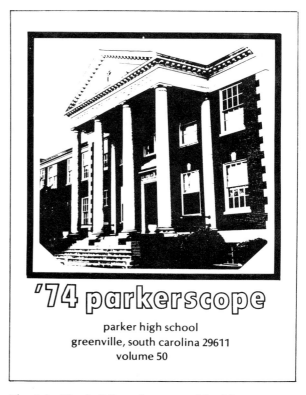

Fig. 1.1—The building picture on this title page was transposed from a halftone photo to a line drawing. Caution: This technique requires special training. (Courtesy NSY/NA.)

exemption proposal is final - ly tested

Every high school student in Austin in the past several years has been only too familiar with final exemption programs. Plan upon plan has been discussed, hoped for, presented to the School Board and always turned down or put off forever.

The topic had become one of boredom or disgust, as students looked back on all the work and talk for nothing. Everyone had just about reached the conclusion that any attempt of this nature was hopeless.

So when the Student Council decided to give it a try, most seemed uninterested. After all, what was the point in everyone's getting excited about the possibility of no finals when they would, like always, end up taking them anyway.

As the year progressed, Dena Chasnoff and her committee worked diligently to win the approval of faculty, parents and students for a very different proposal. Students began to open their eyes—some in excitement and others in horror—when the plan was explained for the first time.

The plan linked absences and grade point average to reward students who came to class. Under the plan, any student could be exempt from three finals if the following requirements were met:

Absences	Average needed
1,2	B-
3,4	B
5,6	B+
7	A-
8	A-

School field trips and UIL events would be excused, however illness and appointments would be counted as unexcused absences.

The plan was presented to the School Board. The Board listened. For the first time, members agreed to accept the program.

Because of the controversy of the plan, it was held on trial at Anderson second semester, waiting to get results before implementing it.

The main controversy of the program was over the absence tie-in. Those in favor of the plan were hopeful that it would cut down the skipping rate. Others felt that the grade average was all that should count. Since seniors were unaffected, most were not interested. And underclassmen, whether they understood the plan or not were delighted at the prospect of possibly being exempt from as many as three finals.

But one fact remains: up until this point, no underclassman have had the chance to be exempt and no other plan has had the chance to be tested.

settling

1. The finals exemption proposal drew many curious interested people including faculty, students and parents to the school board meeting that had the plan on the agenda. Chris Allman, a senior at Anderson addresses the board about her feelings on the proposal.
2. The student council which sponsored the program was represented at the meeting by Nancy Davidson and Dena Chasnoff, the hardworking chairman of the exemption committee.
3. This spring, seniors like Gayle Donnell and Patty Pontegoo were not the only students given the chance to be out in the sun during finals because of the trial exam-nation-exemption plan.

FINALS EXEMPTION REACTIONS

	yes	no
1 Do you like the new finals program?	56.4%	43.5%
2 Do you feel that the absentee system is fair?	50%	50%
3 Has the program affected your attendance in any way?	26.5%	73.4%
4 Were you aware that other finals proposals had been brought before the school board?	43.4%	56.5%
5 Do you feel that finals are necessary in preparing for college?	55.7%	44.2%
6 Do you fully understand the mechanics of the program?	49.8%	50.1%

Thirteen percent of the students were surveyed.

tradition-coated prom
something to remember
in fleeting senior lives

graduates

A basic part of any graduating class is the traditional prom and banquet and the seniors of '74 certainly didn't overlook this memorable occasion.

After untold hours of searching for the perfect formal or the snazziest tuxedo, seniors arrived at Tracor ready for the big event.

A dance floor adorned with a colorful rainbow, balloons, crepe paper and a glittering '74 set the scene as Orion set the pace for the remaining three hours of the prom. During breaks, students drifted out onto the balcony to enjoy the warm night air,

As the band struck its final note, decorations were pulled from the ceiling to be kept as souvenirs of that unforgettable evening.

1. Seniors gather at tables with friends, struggling through stiff formals and cumbersome tuxedos to devour delicious steaks and potatoes. Ben Vega, Melonie Milner, Gina Quick and Jamie Lidington laugh with fellow band students while enjoying dinner.
2. Taking a break from the hot dance floor, Scott Hornaday and Mary Howland get something cold to quench their thirsts.

50   51

Fig. 1.2—A background screen, called a mezzotint, was used with a second color, red, to make the big dominant photo stand out in these pages from the 1974 *Afterthought,* Anderson High, Austin, Texas. (Book was made available through courtesy of National School Yearbook/Newspaper Association.)

6 lettermen return to pace linksmen

Former Bluejay cage star Mike Caruso was coach of this year's golf team.

With six lettermen returning, things looked promising as spring came to Omaha.

Top linksmen were Hugh Hanson, Bill Kennedy, Marty Manning, Jim Fitch, Pat Moriarity and Mark Sheehan.

Fig. 1.3—Silhouette from a Creighton University *Bluejay,* Omaha, Nebraska, creates an effect like that of outlining, or like using a special background. Size of photo dramatizes technique.

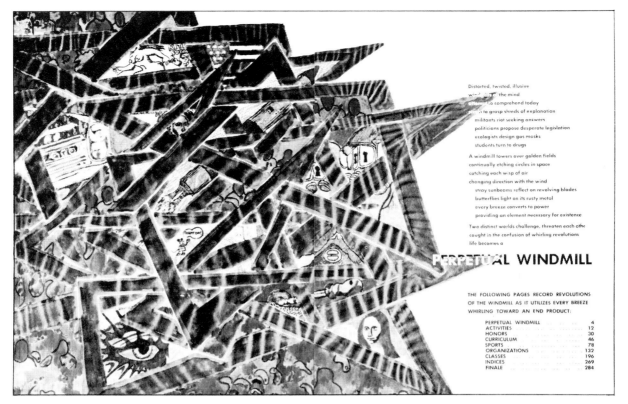

Distorted, twisted, illusive
wind ... the mind
... to comprehend today
... to grasp shreds of explanation
militants riot seeking answers
politicians propose desperate legislation
ecologists design gas masks
students turn to drugs

A windmill towers over golden fields
continually etching circles in space
catching each wisp of air
changing direction with the wind
stray sunbeams reflect on revolving blades
butterflies light on its rusty metal
every breeze converts to power
providing an element necessary for existence

Two distinct worlds challenge, threaten each other
caught in the confusion of whirling revolutions
life becomes a

PERPETUAL WINDMILL

THE FOLLOWING PAGES RECORD REVOLUTIONS
OF THE WINDMILL AS IT UTILIZES EVERY BREEZE
WHIRLING TOWARD AN END PRODUCT:

△ *Fig. 1.4*—A current, dynamic idea, ''Perpetual Windmill,'' and effective copy rescue the art in this spread from unevenness of technique. Table of contents shares the theme spread in this Catalina *Torch,* Tucson, Arizona.

Fig. 1.5—Themes are sometimes implicit, rather than explicit, in modern yearbooks. Thus in the 1974 *Totem,* Chamberlain High, Tampa, Florida, the openers subtly relate students to the world lying around them. (Courtesy NSY/NA.) ▽

Fig. 1.6—Another challenge, ". . . Being Now," was the idea set and followed in the Hazen High, Arkansas, *Hornet.* Here, table of contents is on the theme opener, below a thematic copy block.

Fig. 1.7—"Metamorphosis" was the theme of a modern yearbook, the *Chief,* Greenville Senior High, South Carolina. The butterfly picture below gives support to the motif idea.

Fig. 1.8—The thematic peg for a Griffith (Indiana) *Reflector* was "Name Game." It gave editors a springboard for protest against use of labels. Capitals effectively stress theme words.

Name Game befuddles players

Myriad of rules causes player dropout

No one seemed immune from the game. Labels were invented to fit every type of person. Even time-honored events failed to escape the caustic effects. At cheerleading tryouts, contestants had to deal with not only the usual bugaboo of tension, but also the chant, "Who rah, we rah, we don't want a rah-rah!" In class elections the usual leaders were ousted, despite their records, to make way for a more liberal faction. Students emphasized group association rather than individual merit. Some teased athletes for abstainance from drinking and smoking, while others mocked any wish to excel.

Students voiced opinions about procedures used to select homecoming queen. Signs and paper buttons backed a write-in candidate. Sparks flew but as Homecoming approached, the fires of youth died and the holiday passed without incident.

Fig. 1.9—"Putting the YOU in U-High" was the theme chosen for *U-Highlights,* University High, Chicago. An Indianapolis school yearbook staff similarly spoke of "The IN-thing at Arlington."

Theme or Linking Idea **11**

1. Assign a secretary (maybe the adviser) and hold a brainstorming session. Keeping in mind the ideas you have examined in the earlier parts of this chapter, but trying to modify what you imitate so that it fits your school and year, list as many relevant theme ideas as you can within the next 15 to 20 minutes. Ready? Start!

2. Establish teams of two or three members, and using the three, four, or half-dozen best ideas that came out of this session, agree to come back within 24 hours (a week if this is for a weekly session in summer school or summer vacation) with a rough dummy for a thematic opening page and four to eight opening theme pages, for three or four other division spreads, and for the closing page. Sketch, or at least write descriptions of, the picture(s) you plan. Write headings, and write at least rough drafts of the theme introduction.

Let's look at this assignment more closely. Suppose your theme suggestion was "Central Is a Friendly World." Your opening scenic picture should introduce the idea dramatically, with perhaps a picture of a crowd at some special occasion welcoming new students, or something unusual in your school. Be sure the faces featured are smiling, or at least look friendly.

Maybe it is a picture of a school official noted for his or her friendly attention to new students or visitors. A close-up picture of such an administrator welcoming a new student or showing a visitor around might serve as this theme-intro picture. Or look back at the illustrations and see if one of them suggests something to you.

You will need to introduce various aspects of the school on the opening theme pages (assuming that you have room for such a section). Academics will prove a real test to your theme, perhaps, unless you can think of one course, one teacher, or one special unit in one class that represents the "Friendly World" we are talking about.

Sports as a theme object may also offer problems, unless you can envision an athlete helping another athlete to his feet after a hard play, or an occasion on which one player (tennis?) has just lost to another in spirited tryouts for first position on the team and yet is finding it possible to smile and congratulate the victor. This photo would obviously require much planning in advance. Two or three special pictures in sports, academics, special events, and organizations might be needed.

Now let's look at division pages or spreads. [...] avoid ma[...] tion of w[...] theme pa[...] and be s[...] exhibit va[...] Friendly [...] World of [...] "A Frien[...] lenges"; e[...]

If yo[...] tions, the[...] and copy[...] this year, [...] the Cale[...] the idea [...] jor or ev[...] standard [...] ing to clo[...]

The [...] School in[...] partments[...] nizations [...] with acad[...] maybe the[...] nalism); musical instruction and clubs and groups such as band, chorus, etc.; speech-drama with associated dramatics and debate and speech activities; history and the history club; home economics and its related clubs, etc.

The third section might then be devoted to the people themselves, "Around the School with Individual People," album-style portraits of faculty and students and then the groups as groups, especially those who have no real activity and do nothing that makes a special impact on the rest of the school.

Index and advertising follow logically.

Closing. Don't forget this page or spread or double-spread. A picture shows a senior stepping out of the front door into the world of outside life, maybe still wearing a smile, and his cap and gown. This should get you started.

Copy should be relatively brief on introductory pages, on the dividers, and on the closing page. It should avoid the stilted, fancy, artificial style that sometimes ruins effectiveness of a linkage idea. A subtle hint is always better than blatant repetition.

The magazine-style or cryptic headline that piques interest may appeal more on opening pages and even for division-page headings. Or you may prefer to use narrative or news style, such as most yearbooks now seem to use inside the book. Or these pages may be ideal for trying out the lead-in headline, a form of heading that leads directly into the body block, or may even be absorbed into the body copy, inside the lead sentence.

2. Planning and Organizing

I. Logically, you must first take stock of what your yearbook will contain. Let me offer my ideas as to what parts, sections, or divisions should be included in books of this present age. Don't hold me to the order in which I present them here, and don't even consider that the sectional names are sacred, or that there is only one way of arranging sections. For instance, see my suggestion for dividing the book in the exercise for Chapter 1. But regardless of all that, the superior book of 1976, or 1986, will likely contain these parts:

A. A cover, which you will plan after deciding on the theme or linkage device and which you may not wish to work out completely until you have developed the art and plan for opening, division, and closing pages. Its elements include:
1. The name of the book and the year, at least, on the front
2. Optionally, on the front cover, the name of the school and the city
3. Backbone information: at least the name of the school and the city and the volume number and (if space permits) repeat of the title and the year

B. Opening section, with these minimal elements:
1. Title page
2. Listing of contents
3. Thematic introduction, introductory scenes, typical pictures inside and outside buildings, such as cafeteria, auditorium, classes, labs, recreational areas, front entrances, etc.
   (Note: Take care in presenting the theme or mood or general atmosphere pictures to avoid intrusion into the month-by-month or day-long reporting of the events-features section.)

C. Features and special or outstanding happenings (events) of the year, the important all-school program that is not part of the curriculum, not peculiarly part of what is called extra-curriculars: By "all-school program," we may consider and include school registration, enrollment, first-of-school happenings, assembly and holiday events, centers of campus or school activity not already featured in the thematic or opening pages, homecoming, and many other things, some of which will be mentioned in the chapter on this phase of coverage.

D. Curricular activity: classes and departments, divisions, schools within a college or university, laboratories, special or unusual instructional programs, unusual methods, visits to special places (journalists to newspaper plants, for instance), visiting speakers and guests (the mayor to a class in government, for instance), and adjunct offices, departments, and programs such as visual aids, library, etc.

E. Clubs, organizations, groups, societies, even publications—in general, all extra-curriculars except sports, which usually bulk too large for inclusion in any but a separate section. The action, the accomplishments of the year, and the big events are to be given top billing here, in words and pictures. Minimize static pictures and warmed-over copy. (All this will be discussed in detail in the proper chapter.)

F. Sports or athletics, physical education. You will likely remember the major sports, but remember also to include:
1. Girls' or women's sports, which recent court rulings as well as a sense of fair play suggest should receive equal treatment with boys' or men's sports
2. The organized physical education classes and programs unless they are included in curriculum (as is quite appropriate if all action derives from the credited classes)
3. The so-called minor sports, those that attract fewer spectators and less revenue—tennis, track, swimming, bowling, wrestling, baseball
4. Intramural or playground or gymnasium sports that are not part of the organized physical education program

G. Portraits:
1. Those of administrators and faculty members, sometimes included in the academics-curricular section, but more successfully kept in a separate group at or near the end of the book by increasing numbers of modern staffs
2. Those of students, freshmen through seniors, also most generally presented near the end of the book, after conclusion of all the actual story of the year
3. Honorees, which sometimes have a separate section but more often are included, at least in all but the very

large books, in features or even class portraits

H. Posed or static groups: Here, it seems to me, belong all those inactive or purely honorary groups, whose members are selected because of their individual achievements or activities in a variety of fields—academics, sports, etc.—but which by their nature are not intended to participate as clubs in the life and activity of the school. Historic each may be, and even visible, like the gargoyles above the auditorium entrances or the hundred-year-old school-ground oak beneath which generations of students have gathered to discuss school problems or life in general—like that Eriso-phian Literary Society of my college days, which had been founded for the noble aim of stimulating an interest in reading good literature, but which gradually sank into the custom of meeting just twice a year, once to elect officers and collect dues, a second (and final) time to have the picture taken for the annual. Perhaps you can do as some some editors are already doing, assess such groups a fee for their space, since they in effect do not belong in the pages where the record of the school year is spread. (Group photos will be discussed fully in later chapters.)

I. Advertising: Sometimes divided among the various sections, this part of the book seems better kept in one piece, and in my opinion it still works best at or near the end of the book. Names used vary widely, as I shall illustrate later on, from "Community Friends" to plain "Business Section" or "Advertising." The best editors make advertising coverage and design as lively as possible and integrate it into the book. Design and copy should match or blend into the total book, never stand out in dreary contrast because of bad typography, art, and patterning.

J. Index and closing pages: The index, like the title page, seems to be fairly firmly located by its nature. Collecting material for it should begin the very first day of staff production. Its care, handling, and display are discussed in a chapter at the end of this text, which you may wish to study out of normal order. Maybe that would be a good lesson for next time! Closing must, of course, round out the book, may incorporate editorial acknowledgments and credits or the editor's final message, and at least in the thematic closing spread or pages, should match the opening and division pages closely in photo coverage, copy, and design.

A. Editors have been trying seasonal or chronological methods of organizing the yearbook for almost as long as I have been studying yearbooks, though very, very rarely with anything but disaster to the readability of the book.

   1. A moment's reflection indicates that too much of school life is horizontal, that is, flowing evenly and continuously from the first weeks of the year through the close, and therefore may not logically be assigned to one seasonal section as fall, winter, spring, or summer.

   2. But you might consider this plan:

     a. Organize the first portion of the book on a chronological basis, events from the beginning to the close of the school year, beginning with registration or school opening, holiday events, special all-school programs and assemblies, and sports in the seasons where they fall.

     b. In the second part, interweave academics and all associated organizations, publications, societies, and related events such as musical, dramatic, journalistic, scientific, etc. Drop in the unrelated extracurriculars at the end of this section—service clubs, perhaps student government, honoraries, honors, etc.

     c. The third part would include the static elements—portraits, groups that exist but have no real part in school life, index, advertising, and closing.

B. Simple deviations from standard and usual organization have been tried by successful editors.

   1. The combination of curriculum with related curricular clubs is one of the more logical and interesting variations.

   2. Addition of a full section on fine arts, with illustrations drawn from the various art classes, made one or two yearbooks of recent years more than usually interesting. The section was placed just after the regular curricular division.

   3. A separate musical section offers a method of including both the classes and the organizations associated with them. In a school or college where musical groups are especially strong and active, this avoids a situation in which either curricular or extracurricular activities seem to be dominated by this part of the school program.

C. A more radical change in plan was used in the Arlington, Indiana, book which I mentioned in the theme chapter. The "Quiet Revolution" of the *Accolade* involved telling the story of the year in the first half of the book, then literally flipping the book over to offer advertising, thematic essays, and routine elements in the second, or flipped, section.

D. You may wish to look back at the suggestion made in the exercise for Chapter 1, in which you separate the book into major thematic sections. There I listed the first three of these divisions. I now add the fourth:

   1. "Around the School with Big and Small Events"

   2. "Around the School with the Curriculum"

   3. "Around the School with the Individual People"

   4. "Around the Community: Business Friends of the School"

   (Note: Closing and index would come at the usual places.)

E. As a sort of postscript, let me refer you to chapters on various sections for other planning ideas. Take a quick look, for instance, at the *Hack,* discussed in Chapter 13, "Portraits." This book strings out faculty and student formals at the bottoms of pages of other sections.

nation's leading judges and writers in the field, has suggested that after deducting pages used in opening pages, theme section, index, advertising, and closing pages, you roughly divide the remaining pages by three and give one portion to each of the following:

A. Events, issues, and academics or curriculum
B. Clubs and sports
C. Faculty and student portraits, with the static groups thrown in here as suggested above
(Note: If I were to modify the above apportionment, I would give more weight to events and academics, taking away from the usually overweighted portraits section.)

IV. **An old system of outlining a yearbook, the ladder plan, is hard to improve. In it, you arrange proposed page numbers on each side of a long vertical line, as you intend them to fall, starting with the right-hand side, odd numbers 1, 3, etc., and then the left-hand side, even numbers, like this:**

EVEN			ODD
End Sheet			End Sheet
Title Spread	2	3	Title Spread
Theme, Contents	4	5	Theme-Intro
Theme-Intro	6	7	Theme-Intro
Theme-Intro	8	9	Divider-Events
Events	10	11	Events
Events	12	13	Events
etc.			

V. **It is essential to make the earliest possible start on your book. Here are some suggestions of things to do first. (You may wish also to read an article by Mike Howard in the October 1972 *Photolith*, "How to Get Started.")**

A. Check past issues of your school's yearbook and understand the course past editors have followed. This is not with the idea of slavish imitation of old practices but rather of finding good traditions and practices on which to build. In a sense, the yearbook is one of a continuing series of reports, and you wish your own book to make full use of, pay full tribute to, whatever has gone before, while fitting your own story into the total story to date.

B. Study all available exchange and loan books (as you already have done in looking for thematic ideas).

C. Check past volumes of scholastic magazines. While my past experience as an editor and service director may have led me to turn more easily and frequently in this book to one major magazine source of ideas, there are three national organizations concerned with the yearbook and at least four scholastic-collegiate publications magazines that (in widely varying degree) deal with the yearbook and its problems. (See the list in "The Adviser and the Staff.")

D. Have full discussions with your school or college officials (principal, dean, director of publications, etc.) on philosophy, policies of the school, financial considerations, etc.

E. You will likely wish to go over the yearbook publishing and photography contracts with appropriate officials. It is to be hoped that the adviser, the editor, and the business manager have been involved in the preparation and signing of these important agreements, though such is not universal practice, I am afraid. *(Be sure to read all the fine print.)*

F. Plan an early subscription campaign (see Chapter 15) and a perhaps earlier advertising sales program (see Chapter 14).

G. Consult with both the publisher (actually, the printer) and the commercial photographer to see what help each can provide and what each expects from staff, editor, manager, and adviser. Many customary and expected things are always found in the contract. Emphases on deadlines vary and should be spelled out clearly. So should penalties for lateness, the actual cost of extras—pages, color, special art, etc. You may find that your printer has far more to offer you via consultation and materials than you have expected or known. The photographer may be able to help guide the photo staff or help with development of prints beyond anything given in a written contract. He may even be willing to do some special group pictures not actually specified in the portrait agreements.

H. Learn names and addresses of associations and services and plan now to make full use of them. Let me at this time refer you to "The Adviser and the Staff" in the first part of this book for more detailed suggestions that are applicable to planning the book and to carrying through those plans.

Pictorial Examples

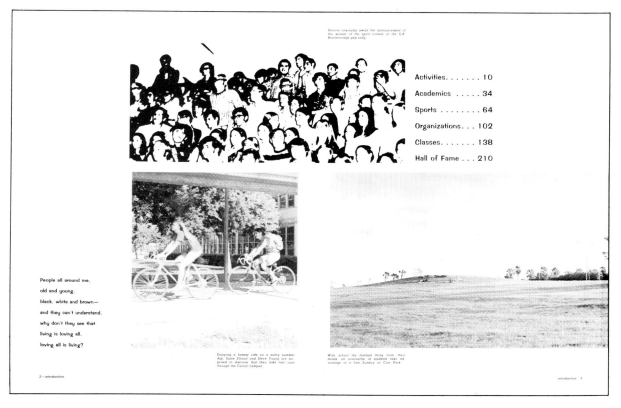

Fig. 2.1—Table of contents from the *Anchor*, of Mary Carroll High School, Corpus Christi, Texas, illustrates a standard method of organizing a yearbook. Pictures show students in local scenes. Polarized photography and copy introduce the book.

Fig. 2.2—*Power*, San Carlos High, California, combines sports, events, and studies into a seasonal plan of coverage. Clubs, portraits, and advertisements have their separate sections.

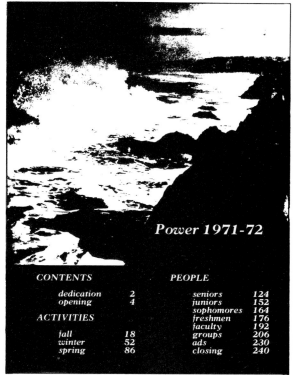

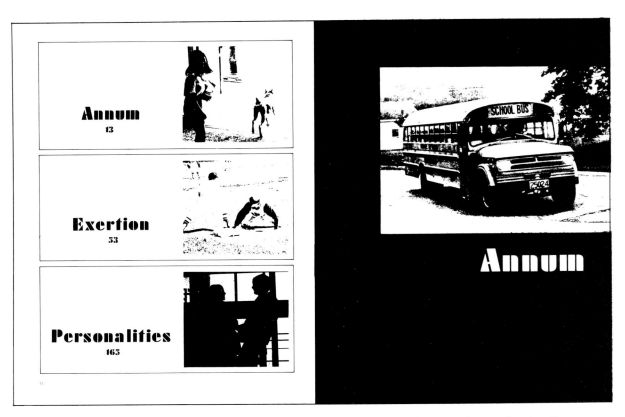

Fig. 2.3—A modern trend toward using fewer, larger sections is indicated by this contents page and accompanying division page from an *Elkonian,* Centerville, Ohio, High School. Sectional titles merely hint at contents.

Exercises

1. After discussion, formulate a ladder for your yearbook based on either standard order or your own thematic variation. (Note that you need not denote the subject of each page or spread as long as you indicate that pages_____through_____will be given, say, to class portraits, clubs, etc.)

Page	Page
	1.
2.	3.
4.	5.
6.	7.
etc.	

2. Explain how the reader will find your pages that cover specific clubs and individual departments or classes if you follow chronological or seasonal order.
3. Assuming a combination of academic clubs with academics, list the names of the subjects and related organizations.
4. Assuming this same combination, tell how you would cover remaining clubs.
5. Assuming a seasonal or chronological order, tell how you would place various subjects, organizations, and publications. If there is a seeming violation of logic in your solution, explain why.
6. Argue the case for or against placing static group shots at the end of the book.
7. Make two lists: one at the left for clubs that are dynamic and active and should, in your opinion, be placed in the "action" part of your yearbook; one at the right for clubs that deserve picturing as groups, perhaps, because they have strong places in the traditions of your school but are almost totally inactive and actually contribute little or nothing to the life or the welfare of the school at large. Be willing to debate

controversial listings and to come to a group decision before making a final staff placement of all organizations.

8. Write in outline form your own suggestion as to how the index needs to be assembled, starting with the first day of production.

9. Leaving out any consideration of the chronological order of arrangement, write in outline form your own preference of the order of the parts of the book, one that is reasonably traditional but not necessarily in accordance with the order given in the text portion of this chapter.

10. Assuming a standard, "vanilla-style" organization, list four or five variations or special arrangements inside sections that would give punch to your book. (Suggestion: Review all illustrations given in the text and pictorial sections of this chapter and in available exchange books. Then think how you might do clubs differently with little change in the order of the sections and what you might do to portrait sections that is out of the usual or ordinary.)

3.
Design
and
Layout
Patterns

I. **Let's consider our terms first.**

    A. *Layout* means the plan you use in laying out pages of your book.

    B. *Design,* whether as a verb or a noun, carries the special meaning of artistic or skillful planning, according to American dictionaries, whereas *layout,* or the verb, *to lay out,* carries more of the connotation of workmanlike planning and performance, without special reference to art or even skill.

    C. For those seriously studying and using this text as you lay out your book, I strongly urge the use of your utmost skill, even high art, in all your plans, and I hope that you will never settle for the drab essentials as stated in the dictionary definitions. Plan to make the yearbook layout as imaginative and creative as you are capable of producing.

II. **The common unit of the yearbook layout is the two-page spread. Exceptional single pages must be designed vertically. These include title pages, dividers, and the sign-off or acknowledgment page.**

III. **Elements to be considered in most layout planning include pictures and art (the yearbook is first of all a picture book); type—headlines, body copy, and cutlines; and the white space, which serves to frame other elements, to provide added emphasis, and to give relief to the eyes from heavy type or pictorial art.**

IV. **In laying out a unit, arrange elements for the most satisfying or pleasing appearance, the greatest readability of word content, and the greatest harmony or simplicity. When I say all this, I am well aware that I am talking in generalities, that judgment and good taste are not given to all persons and in fact must be cultivated by those originally endowed with the qualities.**

    A. Staffs having one or two leaders gifted with the artistic eye, with discriminating taste, and with a well-honed sense of orderliness and unity have treasure beyond all that can be packed into a volume of art principles.

B. When the "plan" shows up too clearly, intrudes into the reader's consciousness to the point that the story line is lost, your layout is a bad one. Remember the adage: "Form follows function."

V. Keep your pictures almost exclusively rectangular.

A. Avoid squares, circles, ovals, and most if not all slants.
B. If you do slant pictures or even employ a rare circle be sure you make the use functional. Let the new shape serve to move the eye in the direction you intend, not obstruct clear visibility of subjects or easy reading in any way.
C. Avoid exotic trimming of pictures into the shapes of stars, moons, footballs, basketballs, and the like.
D. Avoid posing of groups into special arrangements like those the band may form at the half of a ball game, such as musical clefs or letters. And avoid cutting out heads and placing them inside such art designs (those of star football players at the points of a drawn star, etc.).
E. Outlining a picture (cutting out backgrounds and leaving heads and top parts of bodies, for instance) may serve as occasional emphasis for your layout and may give the "dominance" discussed later in this chapter. But when you multiply such devices, you lose rather than gain effectiveness.
F. Layout specialists tell us the vertical form is more dynamic than the horizontal. Use of a vertical picture to contrast with a horizontal one adds vigor to a layout. All-horizontal pictures make for a less dynamic effect. The more they are squeezed down or made arrowlike, the greater the sense of movement.

VI. Type sizes and column widths must be carefully selected for good layout.

A. In most families and styles, 10-point regular type makes excellent body size. In some special types, 9 point or 11 point may be preferred because of variations of design.

B. Make cutlines distinctive from body type. If body is 10 point, for instance, cutlines can be in 8 point. Italic style, boldface, or all-capital type in the same size as body is occasionally used.
C. On the 9 × 12-inch page, minimum column width (approximately 10 point) is about 2¼ inches or 14 picas. On a smaller page, the minimum width is sometimes dropped to 2 inches.
D. Standard maximum column width in body type is 3½ inches (21 ems). Only when the type is 12 or 14 point, as is the case sometimes for special messages, may the width rule be relaxed.
E. Good layout permits use of either a clean sans serif or a Roman for body type, though those more concerned with readability insist that types with serifs (Romans or italics) are easier to read.
F. Body type should not be bold or heavy, since substantial blocks of such type tire the reader and also compete unduly with pictures for first attention. For the same reason, beware also the excessive use of italic type.
G. Don't mix italics and boldface in your body type.
H. Don't use all-capital style for emphasis. One usage, preferably italic or, secondarily, boldface, suffices.
I. Don't run body type around pictures. Appearance and readability are both weakened by this arrangement often found in newspapers and magazines.
J. Count cutlines so that they do not leave "widows" (less than half-line at the end, though sometimes defined more strictly as a quarter-line or less).
K. If body type runs to the top of a column from a preceding column, make sure the first line at the top of the column is more than a half-line long. (Less than a respectable length here is also known as a widow.) You need not worry about so-called widows at the ends of paragraphs of body type, except in this one case.
L. To avoid widows, you must learn to count units of your type. A common way of counting is to consider most small letters, capital *I*, and all numbers but 1 as a single count; most capitals and small *m* and *w*, 1½; punctuation marks, the number 1, letters *l, i, j,* and *t* as ½. Capitals *W* and *M* are

counted as two units. Another way of arriving at a dependable average is to count units and average them for 25 to 50 lines of your own special type.

M. Keep paragraph lengths reasonable. Break them in wide columns on an average of every 5 lines, in narrower columns every 5 to 7 lines. Indent 3 counts for a paragraph beginning. Spacing out between paragraphs is a more wasteful method.

N. Cutline blocks follow the same general rules of width as body blocks, except that 8-point columns may be as narrow as 2 inches without looking too thin. One or two lines of cutline may violate the 3½-inch rule, but break longer cutlines into two columns.

O. Never let a cutline extend beyond the edge of the picture right or left.

P. Maintain a consistent space between all pictures and their cutlines. One-eighth to 3/16 inch is acceptable. I personally like a 1-pica margin best of all. Avoid a crowded look or a gappy appearance.

VII. **Headlines are first of all intended to summarize their stories and to attract the reader's interest. But beyond the functional purpose, headline types have value in making pages attractive, in layout, that is:**

A. Typography experts suggest use of Modern Roman, a few Old Style Romans such as Century, Cheltenham, and Garamond, or sans serif types with strokes of medium weight in yearbook headlines.

B. Scripts; square serifs; cursives; very, very rarely Old English; and a few variety or novelty types may be used in spots to a limited degree. Any of those becomes monotonous if used a second time in a book. (These are illustrated in the pictorial section of this chapter.)

C. Book titles may run larger than any other, perhaps up to 72 point (1 inch), and division heads perhaps up to 30 or 36 point in standard type. These headings, being brief, may even be in expanded type and/or capital letters. Headings inside are rarely more than 30 point, more usually 24 point, sometimes as small as 18 point. All de-

pends on the nature of the type. Most types used in headlines above stories are in condensed style, since it is important to be able to get as many letters as possible into limited space.

D. Never violate an inside or outside margin with a headline. The head may cross a margin inside a page if it spreads to two or more columns.

E. Only a major headline, never a subhead or other type, either for a cutline or a body block, may bridge the gutter of the two-page spread.

F. In crossing the gutter, never split a word (even a compound) or carry only a single word across the gutter.

G. When crossing the gutter with a headline, use half the width of the margin on each of the facing pages, but no more than half. To use more space would be to endanger readability; to leave more would tend to create a gap.

H. The kicker above the headline should be two sizes smaller, as for example, 14 point for a 24-point headline.

I. The kicker line should be of the same family as the headline, or a type that blends pleasingly, like a plain sans serif for a clean Roman headline. (Not all type authorities will agree with me on the latter suggestion, but I like and have used the combination for many years.)

J. If you use a subhead or deck below the main headline, it must be of the same family as the headline and also noticeably smaller, as in the case of the kicker. I do not recommend any extensive use of decks and especially advise against ever using more than one deck in a yearbook.

K. For appearance as well as readability, I recommend placement of the headline above the story it covers or summarizes. Occasional variation is permissible, such as placing the headline alongside the story, to the left of, or very rarely below, the story. But always make the headline adjoin its story.

L. Avoid setting headline type vertically, diagonally, or in wavy or broken lines. Such patterns add neither beauty nor readability. (See discussion of eye-direction later in this chapter.)

M. Prefer the downstyle in headlines, capitalizing the first word and all proper nouns and adjectives, but no others.

1. Avoid the ludicrous stylism of "e. e. cummings" the poet, since it makes reading harder, draws undue attention to typography rather than the purpose of it all, communication.
2. Also avoid, for both appearance and readability, the all-capital headline.
3. Don't imitate the freakish style practiced by at least two metropolitan newspapers, that of capitalizing *every* word in the headline, however small and unimportant. (Articles, conjunctions, and short prepositions are all capitalized in heads written in this style.)

(Rules about headlines that are based primarily on journalism and easy reading rather than on appearance and layout will be found in the appropriate chapter.)

VIII. Let's set up and observe rules about margins.

A. The outer margins serve as a frame for the picture and must be consistent to be effective and attractive.
  1. Outer margins are smallest at the center of the spread, since they double to form the gutter.
  2. Moving from the center, margins increase as they go: larger at the top; perhaps larger still, or at least the same, at the right or left; and widest at the bottom. (Example: center, $\frac{1}{4}$ inch; top, $\frac{3}{8}$ inch; right or left, $\frac{1}{2}$ inch; bottom, $\frac{5}{8}$ inch.)
  3. For the opening section, division pages, and the closing page, greater freedom is allowed in margins than inside the book, but even here, some consistency of format must be observed, and margins must not be wildly excessive.
  4. Inside the divisions of the book, on opening pages, the editor has leeway in setting top margins. Thus the headline or top of the lead picture might fall as far down as one-third page without offending art principles.
  5. Generally speaking, however, all other margins must be set and kept, though the lower margin of the final page of a section need not be precise. Don't try to pad in order to fill space here. (This page does look better when it is at least two-thirds filled.)
  6. Each outside margin must be substantially defined, established, or denoted at least once per side of the layout by a picture of moderate-to-large size or a heavy copy column or block. (A cutline touching the outside margin, for example, is not enough to constitute adequate marginal definition. A narrow column touching the lower margin is of questionable strength.)
B. Inner margins must also be consistent.
  1. Where pictures are clustered, as in mosaic, Mondrian, or modular, set an inner margin such as an em, or perhaps $\frac{1}{4}$ inch ($1\frac{1}{2}$ ems), and never deviate from it, at least not on the same layout or inside one division of the book.
  2. For news or magazine format (old-style) in which cutlines may come between the picture and the body block, set and keep regular margins between the picture and the cutline or ident (1 em is hard to beat) and again between the cutline and body type (this may be somewhat more, but don't let it become so great that what looks like an accidental gap appears). I personally have always liked to keep a regular distance between headline and body, something like $\frac{1}{4}$ inch, but the larger the headline type, the greater may be the distance here. The overline should be somewhat closer to the headline than the head to the story, such as 3/16 inch if the head and story are to be $\frac{1}{4}$ inch apart.
  3. Don't leave excessive or irregular margins inside. Large white gaps or holes tend to "explode" or destroy layout. Irregular margins inside give the justified impression of carelessness and disorder.
  4. Don't expect printers to do your planning of margins or space-outs, or leave things to chance. Chance is rarely happy in these cases, and printers are not paid to be editors.
C. In news or magazine format or design, each cutline is preferably placed be-

neath its picture. In Mondrian or mosaic design, cutlines are clustered.

    1. Try to place one block of cutlines on each page when there are a number of pictures on each page. Balance off the two blocks pleasingly.

    2. If you use ragged-edge or unjustified type, make the ragged edges lie away from the picture(s) and the even edges adjoin the picture(s) the cutline describes.

    3. There is no excuse for varying cutline-picture margins whimsically from one page to the next.

D. White space other than that serving for margins should be placed at corners, preferably outside, except as indicated for opening and closing pages of sections.

IX. Bleeds (elements, mostly pictures, extending to and through a margin to the edge, or across the gutter to the other page) are acceptable under these conditions and rules:

A. Most experts agree that one bleed per side of a layout is acceptable and that using any more becomes questionable form.

B. It is improper to bleed *part way* into the margin. (An exception is with the kind of headline that spreads across the center margins, which, as I have suggested above, does go halfway into each gutter margin.)

C. Only the greatest type experts can bleed *type* effectively. Leave the effort to the experts and to those with the budget to afford to hire them.

D. In allowing for a bleed in a picture, leave 1/8 inch, or perhaps 1 em, for needed trim space. (This is to be allowed in the reduced size of the picture, not the picture before reduction.)

E. Bleeds to the center of the page are less effective than other kinds, since they are stopped by the center fold.

F. In bleeding across the gutter, never allow parts of the face or other essential picture elements to be caught in the fold or binding.

G. In bleeding across the center, be sure enough of the picture carries across ("splashes," or "slops over," as an old friend of mine called it) that the bleed will not seem accidental or uncalled-for.

H. Don't bleed faces, parts of the head or scalp, or other body parts off the page.

I. It is a good rule never to bleed portraits or portrait blocks because of the danger, or rather likelihood, of trimming off parts of faces or scalps in the procedure.

J. Whether you are bleeding or not, **don't** face pictures off the page. (Exception: You might be intentionally showing seniors "marching off into the future," for instance, and thus having the line face off page would be proper and meaningful.)

K. Never bleed pictures together at the center. This gives an effect of a confusingly unmatched single picture.

L. Remember the rule about "defining" margins when you plan bleeds. Of course, if you bleed all the way out a side or all the way up or down vertically, this rule does not apply.

X. It is well for the amateur to learn some of the fundamental art or layout principles.

A. *Balance* is the best known of these.

    1. Newspaper makeup people understand best of all *formal* or *absolute balance*. In this, you divide the page (the layout unit, that is) in half horizontally. Place a picture or heavy type element (headline and body) at the right and balance it off exactly at the left with the same element. Proceed from there, making one side almost or entirely a mirror image of the left. This provides a convenient pattern for layout units like those club sections. In fact, yearbook editors formerly used formal balance in many or all sections of the book. It soon became monotonous and dull. The lack of imagination implied in such repetitiveness made many a yearbook a dreary volume. Some yearbooks have expired in recent years out of sheer monotony resultant from this sort of planning.

    2. Much better layout is *informal balance,* sometimes called *asymmetrical balance*. Elements are approximately balanced on the page, but

the weights are varied enough to offer an interesting combination. Some points to consider in doing informal balance:

a. Pictures at the top of the page are heavier than those at the bottom.

b. The farther a picture is from the center or fulcrum, the more weight it has; the nearer to the fulcrum, the weaker it is.

c. Heavy picture or type tones weigh more than light ones. An average picture generally outweighs type blocks, which as a rule carry lighter visual tones.

d. Because of the principle of eye-direction, discussed later, a picture at the right will outdraw one of equal size and tone at the left.

e. Color pictures also outweigh black-and-white pictures.

f. Vertical shapes are more dynamic than horizontals.

g. Slim rectangles, horizontal or vertical, have greater movement than do rectangles that approach the square in proportions. A square, like a circle, has no motion or dynamic pull at all, makes for poor balance, and weakens layout.

B. *Eye-direction* indicates the way a layout directs the eye. Natural eye-direction (particularly for readers of English) is left to right.

1. What typographical authorities call the primary optical area (POA) is the upper left corner of the layout unit being designed.

a. The deadest area or terminal area is at the bottom right.

b. Some of those who do newspaper makeup have long asserted that the right-hand top position is the most important spot, and that the main story therefore belongs at the right on page 1.

c. For yearbook layout, logic suggests that the point of greatest interest should be top left, and that the main picture belongs there.

d. Whatever is the case, if the reader's eye finds nothing of great interest at POA, it will slide naturally across to right top and thence down and around till it finds the main body of type, if there is one. (See "Dominance" below for more discussion of this.)

2. Pictures having greatest optical interest or drawing power are the first elements in layout.

3. Since type should follow natural eye movement, left to right, diagonal and vertical type (up-down or down-up) should be avoided. So should wavy lines of type, as mentioned earlier.

4. Placement of pictures should lead the reader in the direction you intend him to read, usually left to right, then down, then back and up, though counterclockwise layout is by no means unusual and can be effectively planned.

C. *Alignment,* which works closely with the principle of eye-direction and may even be considered a corollary, is the practice of placing pictures and/or type so that tops of prints or body blocks lie on the same line, as do sides of both, and where practical, bottoms as well.

1. Variations in alignment are allowable where they do not cause art principles to be violated.

2. Thus white areas at the corners of layouts are perfectly allowable, even though alignment may seem to be violated in the process of leaving these "relief" spots.

3. Obviously, the quality of alignment helps attain evenness of inside margins as recommended earlier.

4. Raggedness, as opposed to alignment, gives the appearance of careless planning, distracting the reader from the material to which he should be paying his full attention.

D. *Unity* in the yearbook applies as much to appearance as to the content of pictures and type. This quality makes all parts of the spread, the section, and the book go together harmoniously.

1. Openers, dividers, and closing pages will have a similarity, and in turn, will blend with, though not look precisely like, inside pages.

2. Inside pages of the various sections will all go together in a way to suggest that the entire book was planned by one staff, and that one

editor supervised the entire production. (There is never any nonsense such as "I turned each section over to an editor and gave each one absolute independence of action.") Even where different patterns, as discussed later, are employed in various sections, a method is used to tie all into a common package.

3. On spreads and individual units, informal balance builds unity.

    a. So does the technique known as "spread-linkage," in which the gutter at the center is bridged by a large piece of art, or by a photograph (perhaps the "dominant photo" mentioned below), or by a headline that spreads across the two pages.

    b. Still another method of linking pages is by the "echo" method. A large picture at top right or top left is echoed or mirrored in shape and content by a far smaller picture at the opposite lower position.

4. Throughout the book, a unifying element is the theme idea or motif design.

5. Again, for the whole book, adopting and using a single family of good headline type makes for unity of the book. (Use of proper type and proper sizes is discussed elsewhere.)

E. *Variety* is in a sense the reverse of unity, but it serves to preserve unity by saving it from monotony.

1. The informal balance already discussed is in itself achieved through variation of sizes and shapes of pictures, within the framework of rectangular design for the most part.

2. Dominance, the next layout principle discussed, depends on variety of picture sizes to make it an effective principle.

3. Use of the vertical shape to contrast with prevailing horizontals gives emphasis through variety, just as narrowing horizontals (see discussions under "Balance") create dynamic flow and move the eye along through a variety of shapes. (All verticals or all-alike thin horizontals would be as ineffectual in layout as a collection of exclamation or question marks is useless in editorial style.)

F. *Dominance* is the most important principle of layout, or one of the most important ones. That is why it deserves this final position. As the saying goes, "The eye seeks first the one thing highest on the page or layout."

1. Top left or top right, depending on your preference, is the natural place on the layout for the "dominant" element, usually art, and most usually in yearbooks photographic art.

2. The second picture must never be more than two-thirds the size of the dominant picture, or at least must never have the effect of a 2-to-3 relationship in strength. (Darker or lighter tones and static shaping both affect strength, as does actual size.)

3. The entire left-hand or right-hand page, or a "splashover" picture taking one full page and as much as one-third of the second of a spread, certainly constitutes a dramatic dominant photo and is effective especially on opening and division pages and perhaps closing pages or spreads.

4. A sequence of pictures, together making up a small picture story, may be designed as a unit and so considered. Similarly, a cluster of related pictures may be combined into a unit. Either picture group may then be the dominant art for a layout.

XI. A number of special design patterns have been useful in yearbook layout. Let's look at some of them.

A. The old-timer in the group has been called *news* layout by one writer in the field of yearbook design. Actually, this is the standard old form that magazine and yearbook editors favored for many years:

1. It may carry one big picture, usually at the top.

2. There is always a large quantity of type that, with its "art," fills pages top to bottom in all columns. Type comes inside as a rule, not, as in the clustered-picture patterns, outside the art.

3. There is no effort to relieve the lay-

out with white space, or at least not at corners, though a story may start as low as one-third page down.

4. No special effort is made to keep inner margins even, though editors try not to leave such large gaps inside as to disrupt layout and make the reader uneasy.

5. Cutlines generally go beneath their pictures, but they may, for convenience, sometimes lie above or even alongside. They are usually immediately adjacent, that is, one cutline by one picture. (Exception: When art is doubled up, the cutlines may themselves be doubled up and placed at top, bottom, or even between the two.)

6. Other than cited in the exception above, pictures are never grouped or clustered.

7. This pattern relies heavily on spread-linkage, either headline or art or both crossing the gutter to unify the spread.

B. *Columnar* layout is useful for standardizing type columns. It works well in combination with news patterns, or in fact with any of the designs discussed here. While there are a number of acceptable columnar patterns, such as 3 column, 2 column (regular), 2 column uneven, the commonest is 2 column. Here is how to plan this type of columnar pattern:

1. Set a column width, and don't let it exceed 3½ inches (21 picas).

2. Establish standard outside margins (see discussion above) and decide on an inner margin width such as the ever-acceptable 1 pica.

3. All body type may now be set for this 21-pica width, and headlines will be written accordingly to cover one column or the full page (that is, to fill 2 columns) or perhaps will spread across the gutter to cover a story that runs across.

4. Pictures may be planned for a single column, for 1½ columns, for 2 columns, or now and then for spreading across one page to the other. (Be sure a bleed or splashover runs at least a half column, or even a full column, into the next page. "Thumbnailing" a tiny portion of a picture across looks accidental.)

5. A 21-pica width cutline will serve well for all pictures, since the minimum width is to be 21 picas. If you should adopt 3-column layout, with pictures as narrow as 14 picas (or approximately), two widths might work better, 14 picas and 21 picas. Never go beyond two widths for your book. Remember that *no cutline may ever be spread across the gutter.*

C. The *mosaic* pattern has been around for a number of years in yearbook planning. It built to a climax of acceptance in or about 1970 and has continued to enjoy wide favor among editors.

1. In mosaic, pictures are clustered together at the center of the spread and the layout begins, like most good ones, with a dominant photo at the top, which may or may not spread across the gutter.

2. When it is finished, usually with from three to five pictures, the mosaic pattern displays a clear, informal effect, with variation of picture sizes. Outer margins, except for deliberate bleeds, are inviolate, and inner margins are identical and modest, never gapingly wide.

3. Cutlines are clustered in two blocks, as a rule one on a page, with no cutline too far from its picture. Cutline blocks are pleasingly balanced against each other across the layout. Ample room is left for the headline and story.

4. Surplus white space is left at the corners, with allowance already stated for lowering the top margin or varying the bottom margin in special cases.

D. *Mondrian* (named for a design originated by an artist of the early part of this century) is a form often confused with mosaic and similar to it. It is produced like this:

1. Avoiding the geometric center of the layout both vertically and horizontally, draw two intersecting straight lines, one vertical, one horizontal. Obviously, the vertical line will never coincide with the gutter, and thus pictures will not, as in mosaic, actually cluster at the exact center.

2. Subdivide any or all areas, always

using horizontal-vertical lines to make areas for pictures and type.

3. It is recommended that one vertical line and one horizontal line be left to extend uninterrupted from side to side, top to bottom, preferably the original lines. Now plan your art and blocks inside the areas you have delineated.

4. Allow and dummy four or five pictures, remembering rules for leaving the dominant picture at the top, making it half again as large as the next largest picture, etc.

5. Mondrian style permits use of some of the layout areas for type. It is my own recommendation that copy blocks and heads be given outside position, perhaps even outside the so-called Mondrian design itself.

E. *Modular* pattern may owe its origin to the now defunct *Life* and *Look* magazines, both of which had excellent overall design.

1. The pattern of modular layout is a large and relatively narrow rectangle. Headlines and, usually, stories will lie outside.

2. The "module" may lie across the spread, left to right, and may bleed or not, as the designer prefers.

3. Alternately, the pattern lies vertically *along and on both sides* of the gutter, and again it may bleed *top and bottom,* at *top or at bottom,* or *not at all.*

4. Break the big rectangle into rectangular subdivisions. These may range from three to six, and the shape of the large dominant photo may determine whether your pattern will be vertical or horizontal.

5. As with Mondrian, you may use one or more areas for copy, though this is not always easy to do with the greatest orderliness or tonal evenness. (One occasional technique is to reverse type on 100 percent screen in one of the middle-sized rectangles.)

6. Modular patterns have been effectively used for openers, dividers, and closing pages, especially when other pages of the book are designed with another modern pattern like mosaic or Mondrian. There is suitable contrast, yet enough similarity that unity is not disrupted.

F. These are only the major patterns that occur to me at this time. Other forms are being invented every year, and some have no doubt been developed since I began assembling material for this book. Some other ideas that may or may not be of value include these:

1. The author of a recent layout book mentioned one pattern that is really a variation of mosaic. It is *pinwheel,* and the shape is developed by dropping one picture area on each side to or near the margin or off the page, away from the line of other pictures on the side or top and bottom. This pattern makes it difficult to find room for copy, cutlines, and headline.

2. *Doric* layout was suggested in an article of a few years ago by Adviser Ron Phillips of Black Hills State College (*Photolith,* October 1971). It is distinctive in that it depends entirely on vertical shapes running across the layout unit, left to right. The originators thought that the design looked like Greek Doric columns. The form is a bit complex and would work mostly to set off division and other thematic pages. As far as I know, it has had very limited acceptance to date.

3. *Montage* is a form suggested by Jim Rodman Lowe in a book named *Contemporary Layout Design.* In it, a large picture, full-page or bleeding across to the second page, is set in contrast with what the author calls a montage of three to six smaller pictures arranged mosaically across the spread.

4. *Isolated element* is like montage except that here one picture is pulled from its Mondrian, mosaic, or other pattern and reduced in size, perhaps changed in shape, and moved across the spread for a special effect. Balance is achieved here by placing the small element farther out from the "fulcrum," in the manner of the similar "echo" technique previously mentioned.

5. *Skyline* is a development of the mid-seventies, allowing elements of type and photography to violate the top margin, creating the effect of a city's skyline. Like most variations from standard form, this pattern

requires application of an artistic eye to be successful.

6. *High profile* is another recent adaptation to yearbook usage. In planning it, the layout editor or artist increases the lower margin dramatically, though keeping it fully defined. He may make the upper part of the layout distinctive while actually defining the margin at least once.

XII. Color has much to do with appearance and thus in layout in the modern yearbook. See what your printer suggests and can offer. But keep these facts in mind:

A. To be effective, a second color must blend with other colors used in the book. Get help from someone who knows color combinations and consult a color chart before making firm decisions.

B. Using too much color does nothing but add to your cost without beautifying. Some authorities say that more than two touches of the second color on a page are per se excessive.

C. Throwing together three or perhaps four colors, even if they are relatively congenial, does not assure added beauty commensurate with added cost. The result may be a clown's suit where you hoped for formal beauty.

D. If your budget will permit a four-color process, be sure that the place you intend to use it fully justifies the added emphasis. And be sure your four-color photography is of the best quality before investing in color separation and the added press runs that are required.

E. If you purchase a second color, be sure to plan so that you get the most possible advantage out of it. *Remember that you have access to the second color on four to eight pages of the signature* (depending on the method of the run) *for little or no cost above what the color costs on the very first page.*

F. And finally, if your budget will not stand added color, remember that action photography, well planned and in strong black and white, is hard to beat for effectiveness of layout or overall appearance.

XIII. In the limited space of a chapter, it is impossible to discuss or even mention all aspects of layout and design as they apply to a yearbook. Let me mention or, in some cases, emphasize a few points that bear strongly on layout and design:

A. Don't let the printer fill out a headline to the full width desired by leading it out. The result is confusing and unattractive, as a rule. (The way to avoid this is to write heads to fit the intended space.)

An editor with room for 24 counts tried to get by with this:

52 on Honor Roll

The printer, with all good intent, spread it to fit, like this:

52 on Honor Roll

The editor should have written it more like this:

52 Listed on Honor Roll

B. Similarly, don't ask the printer, or allow him, to lead out a body block that was intended to fill a certain space but did not run long enough. (The solution here is obvious: Write copy to fill space, or redummy the page so that less copy is needed. Sometimes this can be achieved by moving a picture inward, leaving surplus white space at a corner.)

C. And above all, don't write so much copy for a dummied spot that the printer must set the copy in a smaller type, or as my old newspaper printer used to threaten my staff, "set it in rubber type and compress it." All body blocks, it seems obvious, should be set in type of the same size.

D. Beware the temptation to use clumsy hand-lettering. This is in the same category as clumsy or even relatively neat cartoons, which I have discussed fully in the first chapter. If you need something fancy in a type face, consult the printer. If he cannot argue you out of it, at least he will likely find a face that can be printed and will not look like something done by doodlers or amateurs. (Reread in Chapter 1 what has already been said about cartoons and amateur drawings, sketchings, etc.)

E. Avoid (for about the same reason) re-producing logos of clubs, titles from mastheads of other publications, etc.

F. Crowded pages may seem more economical, but for better effect, select material with greater care and trim art and edit copy with discrimination to allow more room to breathe, especially at corners.

G. The same caution as the one given immediately above applies to individual pictures: *A limited number of subjects are more interesting than a mob,* unless the object of the picture is to show a mass of persons in a hall, at a ball game, etc. Crowded pictures generally make for bad layout.

H. Avoid distant and indistinct pictures.

I. You can enhance layout as well as interest by placing action pictures on opening pages and in early sections of the book or at the tops of individual spreads, and static group shots at the end of the book or in the least conspicuous places on layouts. (This point is fully discussed elsewhere, perhaps more than the average reader might wish.)

J. Give portrait spreads increased appeal by using lively action pictures in prominent spots.

K. Do the same for the index section itself.

L. Look for other methods of relief of dullness in reference pages and portraits spreads: headlines and variation in size and shape of portrait blocks are two suggestions. But your imagination can come up with others.

M. Avoid cap-and-gown pictures for seniors, and use rectangular shaping for all portraits, never oval.

(Note: As stated above, some of these points will be discussed in more detail in later chapters.)

Typographic and Pictorial Examples

Fig. 3.1—Typography.

A. Type to show the groups

ROMAN (Old Style): **Curriculum Changes Mark Year**

ROMAN (Modern): **Service Clubs Aid Child-care Centers**

SANS SERIF: **Bears sweep district in tennis**

SCRIPT: *Pen Valley Club*

CURSIVE: *It was a year to remember*

SQUARE SERIF: **Historical Notes**

OLD ENGLISH: **Memories**

30

NOVELTY TYPES: **LEADERSHIP** LEADERSHIP
LEADERSHIP LEADERSHIP

B. Type for proper and improper headline styles

TWO STYLES COMMONLY USED

1. Up-down (everything capitalized but "weak words" like short pronouns and occasional articles):

**Ecology Club Joins with East End Lions
In Planning an All-community Cleanup Drive**

2. Downstyle
nouns capi
letters):

STYLES NOT GENERALLY RECOMMENDED

1. All capitals:

BASKETBALL TEAM WINS CITY RACE

2. All lower case:

**junior civitans, civenettes unite
form single bhs citizens club**

style (first letters of *all* words capitalized):

niors Cast In All The Key Roles

After being ripped up to the net Herman (82) James, Fort (84) and Eskew Moore (83) close in on an Eastside ball carrier (right).

Below: After making a long run Steve Arnold (78) is hauled down by an Eastside defender.

Bottom: After a full season of use varsity football equipment hangs in place until next year's practice begins.

VARSITY

The Greenwood Eagles flew by Parker 35-0. A strong Eagle offense crossed the goal line five times during the game. The Tornadoes record fell to 0-8.

ENDS

Parker's ninth loss came by the hands of the Eastside Eagles 21-7 in the annual Homecoming game. Parker lead 7-0 at the end of the first quarter but a strong Eastside offense scored 21 straight points to hand Parker the defeat.

PERFECT

In the battle for last place the Tornadoes lost again to Hillcrest, 10-0. The Parker offense couldn't muster any sort of drive against a strong Hillcrest defense.

SEASON

Parker ended a perfect season by losing to Greenville 21-0. A strong Raider offense gave Greenville a three touchdown lead after three quarters.

The Tornadoes then started a drive at their own eighteen. On first and ten Steve Arnold attempted a pass to Allan Childress that fell incomplete.

Following an argument over a pass interference call, a fight broke out. After the field was cleared the ancient rivalry was called with 8:33 showing on the clock. This ended a long, dull season for the Golden Tornadoes of Parker.

VARSITY FOOTBALL
0-11

PARKER		OPP
7	Byrnes	3
0	Carolina	2
	Easley	

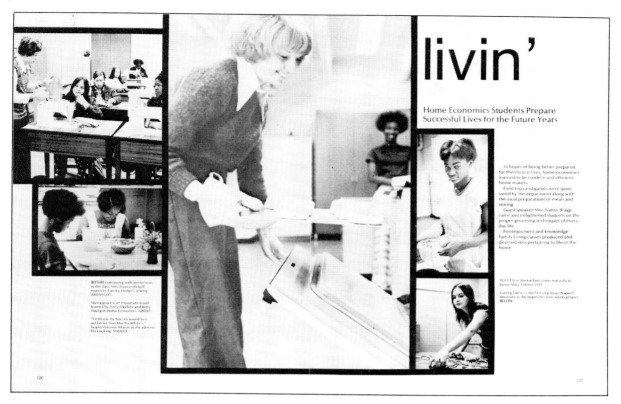

Fig. 3.9—Experiments in patterning, such as the uneven design seen here, have become relatively common in modern school and college yearbooks. These pages from the 1974 *Parkerscope,* Green-ville, South Carolina, might be designated "sky-line" layout. The black borders recall early Mondrian art. Strong photography gives sup-port to dramatic design. (Courtesy NSY/NA.)

Exercises

1. Discuss this suggestion: "If one star or slanted picture or outlined picture is ap-pealing, then it is obvious that as many as 25 such shapings on a page or spread will be many times as attractive." (Hint: Com-pare the above idea with the suggestion that if one aspirin helps relieve a headache, 25 might well provide a permanent cure against all headaches. Or that if hearing a funny joke once is amusing, hearing the same one 25 times would be many times as hilarious.)

2. Discuss the use of all-boldface type for the body in a yearbook.

3. Select a typeface in 8 point. Take three cut-line widths—14 picas, 21 picas, and 29 picas —and determine the maximum count for single lines. Use the type found in last year's book in your school, or use Century Schoolbook (a plain, readable, rather ex-panded type). One typesetter says that 2.89 counts of the Century Schoolbook he offers go in each pica. (Remember, in computing lines from last year's book, the counts given in the main section of this chapter are ac-curate enough. Review them.)

4. Take 10-point body type for 14-pica and 21-pica column widths. The same typogra-pher mentioned above sets 2.5 counts per pica of Century Schoolbook. What does this figure per 14-pica and 21-pica columns? Use at least 10 inches of body copy from last year's book for each computation and determine the maximum count for 14-pica and 21-pica columns. (If last year's book had columns of different widths, you may have to do some intelligent improvising.)

5. Measure the margins of last year's book. How do they compare with suggestions made above? What margins do you suggest for the book you are now planning?

6. Take the headline style used in last year's book on inside pages and count average units of width for 14-pica, 21-pica, 29-pica, and 44-pica heads. Use the same allowable counts per unit as in body type, except that in most types you may need to allow ¾

count for *l*, *t*, and maybe *j*, rather than ½ count. Variation per column should be figured at no more than 2 counts; that is, if maximum is 18 counts, the range is 16 to 18.

7. Plan a *mosaic* layout, with no more than four pictures. Let the first picture spread across from top right or left to occupy at least half the opposite page horizontally. Let it occupy somewhat more or somewhat less than half the depth of the layout. (Avoid exact division.) The second picture must not be larger than ⅔ the size of the dominant photo. Leave space on the outside for headline, body, and cutlines. Set and observe carefully an inner margin of no more than ¼ inch. Observe the principle of alignment at all times (see above). From an old magazine or newspaper, cut two 21-pica columns or three 14-pica columns, a 24-point to 30-point headline (¼ inch to 5/16 inch deep) for the purpose of your dummy, and two 14-pica cutlines, each approximately ¾ inch deep.

   Now ask yourself these questions:
   a. Have I bridged the gap with my dominant photo fully enough that the effect does not seem accidental and is more than a mere "thumbnail"?
   b. Is the dominant photo, as planned, worthy of its position by its nature? Is it at the top of the layout? Is it 1½ times the size of the next largest photo?
   c. Does the variety of sizes of pictures seem pleasing, or is there a sameness in effect among lesser pictures?
   d. Do pictures align properly? How about type and top picture?
   e. If you have bled any picture or pictures, have you properly allowed for full bleed, including trim? Are you sure there are no pictures or type blocks that butt into margins?
   f. Does your layout give the appearance of informal balance now that it is finished? Have you left surplus white space at corners, *not* inside?

8. Following the directions for *Mondrian* layout given above, produce a layout with either four or six major areas. (To make six areas, you will draw one vertical or horizontal line through to both edges of a layout, bisecting two of the original four areas, though not necessarily in exact halves.) Be careful not to disturb plans and positioning of the dominant photo. Use pictures and type clipped from old publications, or sketch in art and line in type.

9. Repeat the above exercise, using one of these patterns: *news, modular,* or *columnar.* (You are allowed to experiment with another format, with the teacher-adviser's approval.)

10. Mark the following *T* or *F*. Feel free to refer to the text. Time yourself and put time for completing the exercise at the top of the "test."

Score: _____ *Time:* _____ *Min.*

   a. _____ All layout forms are set and final, allowing no variation or experimentation.
   b. _____ The more color you can afford to use, the more attractive the book will be.
   c. _____ When you have space left over inside, the best filler is a cartoon.
   d. _____ Since the yearbook is educational, hand-lettering and art are preferable to printer's type and photography.
   e. _____ The more people you can crowd into a picture and the more pictures to a page, the better your book will be.
   f. _____ Write copy blocks short so that printer will space out, leaving air between lines.
   g. _____ You, not the printer, are responsible for fitting headlines to space.
   h. _____ Try to get a nice doughnout hole in the center of your layout.
   i. _____ Reproductions of newspaper type and pictures add to the beauty of the book.
   j. _____ The alert editor throws in an abundance of ovals, slants, stars, and other exotic shapes to relieve stodgy rectangles.
   k. _____ Informal pictures clutter up portrait sections and distract from the formal pictures. Avoid them like sin.
   l. _____ It is a sign of backwardness and lack of imagination when you rely on black-and-white pictures in this "age of color." Borrow at the bank if you need to, but have color.
   m. _____ Modular layout is recommended for division pages.
   n. _____ Columnar layout allows a wide variety of column widths on every spread.
   o. _____ A "widow" is a short line at the end of a paragraph and must be avoided at all costs.
   p. _____ Cutline "widows," while common, indicate that the staff failed to take time to count units.
   q. _____ It is a sign of wastefulness ever to leave white space unused.
   r. _____ A dominant photo can go anywhere on the page with equal logic.
   s. _____ Absolute balance is the best balance of all.
   t. _____ Standard margins generally allow the largest space at the bottom of a layout.

4.
Editorial Content

IT SEEMS obvious enough, but it needs to be said again: In the yearbook as in all media, the first purpose of words is to communicate ideas, whether in titles, running heads, standard headlines; in commentary inside thematic pages; in body blocks or story; or in identifications, captions, or cutlines.

In the preceding chapter on layout, I have discussed the typographical units that constitute the form of words. Now, even at the risk of repeating points already made, let's consider the primary role words play—that of communicating with your readers.

I. A yearbook worthy of its name must have a story in words. The story is in copy blocks (justified type, unjustified, ragged edge, poetic style, or standard prose). Copy will normally appear on all spreads, with these exceptions and special allowances:

   A. Opening thematic pages, though a running story here normally adds strength to coverage. This running story may be in staccato or headline style.

   B. Dividers definitely need at least intro copy, though leeway is far greater for the format used here. Staccato, poetic, or even running headline style is acceptable, in declining order of preference. (See Chapter 7.)

   C. For a variation technique, but definitely not for regular use, an occasional picture story can be fully told in accompanying cutlines.

II. Copy for the yearbook is normally brief while yet covering periods of time up to 12 months. It must follow established journalistic principles of good newspaper-magazine writing. The stories will more nearly resemble news features or regular feature stories than actual news, since the yearbook almost never actually breaks spot news.

   A. Stories for the yearbook may be gathered and written at a far more leisurely pace than those for either the newspaper or the magazine. Staff members should be expected to take the greatest care in gathering news, in writing their stories, and in checking for accuracy, whether of fact or of spellings, punctuation, or grammar. Editors and advisers should both instruct staffs and insist that they follow established procedures as carefully as airline pilots or skilled electricians apply their respective skills.

B. Avoid rehashing of old stories, use of historical data, and recitation of aims, goals, purposes, or mottoes, unless such material is very subtly tied into the current year's story.

C. Limit editorial comments and opinions mostly if not entirely to the opening and closing pages. At the start, the editor may reveal plans, discuss the theme, and generally be as subjective as he or she wishes. In the closing, it is appropriate to acknowledge those who have been of service to the editor and staff, and to round out the theme appropriately. Here are some cautions and supplementary points:

1. It is best to avoid evaluative statements or superlatives in regard to clubs and organizations as well as people. You do nothing but embarrass a teacher (and you certainly do not endear yourself and the staff to other teachers) by calling one favorite "the most popular" or "the best teacher in school." And it is best to leave it to an evaluative agency to determine which organization is "the most valuable club in school" or has "done most for the school."

2. The same rule applies to statements that "our school" has more "school spirit"—whatever that intangible is—or any other unmeasurable quality, except as attributed inside quotation marks to someone willing to garner local favor at the expense of sounding silly. And go slow in saying that you have the "best" principal, the "most successful" or "most understanding" superintendent.

3. If the sports editor feels compelled to express personal opinions about the various seasons, the coaches, the effect of weather, officiating, youth—or whatever—on the course and the outcome of a season, he must use a byline either at the beginning of the story or as a signature at the end. (Let me add here that this is by no means either a recommendation or even approval of such a practice. I do most earnestly recommend against inclusion of sports stories that apologize in any way for poor seasons or games, criticize coaches or blame weather or officiating for losses, or make inde-

fensible or unsupportable statements that "while the boys did not win many games this year," they displayed "unusual character," or "grit," or "promise," or other such qualities that unhappily do not show in the statistics.)

4. Sports editors may quote opinions from authoritative or official sources, such as coaches, principals, officials of sports conferences, and others. The same privilege is given to editors of other sections, of course. Be sure you have the permission of such people to quote their opinions and have them check your language. (You have no more right to be sensitive about your journalistic prerogatives than people in the public eye have to be about their reputations and jobs.)

D. Don't invite school officials to write "messages" to the students or to the senior class. This imposes an undue burden on these people and almost forces them to offer standardized, meaningless, cliché-laden material that neither enhances their standing nor adds to the value of the book any more than does the student newspaper editorial urging greater "school spirit" or less littering, or that usual commencement speech beginning "Now as never before. . . ." Besides, why should principals and others do your work for you any more than for athletes, public speakers, or school musicians?

E. Don't invite club secretaries to write final copy for the yearbook. Don't use their reports except as source material. The good editor and writer will combine interviews with people in authority, research, minutes of meetings, and even the secretaries' summary reports of the year in preparing the final stories of clubs and organizations.

F. In short, tell the reader the story about the current year, stating the facts in order of decreasing importance, interest, or both. (The editor can trim copy from the bottom with least damage to completeness when it is written in this inverted-pyramid style.)

G. This brings us to the lead. It should feature (tell first) the most important or most interesting fact in the story. The old journalisic rule is that the lead must contain, in order of declining importance, a summation of the *who*, the *what,* the *where,* the *when,* and usually the *why* and the *how.* The lead may report first the highlight event of the school year for an organization, the most significant accomplishment of the school administration, the big contribution of a service group, the top achievement of an athletic team, the greatest change in a publication (such as the newspaper's becoming a semimonthly or weekly during the year, the yearbook's adoption of a new 9 × 12-inch format and going to an increased number of pages). It may seize attention or perform its function as a lead in a number of ways:

1. Feature one of the parts mentioned above in such ways as these:
   a. *Who:* A notable person like the mayor or the governor who may have appeared as the speaker at a major assembly program
   b. *What:* Construction of a new gymnasium: "A new $150,000 gymnasium will be erected this next year on the site of . . ."
   c. *When:* "On September 12, 75th anniversary date of the founding of old Central High, . . ."
   d. *Where:* "Standing on the very spot where, 75 years before, the pioneer citizens of New Hope had dedicated a plot of ground for education . . ."
   e. *How:* "Kicking a field goal for 50 yards as the last seconds of the game ticked away . . ."
   f. *Why:* "Because they wanted to do something, not just talk about it, a group of students of biology, health, and home economics banded together to form the new Environmentalists Club this past year . . ."

2. Without pretending to exhaust the kinds of structural, rhetorical, or grammatical methods of starting a lead, I would like to present some of the more interesting and promising ones for yearbook journalists:
   a. *Startling statement:* "'A college is worth ten producing oil wells to the community,' President Wellington Biddle told chamber of commerce and civic leaders at the start of a sustentation drive last fall . . ."
   b. *Direct quotation:* Startling statements like the above make good direct quotation leads. Avoid putting routine remarks inside quotes or at the first of the lead: "'No basic changes are planned in curriculum or schedule this year,' Principal Osgood White told students at the year's first assembly . . ." (That simply does not justify the quotation.) Unusual opinions or controversial comments make good features, however: "'A State championship in three years' is the prediction of Coach 'Rocky' Johnson, Midvale's new athletic director . . ." (Believe me, *there's* an unusual word from a member of the world's most cautious profession!)
   c. *Indirect quotation:* Unless the statement has special wording or unusual color, it can sometimes be boiled down, given increased punch by a good writer, and still serve as a feature lead: "Declaring *that Central deserves the best facilities possible,* Principal Adam V. Mudge told a crowd attending groundbreaking ceremonies for the new gymnasium in February *that this should be only the beginning of good things for the historic school* . . ." That could be a bit overloaded, but it carries much strong material. (Note: The indirect quotations have also illustrated the noun clause. Two noun clauses are italicized in the above lead. Either might have been featured.)
   d. *Question:* "How shall we improve reading skills in an age of television and movies? This was a question the English department met head on the past school year . . ."
   e. *Exclamation* (which may also be a startling statement, as discussed above): "'Never say die!' This trite slogan was the guiding principle of Central's sophomore basketball team . . ."
   f. *Literary allusion, song title, paraphrase, truism, familiar saying,* or *parody* (a humorous takeoff):
      (1. "'To be, or not to be' was a question faced bravely this year by the Central Service Club, as its members rebuilt lost prestige . . ."
      (2. "*A Tale of Two Cities* took on

meanings that would have amazed Dickens this year as perennial rivals West Byron and East Hilldale opened a co-operative program of . . ."

(3. " 'Singing in the Rain' was the sad fate of Midville's choral clubs this year. On six different occasions, they found themselves performing in various degrees of moist weather."

(4. " 'A stitch in time'? Yes, that was the unusual experience of home economics students this year as they added background music experimentally to some of their lab projects, including sewing . . ." (As funnyman Jimmy Durante used to say, "I've got a million of them." And you can devise them till you and readers weary of your cleverness. Use them with caution and restraint.)

g. *A summary of big points:* "*Panther Paws,* the school newspaper, made history five ways this year: it went from monthly to semi-monthly, changed to tabloid size, with four columns, adopted magazine format, and redoubled feature and in-depth reporting . . ."

h. *Special grammatical forms* include these:

(1. PARTICIPIAL PHRASE, which often permits "tying in" two or more big ideas in the first sentence, very much like the summary lead mentioned above: *"Leading the state in offense and placing third in defense,* the Tiger football team went to the state finals this year for the first time ever . . ." (Note: The italics are my own.)

(2. GERUNDIVE PHRASE: Don't confuse it with the participle. The participle is an *adjective* formed on the verb, whereas the gerund is a *noun* formed on the verb. The gerund can stand alone as subject or object, but the participle needs a noun to modify or "lean on." A proper illustration of the gerund phrase: *"Speaking Spanish* was the goal of this year's Spanish Club . . ." An awkward method:

"Earning letters this year were . . ." Here, the gerund or participle, "earning," is used in a way that makes it impossible to diagram, since the names following the linking verb "were" are obviously not predicate nominatives; that is, they are not the same as "earning." Try this: *"Earning letters by playing ____ minutes or more during the season,* these athletes were honored: . . ." Or try: *"Earning letters for time played and by services to the team,* 22 football players were recognized at the annual . . ." (We have made honest participles out of "earning" in the last two examples.)

(3. INFINITIVE PHRASE: *"To earn money* needed for their annual convention, members of the Student Council sold programs . . ."

(4. PREPOSITIONAL PHRASE: *"Without missing a beat,* East's new marching band appeared this year at fourteen public events . . ."

(5. ADVERBIAL CLAUSES (cause, condition, time, etc.):
(a. *"Because injuries kept three star players from the final game,* the Tigers . . ." (Be careful not to indulge in "cry-baby" techniques of reporting.)
(b. " *'If winter comes,* can track be far behind?' Here at East, the answer to that is always a resounding 'no!' . . ." (Note that this also illustrates the paraphrase method mentioned above. "If winter comes" is part of the famous line of a well-known poem.)
(c. *"When the Boosters counted their profits this year,* they found the All-School Fair had brought in $750 to be applied on school projects . . ."

(6. STACCATO: This is perhaps as well classified under "grammatical forms" as anywhere else, though when used by fad-

40

dists and lazy or incompetent writers as a substitute for full sentences and paragraphs for all body copy, it might more accurately be called "ungrammatical." As a feature-lead style, it serves rather well to change pace. In fact, it is much like the summary lead except that it permits replacement of understood words with ellipsis marks (. . .): "Tedious hours of practice, even into the night . . . long, uncomfortable bus rides . . . loss of sleep on long trips . . . marching in sun, rain, mud, snow . . . lugging heavy musical instruments—all these experiences represent a side of the marching band few but members really know." (See below for discussion of the technique in thematic passages.)

i. *Figures of speech:* These offer variation devices for the features of leads. But be careful not to overuse them. They are spices, not nourishing food. In moderation, they intrigue, like the subtle theme.

(1. ALLITERATION: Perhaps the oldest method, this was used by the ancient authors of the epic poem, *Beowulf*. It is the garlic of rhetoric! Try this: "Modern *m*ath, a *m*iracle *m*ethod—or just *m*ore *m*od *m*adness? Central teachers and students pondered the question this year as new texts were introduced into . . ." (Note: again, obviously, I have added italics above.)

(2. SIMILE: This compares two persons or things by use of the words *like* and *as* and sometimes *than:* "*Like Knights of old* seeking the Holy Grail, Midtown's Red Knights went on their own quest this past season . . ." As is true of other tricks or devices of style, this sort of thing can get silly rather fast, if overdone.

(3. METAPHOR: In this figure of speech, you omit but imply the *like* or *as*. The problem is to say something fresh and appropriate. Sportswriters are often the worst offenders against good taste, using metaphoric winds, storms, and various animals. But try this: "*Modern English* is a river that's fed by myriad small rivers, creeks, and rivulets of older languages. This fact gave members of the Literary Club its basis for study during the year."

(4. HYPERBOLE: This is an extreme exaggeration through which the writer aims at startling or impressing the reader or, sometimes, making the reader laugh. Sportswriters, seeking new ways to report old facts, have once more been great offenders in the overuse of hyperbolic clichés. (Some quiet little speedster may be said to "roar down the field," for instance, presumably in the manner of a tornadic wind. For many years in radio reporting, a football player seldom made a touchdown, but rather, he "hit pay dirt," a metaphoric hyperbole suggesting that he was a gold miner who had struck it rich.) Don't try to use hyperbole more than once or twice in the book. Study this example: "For an entire evening, grandparents, parents, and teenagers all dropped the years and became children again as they watched the senior class production of *Alice in Wonderland* in the auditorium on the evening of March 15· . . ." (Here the exaggeration is a rather subtle hyperbole, just as "His mouth fell open like a garage door" is a quite hyperbolic simile.)

(5. PERSONIFICATION: Actually a kind of metaphor, this figure gives human qualities to inanimate objects or lower animals, incidentally using hyperbole or exaggeration for humor or other effect: "*Reaching out with inimical hands,* the artificial turf of Arden Park seemed to deny the Lions the victory over their major rivals . . ." (Let me caution sportswriters again: No "crying towels" or unbeliev-

able excuses! This manner of writing might get by with friendly readers, however.) What has long been known as the "pathetic fallacy" attributes the moods of people to the elements or to natural objects: "East's first outdoor graduation was a success, officials agreed, pointing out that even the *skies* smiled for a day, interrupting a week of almost steady showers . . ." (Not brilliant, but serviceable.)

    (6. APOSTROPHE: In this, the writer addresses that which is absent as if present or the inanimate or nonhuman as if having human qualities: " '*Oh, Mouse*,' " said Alice, " 'I wish you could talk.' " Or as you might write it for the book: "*Alumni of 1895*, were you listening when President Horace Carter asked seniors last fall to give tribute to those who went before them? . . ." (Needless to say, this is a tricky type of lead feature that can get rapidly out of hand.)

  j. *Freak or Novelty Leads:* The only limits here are the imagination of the writer and the tenets of good taste. Let's sample just a few random examples:

    (1. CLASSIFIED AD FORMAT: " 'Wanted: students ready to venture forth on a precarious journey of nine months. Little recognition or honor. Long hours. No pay. But rewards will be yours in the satisfaction of a job well done, in self-improvement, in the appreciation of the entire school.' With that announcement in the school newspaper, this year's yearbook editor started a job that, it is hoped, will go down in history . . ."

    (2. VERSE (original, or a parody of a well-known poem): This is original:

      "Many there were who pointed to the need;
      And many who saw it clearly also cared.
      But only one of all this many dared

      To meet the urgent problem with a deed.

      "This verse points up what Student President Hal Browning did this year when suddenly confronted with . . ."

    (3. Other possibilities: a math or algebra problem or symbol, a cartoon, a slogan. As I said, the possibilities are almost innumerable. The secret is to make them seem credible, not contrived.

H. Copy style inside the story deserves your own special stylebook. Perhaps you can develop such a book cooperatively with the newspaper staff, as a class or joint-staff project. Remember these basic facts as you begin:

  1. Paragraphing is a special art. I have always suggested that editors break copy blocks for yearbooks as for newspapers, not by actual thought units, according to rules of English composition, but at arbitrary intervals, for the sole purpose of resting the reader's eyes and making reading easier.

    a. You may paragraph unjustified lines or poetic style by skipping added space between lines.

    b. Or you may use the standard method of indenting three counts to denote a new paragraph.

    c. An average of 5 lines in 21-pica columns or 7 lines in 14-pica blocks seems reasonable. Don't go to extremes to make paragraphs come out exactly as recommended. Alternating between long and short paragraphs, with a large number in between, looks more natural and will prevent breaks that damage thought unity.

  2. "Keep sentences to an average of 20 words," advised style authority Robert Gunning. I agree with him, but put the emphasis on the word *average*. Variety in length, as in organization and order of parts, makes for easier, more interesting reading. Sentences may thus vary from 1 or 2 words to 35, 50, 75 words, and still average out at 20.

  3. In general, prefer the plain word with Anglo-Saxon origin to the word with a Latin root. Doctors, pharmacists, scientists, lawyers—all have their rea-

sons to use the Latin-root word. But those of us who prefer clear communication, and like being understood more than we aspire to rouse a sense of wonder or a state of confusion, will say *man* rather than *homo sapiens*, *house* rather than *domicile*, *use* rather than *utilize*, that favorite of pedants.

4. Prefer short words to polysyllables (words of more than two syllables). Compounds and words with added endings do not count as polysyllables, incidentally. The same politicians, pundits, and pedagogues who indulge without cause in Latinized expressions are the ones who are likely to say *perspire* for *sweat, proclaim* or *annunciate* for *say, veracity* when they mean *truth, exonerate* when *clear* would serve as well, *terminate* when *end* would do better.

5. I am only broadening the above rules when I add this: Keep as close to a conversational style as possible. Try to avoid a pompous style, the pretentiousness of some authors of text books (except journalism texts, naturally!), and the seemingly deliberate efforts certain government bureaucrats, lawyers, and a few other "experts" make to confuse and overawe the layman. These people write long, involved sentences, refuse to break paragraphs, and often violate the rule against "Latin-ese" and polysyllabic language. Sometimes they add their own jargon, usually without bothering to translate it.

6. Avoid use of "glittering generalities" or even "plain old" generalities. Write in specifics. "A slight increase" in number of graduates is less informative, less interesting than "an increase of 35, which brought the class to 471, the largest graduating class in the history of Central High School." Facts, of course, may require research, interviewing, verification. Don't allow writers to speak of the Tigers as "overwhelming" the crosstown rivals, when actually the game was decided on a field goal in the last quarter and the opponents were on the one-yard line of the Tigers at the final gun. Rapturous or slanted and unfair adjectives are among the "glittering generalities" to be most carefully avoided. Let the facts speak for themselves.

7. Avoid unnecessary words. "Think thin," as the dieters say. Use appositives instead of relative clauses, one word rather than a phrase, a verb that carries an adverbial meaning inside *(chuckle)* to a verb plus modifier *(laugh with amusement* or *laugh appreciatively)*, a noun carrying adjectival meanings rather than a noun plus modifiers *(homily* is a simple word for *solemn, moral talk*, for instance). Get by on as few adjectives and adverbs as possible. We have been reminded by the Watergate hearings how much some politicians and officials of various sorts like to indulge in roundabout phrases such as *at this* (or *that*) *point in time*, for *now* or *then*. The stiff expression wastes 13 or 14 letters without adding anything whatever to meaning. The effort at economy of wording need not deny us occasional repetition for effect or for added color or force, but even here, we must beware the use of whiskery clichés like *tired and weary*.

8. Spell American style, not British. Use *judgment*, not *judgement; labor* and *favor* instead of *labour* and *favour*, etc. (Canadian and British publications and their writers are, obviously, exempted from this rule.)

9. Use the active rather than the passive voice in verbs: "The chairman banged his gavel," rather than "The gavel was banged by the chairman," or "Student Council revised the constitution and presented revisions to the students for a vote," not "The constitution was revised by Student Council and a vote by students was called." Obviously, the active voice is clearer, more direct, more specific. (You might even wonder who called for the student vote in that second illustration.) There are exceptions to this rule. It would be awkward to write this any other way: "Funeral ceremonies for students killed in the accident were held . . ."

10. Capitalize proper names of persons, cities, schools, etc., and first words of sentences.
    a. Don't capitalize names of departments or common names of subjects like history, social studies,

mathematics, home economics, etc. (English and Spanish and other names of subjects derived from proper nouns are, of course, excepted.)

b. Do capitalize and enclose in quotation marks the names of specific and special courses: "Modern Living," "History of the United States," "Art for the Homemaker," etc.

c. Capitalize regional names (the Southwest) but not directions (east or northwest, for example).

d. Don't capitalize seasonal names (spring, fall, etc.).

e. Capitalize titles of respect preceding names, initial degrees or titles following names, but not full word titles following names: President John Bunker, State Treasurer Harry Briscoe, Secretary of State Henry Kissinger, John Bunker, LL.D., Robert Gowens, M.D., etc. Note that titles of national officials, being unique, have traditionally been capitalized (Henry Kissinger, Secretary of State, The Secretary of Commerce, The President, etc.). But titles become functional designations in other cases where placed after names (Oscar Prebble, mayor of Big City; Philip Whitten, principal of South High; Dr. Gabriel Hammerhill, superintendent of schools, etc.).

f. Functional designations, however honorable, are not capitalized (physics teacher Kepler H. Brown or Kepler H. Brown, physics teacher). There is a gray area where your stylebook must take over. Will you capitalize (as most people do) *adviser* or *moderator* before the name of the person? I suggest it, though the logic is rather thin for excluding designations or titles of similarly honorable people, like teachers, lawyers, etc., from similar treatment. As I said in an earlier chapter, I applaud the chivalric gesture of one scholastic editor who always capitalizes *Adviser*. But there is no more defense of the practice than of the common military practice of capitalizing (in press releases and official publications) titles of rank, wherever placed. And there is no defense whatever for writing it this way: Librarian, Mrs. Mary Falkenberg or Yearbook Editor, Susy Clegg. (That last comment belongs under the discussion of punctuation, but I will let it stand here with its brethren.)

11. Punctuate in a way to make reading easy. Display your casualness, your "mod" nature, your cleverness in some other way, maybe on a program in which you promote the yearbook to the student body, or in posters announcing advance sales.

a. Don't place a period at the end of an incomplete thought. (Avoid: "Without a moment's delay.") Admittedly professional writers occasionally elide words, and write "half-sentences," and do it effectively. But the rule stands for student writers and editors, and most of the rest of us most of the time.

b. Don't try to use the comma instead of a conjunction, as a substitute for the comma and the conjunction, or instead of a sentence-ending period. This has long been known as a "comma blunder." It is true that the best writers do it now and then, and with great effectiveness, as in this sentence: "The storm roared, trees bent to the ground, the entire island seemed about to rise from its moorings and fly into the sea . . ." But I would still recommend placing *and* between the next-to-last and last clauses above, just for clarity, even at the slight risk of detracting from the dramatic style of the original form. Usually the omission of the conjunction or the period gives the appearance of error: "The Student Council voted on amendments, they next turned to selection of officers . . ."

c. Commas are used between words and phrases in a series, except that in compiling a stylebook the staff has an option as to whether to place a comma between the last two parts of the series (seniors, juniors, and sophomores or seniors, juniors and sophomores). My own preference is toward keeping the final comma too, but the only firm

44

rule is to make your own rule and stick to it.

d. Use a comma after as well as before the appositive phrase ("Mary Smith, runner-up for beauty queen, served as . . .")

e. Apply the same good rule to non-restrictive adjective clauses ("Mary Smith, who was elected senior president in a close vote, withdrew in favor of . . ."). But restrictive clauses need no commas at all ("Floats that got more than one judge's vote included . . ." or "The one new section that won unanimous approval was . . .") As a caution, let me suggest you try to substitute appositives or participial phrases for relative clauses when possible: "The girl *receiving* most votes" rather than "the girl *who received* most votes," etc.

f. Remember to use the hyphen for compound adjectives like "heavy-hearted" or other compounds formed of nouns that precede the modified word ("Pianist-author-TV performer Steve Allen was . . .")

g. Remember to use the apostrophe for possession in nouns (John's, James', Miller and Harris' grocery, etc.).

h. In pronouns, the apostrophe is used to denote ellipsis, not possession (*It's* for *It is,* and *its* as in "The club revised *its* rules").

i. Avoid use of the semicolon when it is possible to use a period or the comma and a conjunction. (Consider this: "Times have changed, but the interschool rivalry remains strong." Or consider: "Times change. The interschool rivalry remains . . ." rather than the more formal or perhaps literary style: "Times change; the interschool rivalry remains . . .")

j. The dash is useful in marking an abrupt shift in thought or a parenthetical statement. It has special value in direct quotations, since conversation often makes quick changes in direction or complete stops. Don't get into the habit of using it to excuse careless style.

k. Ellipsis marks (. . .) are appropriate in staccato leads and elsewhere to show that words presumably clear to the reader have been omitted from inside sentences in the interest of brevity and vigor. (See the illustrations under "leads" [II-G] above.) In quotations, the marks also permit you to let the reader know that complete sentences or even paragraphs are taken from a longer quotation. They show exactly where parts have been removed.

(Note: Obviously, this is not intended as an exhaustive treatment of punctuation, though it hits on some points I have observed to be most bothersome to student journalists. Consult a complete book of grammar and style for problems not considered here.)

I. Relate introductory passages, copy on the dividers, and sign-off remarks as closely as possible to the theme. Be terse. Staccato style is acceptable in all these places or may be used to set apart the division pages only. Ragged-edge or unjustified lines are often used in thematic copy to set such passages off from the rest of the book. Some editors have even attempted a sort of poetic style in these parts. But well-written prose can do the job acceptably, with standard punctuation and justified lines.

III. Cutlines or captions and identifications (often called *idents*) are important complements to pictures in the yearbook, as in all publications.

A. Two kinds of pictures are often left with little or no explanation:

1. Large posed groups with numerous subjects, perhaps the marching band, may properly be left without identifications of persons shown. A caption ("The Marching Band") may be needed even here.

2. Many experts maintain that there is no need to caption, or even identify, thematic introductory or division-spread pictures. My own advice to editors, which is supported by some highly respected and experienced advisers and authorities, is that you improve readability and increase interest if you at least identify persons clearly shown. Exception might be made for mob scenes in which faces

are subordinate to the idea illustrated or the action being shown.

B. Posed groups with a manageable number of faces are, and should be, identified, whether they appear inside the main sections or in the index part of the book. While there are many common and correct ways to identify persons in these pictures, editors should consider two or three and settle on one system. Put this method in your stylebook and follow it consistently. Let me cite three familiar methods worthy of consideration:
1. "Left to right, first row, Joe B. Jones, etc.; second row, Mary Brown, etc. . . ."
2. "First row, in usual order, Joe B. Jones, etc.; second row, Mary Brown, etc. . . ."
3. "Band members, l. to r., bottom row, John Henry Black, etc.; middle row, Harvey W. Blank, etc. . . ."

C. Captions are defined by the New World Collegiate Dictionary as the "lines above pictures" or "above the story itself." In the sense of overlines above pictures, these are rarely used in yearbooks, since headlines over stories (never referred to as *captions* by yearbook editors) serve to introduce pictures as well as copy. Then, too, yearbook editors must conserve space, and such lines are wasteful of space.
1. However, when used, such lines may pique curiosity, introduce, identify, or do all three. Here are three samples:
"Where the boys are . . ."
"The White Station Chorus"
"The cafeteria: social center of East High"
2. If you do use such overline captions, follow a standard system of positioning. Center them inside outer bounds of the picture or start all flush left with the edge of the picture.

D. Action pictures in the yearbook demand full explanatory sentences, which are either placed below individual pictures (as in old news-style layout) or blocked and placed conveniently near the picture block in mosaic and other modern cluster-style layout.
1. Although these lines are sometimes called *captions,* by transference from the name properly assigned to overlines, they are usually known as *cutlines.* The prefix *cut* means engraving. Invented by editors in the days when letterpress was the common method of printing yearbooks as well as newspapers and books, the word has lost none of its popularity even though almost all modern yearbooks are produced by lithography and of course never use engravings at all. (Strangely, neither the Random House nor the World college dictionary recognizes the existence of the term *cutline,* not even as printing language or journalistic slang. But all editors know it.)
2. In writing the cutline, be sure the feature, that most important idea or that most interesting fact, comes first. Sometimes an interest-arousing phrase is set in capital letters or italics before the rest of the cutline, much like an overline caption:
a. "'A DAY TO REMEMBER': Homecoming this year featured the theme, 'memories,' and Joe Howard, '57, and Edith Kershaw, '65, were among the scores of returning ex-students who dressed in the clothes of their own times . . ."

(NOTE: The introductory words may also be integrated more closely into the first sentence, as in the second illustration.)

b. "*Central's oldest living grad,* Dr. Philip Elder, class of 1901, rode in the first auto of the Homecoming parade."
3. Keep the cutline brief, but do include facts the reader will be curious about. Remember that a good lead carries answers to the five *W*'s and the *H.* Those are good questions to remember in writing a cutline. Whatever photo fanatics say about their art, almost no picture tells all a reader wishes to know. If pictures were enough, the human race would still be communicating with hieroglyphics or perhaps with the sort of art found in ancient caves.
4. Don't say, "Pictured above . . ." or "Shown here . . ." or describe anything that the picture itself clearly shows: "Mary Smith smiles at Herbert Hill while Harry Walters looks on with a quizzical frown at the Senior Class Play. . . ." Most of this should be clear to the reader. Spend

your words telling details the picture does not show: "Mary Smith was lead actress and Herbert Hill lead male in the Senior Play, *Night of Confusion*. At right above, Harry Walters, as the butler, registers confusion because of what he has just heard Herbert tell his fiancée."

5. You are allowed to omit articles not essential to clarity and otherwise to follow telegraphic style in cutlines without damage to readability.

6. You are expected to count units in cutlines so nearly that no widows (very short lines) will fall at the end. Normally, a widow is defined as $\frac{1}{4}$ line or less. I hope you will aim at never dangling $\frac{1}{2}$ line or less, since counting is no big thing, once you learn the proper counts and set the standard lengths, preferably never more than three for a book. (Restudy the discussion under "layout" in Chapter 3.)

IV. Headlines are almost universally used in the better yearbooks, as in newspapers and magazines.

A. Newspaper style, whether news head or feature head, is quite appropriate.

B. Many special efforts have been made to modify this style or to deviate from it, usually with harm to readability.

C. Yearbooks that omit heads entirely are risking readability and the goodwill of readers.

D. Let's review basic kinds and parts of the headline:

1. The banner or streamer is the head that spreads across a page or two pages. It will naturally be in somewhat larger type than single-column heads and other shorter headings, perhaps 36 point of a condensed type.

2. One frequently used headline device is the short label, or brief part-line, lying above the main head and called variously the "kicker," the "tag line," or the "squawkline." Frequently underlined and always in at least two sizes smaller type, this line teases the reader into reading further, often supplements content of the head, sometimes serves to pin down the subject, whether a course, a club, a sport, or whatever. It may read directly into

the head or may stand alone and point forward. It is often followed by a colon:

FOOTBALL:
Tigers earn 4–4 seasonal split

or

SHOCKING REPORT:
Physics Club experiments with electricity

or

COACH WILDER REPORTS,
'This was a season of surprises'

(Note that the kicker is generally flush left, the head either the same or centered below or merely indented two or three counts.)

3. The deck is a relatively little-used subordinate headline that may add a summation of a secondary feature of the story. Once used extravagantly in large city papers, decks have been known to extend down to as much as half a page, to three, four or more additional units in decreasing type sizes. They can serve, if used in moderation, to supplement big seasonal sports headlines:

Dragons win District I championship
(main headline, perhaps a streamer)

18–3 basketball season sets
new school sports record
(deck, flush left or centered)

or

Band wins top honors
in Region IV contest
(head)

Invitation to Mardi Gras
rewards group for success
(deck)

4. The jump line or jump head is normally a key word or phrase, a repeat, in smaller type, of the original main head, or a rewrite in different words, perhaps focusing on contents of the jumped part of the story. Not of

course needed as often in yearbooks as in newspapers and magazines, the jump head is useful in carrying thought into the second part of a long seasonal sports story, or perhaps a running story through a seasonally handled events section:

Beavers compile . . .

or

Football season (continued) . . .

or

**Beavers close season
with 3 big victories**
(Continued from preceding page)

or

**Winter continues great
assembly programs . . .**
(continued)

(Note: Adopt and follow a style on the continuation lines in your book, whether to use *(Continued on page _____)* and, on the page to which the jump is made *(Continued from page _____)*, or *(Continued)* in both spots, since the jump is only from one spread to the next as a rule, or *(see next page)* and *(continued from preceding page)* or just *(Continued)* on the page of the jumped story. Methods are numerous, and as long as they get the reader from one place to the other with minimal effort, all are good.)

E. Now let's consider some rules for writing headlines, with attention first to the kinds of headlines frequently used:
1. Flush-left style is the commonest because it is simple to write and easy to read. Start line or lines at left and keep multiple lines within $1\frac{1}{2}$ to 2 counts of each other, taking into account varying unit counts:

History club compiles
(about $19\frac{1}{2}$ count)
story of Jones City
(about 18 count)

(Obviously, in writing headlines, we must know the type style and the al-
lowable maximum count for the headline before we can even begin. I have assumed a type here that allows 20 maximum count in the column. It will fit rather well.)

2. A single line may be centered in its column of whatever width. This sort of head always appealed to me more for editorial commentary at opening or close of book. (Decks are also frequently centered.)
3. Less frequently used and less modern styles are inverted pyramid and drop-line or step-down heads.

   a. Inverted pyramid:

   Hope of baseball glories
   (about 22 count)
   depends on freshman
   (about 19 count)

   (The three-liner seems impractical for the yearbook.)
   b. Step-down or drop-line:

   **History club makes own history
   with book on school's past**

   (Note: Hanging indention is a style once used in newspapers but hardly practical for the yearbook editor. Its first line is flush left; the second and possibly the third are each about two counts shorter and indented two counts to the right, being flush at the right with the first line.)

4. While every style of type has its peculiarities and there are variations between types as to widths of letters, it is useful to know a standard system for counting headline type. (Incidentally, it is also applicable to cut-line counting.) Try this: 1 count for most small letters, all numbers but 1, and the *I*; $\frac{1}{2}$ for punctuation marks and for *i, t, l,* and *f*; $1\frac{1}{2}$ for capitals except *M* and *W,* and for *m* and *w*; 2 for *M* and *W*. Note that in some types an *l* and an *f* and maybe a *t* will actually spread to $\frac{3}{4}$. I combine two of these for $1\frac{1}{2}$ in my counting, since it seems easier to do so.
5. Your narrative or news head should summarize the big point, feature, or features of the story, and presumably its content reflects the first part of the lead sentence or paragraph. The deck,

if used, reviews a lesser point or lesser points.

6. Each line of the headline should be a thought unit, and the first line needs both a subject and a verb:

Skits brighten year's assemblies

Avoid an ellipsis that gives a false impression:

Make assemblies brightest ever

(Here, the reader may understand a command, rather than the statement that was likely intended.)

7. Since the headline should instill a desire to read the story and attract reader interest, the verb and the subject should be as vigorous and as colorful as possible:

Debaters talk their way into state finals

or

Swimmers splash to district honors

a. Avoid "say-nothing" heads and generalities:

Debate team has successful year

Prefer:

Debate team sweeps district

b. As in copywriting, avoid the passive voice; prefer the active wherever possible. Obviously, the passive is unavoidable in some cases, or at least seems more appropriate:

Funeral services held for accident victims

(This is a newspaper head, and by the time you do yearbook copy, you very rarely need the form.)

But, in general, active voice tells it more directly. Compare the first two below with the second pair:

Auditorium refurbished by service club

Honors attained by band at annual contest

APO service club redecorates auditorium

Band takes first rating at state meet

Don't become so determined about the active voice that you cannot see situations in which stress needs to be placed on the subject, requiring use of the passive verb:

School chorus acclaimed as city's best

c. Avoid use of forms of the verb "to be":

Dramatists *have been* busy this year

Tennis team *was* in building stage

(Tell the BIG thing the dramatists did and tell a key activity or ray of rebuilding hope for the tennis team.)

8. For the sake of both unity and vigor, observe these cautions:
   a. Don't end a first line with a preposition. Avoid this:

FHA members learn *from* new visitation program

Improve it like this:

FHA adds new program of visits to local cafes

(I have made it a little more specific in the process.)

b. Don't end the line on an adjective that needs a noun in the next line to complete its meaning:

School bond vote brings *happy* smiles to faces of officials

Improve the headline this way:

Victory for school bonds promises prompt start of building program

(Note that the second head is in better form and also adds some needed facts.)

c. Don't split a verb between lines:

Cap and Buskin plays *have been presented* to statewide groups

Even if the writer used the passive voice in the interest of featuring the name, itself a somewhat debatable practice, it needs changing because of the split verb. Try:

**Cap & Buskin gives one-act plays
to 23 state audiences during year**

(Here, I have added some needed specifics, changed to active voice, and avoided that verb split too.)

d. Don't break a compound word, parts of a name, or parts of an abbreviation.
Avoid:

Five student leaders attend a *Mid-Tennessee* meet for club officers

Try this instead:

**Five student leaders take part
in officers' seminar in Nashville**

Avoid:

**Rally on ecology at *NW
HS* draws 500 from East**

Improve it like this:

**500 from East attend
ecology rally at NWHS**

(Besides correcting the split, the above head places your high school name in the top line.)

Avoid division of a name here:

**Yearbook staff honors *Mary
Johnson* at surprise assembly**

You may have to give up something here to fit space:

**Staff honors yearbook editor
at special surprise assembly**

or

**Mary Johnson honored
at surprise assembly**

(The latter does not really tell the full story, but then few heads can. It also uses passive voice to feature the name.)

9. Observe newspaper rules in use of tense of verbs:

a. Past tense is always indicated by present tense verb in headlines.

Efforts to raise school levies *fail*

Caution: Don't use a seemingly contradictory phrase with your verb:

Central *adopts* double-schedule *last fall*

b. Future is designated by the infinitive or by the future tense:

East Jonesville *to combine* with Central

or

East Jonesville *will combine* with Central

10. Most numbers in heads are written in Arabic numerals. Where there is space, you may spell out *one* to *ten*, though some numerals, such as time of day, space dimensions, track records, etc., are never written out.

11. Abbreviations and initials are generally avoided, except for commonly understood names like YMCA, PTA, and FHA. Spell out names of months, for instance, except when before designation of the day.
This is right:

School opens *Sept. 12*

This is wrong:

School to open in *Sept.*

Spell out titles unless followed by names.
This is acceptable:

Gov. White visits campus

But never say:

Gov. visits school

or

Supt. announces new schedule

And never use:

Mon. called longest day

or

Pix shown in assembly

or

Prof. from Harvard speaks

(Note also that abbreviations like Co., Assn., or Corp., may be used as parts of names.)

12. As stated previously, the commonest style today is downstyle. In this, you capitalize the first word and all proper nouns:

Mary Smith, Spanish teacher, elected president of state language teachers

Of course, most headlines would have fewer proper nouns than this one above. Two extreme styles are the all-capital style (upstyle) and the rarely used form of the downstyle in which all letters are small, even initial letters of proper names and of the first word in the headline. The former capitalizes every word, including small prepositions and any articles or conjunctions that may be used:

State Officials See An Increase In Enrollment For A Decade

The latter style confuses readers in another way:

central warriors tie west in race for dist. iv title

The old standby, still used in many newspapers and yearbooks, capitalizes words that start lines, and all other words except short prepositions (in, into, even through, but keeps capital letter for Without, Throughout, etc.). It is up-downstyle.

Playing Without a Coach, Team Finishes in Cellar

13. Except when the ease of understanding requires it, as in the second and fourth headlines of the previous rule, avoid use of articles in headlines (a, an, the). That is, keep to terse, telegraphic style. Reread the heads of your daily newspaper to see how writers do this. Examine headline illustrations above. Then note how sometimes the omission or retention of an article depends on whether space will allow:

Present building site defended as sensible 'bird in the hand'

To leave off *the* (above) would to an extent impede readability of the line.

14. Substitute a comma in headlines for the conjunction *and*. Here are two illustrations:

Bowlers reorganize, enter 6 meets

and

Two new school officials, 13 new teachers named

15. Punctuate headlines clearly:
   a. Use commas as you do in sentences, with the added use mentioned immediately above.

   b. Use a semicolon to balance off two separate thoughts, preferring placement at the end of a line rather than inside it.

New schedule opens year a week early; Christmas, Easter vacations extended

   c. Periods are not used after heads, kickers, or usually in or after decks.

   (In some magazine and yearbook styles, the period is used after complete statements inside and/or at the end of the deck or secondary head.)

   d. Single quotation marks, as used in newspapers, are recommended for the yearbook.

Coach Jones calls it 'the year of the Tiger'

16. Avoid repetition of the same or similar words from the kicker to the head or from the headline to the deck:

Basketball squad places two on all-state team

(Head)

Bill Ott, Toby Waters *placed* on honor squad

(Deck)

Do this over, somewhat as follows:

Two members of basketball team win places on all-state squad
(Head)

Bill Ott, Toby Waters receive trophies in Austin ceremonies

(Deck)

(Note that the second effort has not only avoided repetitiousness, but has also added more details. I am not suggesting that this is the best form possible. Maybe the names of the honorees should go in the top head, for example.)

17. While cleverness and variety have as much place in heads as in leads, let me offer some cautions against mistakes even the professionals fall into.

   a. Think twice, maybe three times, before using a pun. Then reexamine it to be sure it is as fresh and as clever as you first thought. Usually it is not.

   Consider these three efforts:

   Cyclones prove gentle western zephyr

   Tigers purr like pussycats

   Lions are kings of District IV jungle

   (Play on the school mascot-symbol has been tried and retried so often that it all sounds like a miserable, worn-out family joke when you trot it out again into a new issue of the book or newspaper.)

   b. Beware "hashed" or mixed metaphors, unhappy alliterations, accidental double meanings:

   East *racers whitewash* rivals as they *coin* many new records

   (Was it track, football, boating—or "paint-your-opponent," or did it have something to do with minting coins?)

   Bears roar like winter *winds*, *burying* all district opponents

   (Was it at a zoo, on the windy plains, or did it happen in one of those late movies, with ghouls on the burying detail?)

Cats are dogged by many injuries

(That had to be a horrible slip made very late at night.)

V. Copyreading (let's spell it this way, though authorities are divided as to whether it is one word or two) is the big editing job, since members of the yearbook staff have relatively ample time to read copy, if they are on schedule, and especially since time limitations and the very nature and method of producing yearbooks minimizes or eliminates the opportunity to read proofs.

A. Adviser and/or editor-in-chief should begin the work of getting good, clean copy by urging and insisting (as far as is practical, that is) that the staff reporter-writer use the most possible care in gathering information and in double-checking facts. Trouble spots include numbers in a club, dollars earned or spent on a school project, specific statistics issued by the sports department, and spellings of names.

   1. Insist that staff members take notes and that the notes are clear enough to be interpreted even a week later.

   2. Reporters should learn also to be willing to repeat questions to interviewees or to ask questions a second time when the first response seems inadequate. They should feel no embarrassment whatever in allowing the interviewees to check written notes for complete accuracy. (A little embarrassment here is of no consequence when compared with big, roaring problems that result from errors congealed in type.)

   3. Those who read copy have a right to expect that every staff member who prepares copy is able to write clearly, grammatically, and in complete, properly punctuated sentences, at least most of the time. Nor is it too much to ask that writers, from freshmen to seniors, keep at hand for reference the stylebook, a dictionary, and perhaps a grammar reference book.

   4. It would be ideal if all staff writers could type, but at least they should learn to print clearly, double-spacing all copy. (Of course, all copy will be typed before being sent to the printer.)

B. The copyreader's first job is to read the story presented by the writer for its total content and general form, and then concentrate on the lead.

    1. He will ask: Has the most important thought, the most interesting achievement, the year's big activity or event been featured (placed first)?

    2. If the answer is negative, the editor should be willing to rewrite the lead and bring it up to expectations in this respect.

    3. For that matter, if the lead is entirely too drab in form, even though featuring the proper material, he may wish to consider whether to ask the writer to try to enliven it in one of the methods suggested earlier in this chapter or, in an emergency such as an impending deadline, to redo it himself. Obviously, since the yearbook is a staff venture, no editor should redo every lead or rewrite all copy to the extent of destroying staff incentive.

C. The next job is to check figures and spellings, especially of proper nouns, when there is any reason whatever to doubt what has been written. (The good copy editor, copywriter, editor, by whatever name, must develop a suspicious nature about such things.)

D. If there are any editorial comments or words and phrases that (in an unsigned article) do more than add color, the editor may wish to ask the writer to delete the unneeded words or do a rewrite. Or he may make the corrections himself, preferably after explaining it to the writer.

E. A next step is to observe the sequence of copy and to make sure that the facts are told in order of *declining* importance.

F. This is a good time to glance at paragraphing, marking copy so that the average length of paragraphs is 5 to 7 lines, as suggested earlier. (Many editors paragraph almost automatically on the very first reading of copy.)

G. Next, the editor may wish to look at paragraph beginnings to see whether they afford clear transitions from thought to thought and are themselves interesting and varied. The very act of breaking into more frequent "grafs" may have caused some problems in these respects. And, by all means, do something to avoid monotony of beginnings. "The" and "A" openings in paragraphs can be as deadly as "er-um" or "ah" interjections in oral speech.

H. A next point that needs examining is variety of sentence length and form throughout the story.

I. And finally, or nearly so, the copy editor will wish to reexamine the entire story for typos that may have been missed; for slack grammar; for misspellings that slipped by earlier readings; for bad sentence structure that slipped by all previous double-checking.

J. Knowing the spot to be filled, the editor will next figure length of copy in lines of type, and if it is too long, cut out expendable words, phrases, and sentences. If the story was properly written, trimming can readily be done at the end. In the unusual case in which there is too little story for the space, the editor may expand parts that have been slighted or handled sparingly and may add minor points that have been omitted. Sometimes the art may be enlarged to fill the space.

K. Follow standard copyreading symbols found in any editor's manual or journalism text. (A simple form is included on page 56.) If you come up with what seems too many changes or marks for the printer to interpret with ease, retype.

L. Reread the final typed copy, being sure that every paragraph is marked with the right-angle symbol facing inward. This tells the printer at least that the story has had a line-by-line editing and is ready for him to set.

M. Of course, there is always something you can do with copy before you turn it loose. Whenever you have the time to do so with any story, reread it one final time and ask yourself whether the writing is as clear as it can be; as tightly written as possible; as interesting; as sharp, with vigorous verbs and nouns that contain descriptive connotations and as few adverbs and adjectives as possible. In short, ask yourself whether it reasonably fulfills the injunctions mentioned above under "style." Now and then, you may decide that there is leisure enough, and urgency enough, to justify a complete rewrite. Maybe the editor can help a writer and the book by sitting down and doing such a revision.

VI. Proofreading, while not always practical for the yearbook, because of tight deadlines, and also because most printers are located many miles from the school and because slow mail service can further delay production, is in itself an art and a skill quite distinct from copy editing. Consider these facts when you are asked to read proofs:

A. This is not the time for rethinking and rewriting. If you are tempted to do actual rewriting to improve thought or style, ask yourself whether such revision is more important than keeping your agreements with the printer, maintaining a schedule, staying within a budget (resetting type is an added cost that the purchaser—you—must pay). I suggest that you forego changes intended to make the story slightly smoother, to make the editors seem cleverer, even to correct minor style errors (spellings that violate your stylebook or a capital where a lower case letter would serve better, a comma where your own rules suggest no mark, etc.). Grit your teeth and pledge to do better copy editing next time.

B. You should, if allowed to make corrections at all, change misspellings of names of teachers, school officials, and students, even if you let the errors slip through previous editing of copy. (We are not all perfect.) If it was a staff error, expect the correction to be added to your bill, and pay it as cheerfully as possible.

C. You may and likely should make changes in content that would, as you read it in clear, bold type (all errors are printed in bold face, I have observed), seriously embarrass someone, or maybe even evoke the ugly word "libelous." This may be a hitherto unnoticed double entendre, an embarrassing nickname used perhaps in private conversation in the locker room, which might arouse ridicule or lift eyebrows when the printed book reaches friends outside school or those at home. Material in headlines and pictures should be examined as carefully as body copy and cutlines, incidentally. I have known of a situation in which a doctored photo roused a mother to the point of threatening suit; another in which an overly revealing photo caused a school yearbook to have a page removed, a new page pasted in by hand,

book by book, after the volume had been printed and bound.

D. The main purpose of proofreading is to check the type the printer has set in copy, cutlines, and headlines to see that no "typos" occur, such as changes in wording, omissions of words, phrases, and sentences, misspellings, alterations of figures, etc. While all yearbook specialists assign skilled people to read type after it is set, compare it with original copy, and correct typos before galleys and/or pages come to you, some few errors continue to slip through. (Alas, even after careful page proofing, the printed book will reveal glaring mistakes you cannot believe you overlooked.)

E. If your contract calls for the staff's reading and examination of "browntones" (by whatever name), you will have the rare and valuable chance to compare the way the printer placed headlines in relation to stories, cutlines in relation to pictures; and to see whether pictures touch the margin or fit the space for which intended or bleed properly into margin, if a bleed was intended.

F. Since time is always at a premium here, it is essential that the editor put himself and his most trusted assistants to work promptly, dropping everything else until the proofs are back in the mail on their way to the printer. One good method is to have one person hold copy, a second the dummy, and the third the proofs, in whatever stage. The old and time-proved method is to read aloud while proofing, though this may not always be practical.

G. Whereas in copyreading you either make corrections directly on the copy or insert corrections so that the compositor can read the finished copy, in proofreading you are marking proofs so that the corrections will catch the attention of the compositor. Using the symbols of proofreading (some of which are quite different from corresponding copyreading and editing marks) mark each correction or make it inside the galley or the page; then draw a line to the outer margin and indicate the correction with the proper symbol (wf = wrong font, lc = make small letter, etc.). See the simple proofreading chart and illustration in the next part of this chapter.

Fig. 4.1—Headline, ragged-edge body, and cutline type in the 1973 *Reflector*, Griffith High, Indiana, look ultramodern. The head is well placed over the story. Overall layout style is older magazine-news pattern (see pages 26-27).

Fig. 4.2—Headline and copy block, like pictures, tell the year's story in this spread from the *Torch*, Catalina High, Tucson, Arizona. The body and cutlines lie outside the mosaic pattern. Head and story feature highlights of seasonal events.

Unique December snow ushers in festive holiday season

Early in December a record-breaking snowfall caused a break in school routine as students built snowmen and threw snowballs. Several-hundred members of the student body were absent while the remaining few found study impossible.

Put in an early holiday mood by the unusual weather, Student Council sponsored a canned food drive while DECA and Red Cross collected for needy families. Many homerooms adopted families or donated to organizations.

'Old Fashioned Christmas' on the 16th provided students their

families and the faculty an opportunity to decorate trees, sing carols with the Minstrels of Troy and make personal requests to Santa Claus. The festivities were ended as Steve Baquet and Kathy Morgan were crowned Torch King and Queen. Runners-up were Anne Amburgey, Lissa Peirce, Dave Robertson and Randy Wronka.

On the 15th the choirs and orchestra combined to present the Christmas Concert. Portions of the program were featured at the holiday assembly on the 17th, the last day before

ABOVE: Pepinaders entertain at a Christmas-time game with new outfits and routines. TOP: Brian Anderson prepares to hit Jenis Kuster with something near to Trojans—a snowball. ABOVE RIGHT: Two members of the International Club sell Christmas cards to a customer. RIGHT: Senior Sylvia Leon wraps packages for her homespun family.

	HOW THEY ARE USED	WHAT THEY MEAN	HOW TYPE IS SET
TYPE SIZE and STYLE	Lansing, mich.--	Capitalize.	LANSING, Mich.—
	College Herald	Small caps.	COLLEGE HERALD
	the Senator from Ohio	Change to lower case.	the senator from Ohio
	By Alvin Jones	Bold face.	**By Alvin Jones**
	Saturday Evening Post	Italicize.	*Saturday Evening Post*
PUNCTUATION and SPELLING	"The Spy"	Emphasize quotes.	"The Spy"
	Northwestern U.	Emphasize periods.	Northwestern U.
	said "I must . . .	Emphasize comma.	said, "I must . . .
	Johnsons	Emphasize apostrophe.	Johnsons'
	picnicing	Insert letter or word.	picnicking
	theatre	Transpose letters.	theater
	Henry Cook, principal	Transpose words.	Principal Henry Cook
	days	Delete letter.	day
	judgement	Delete letter and bridge over.	judgment
	all right	Insert space.	all right
	those	Close up space.	those
	Geo. Brown	Spell out.	George Brown
	100 or more	Spell out.	one hundred or more
	Doctor S. E. Smith	Abbreviate.	Dr. S. E. Smith
	Six North Street	Use numerals.	6 North Street
	Marion Smythe	Spell as written.	Marion Smythe
POSITION	Madison, Wis.--	Indent for paragraph.	Madison, Wis.—
	today. Tomorrow he	New paragraph.	today. Tomorrow he
	considered serious. Visitors are not	No paragraph. Run in with preceding matter.	considered serious. Visitors are not
	But he called last night and said that he	No paragraph.	But he called last night and said that he
		Center subheads.	**Jones To Conduct**
	ful	Bridge over material omitted.	He was mindful
		Kill corrections.	one **student** came
		Story unfinished.	
		End of story.	———————

editing symbols and marks
rs. Note that there is
y-editing and proofreading
arks are made on the
manuscript corrections.

	SYMBOL	EXPLANATION	EXAMPLE	
			MARGINAL MARKS	ERRORS MARKED
TYPE SIZE and STYLE	*wf*	Wrong font.	*wf*	He marked the proof.
	×	Burred or broken letter. Clean or replace.	×	He marked the proof.
	ital	Reset in italic type the matter indicated.	*ital*	He marked the proof.
	rom	Reset in roman (regular) type, matter indicated.	*rom*	He marked *the* proof.
	bf	Reset in bold face type, word or words indicated.	*bf*	He marked the proof.
	≡	Replace with a capital the letter indicated.	≡	he marked the proof.
	lc	Set in lower case type.	*lc*	He Marked the proof.
	sc	Use small capitals instead of the type now used.	*sc*	He marked the proof.
	ᓂ	Turn inverted letter indicated.	ᓂ	He marked the proof.
PUNCTUATION and SPELLING	ᓝ	Take out letter, letters, or words indicated.	ᓝ	He marked the prooof.
	#	Insert space where indicated.	#	He marked theproof.
	ɩ	Insert letter as indicated.	*ɩ*	He maked the proof.
	⊙	Insert period where indicated.	⊙	He marked the proof
	⋀	Insert comma where indicated.	⋀	Yes he marked the proof.
	⋁	Insert apostrophe where indicated.	⋁	Mark the boys proof.
	/=/	Insert hyphen where indicated.	/=/	It was a cureall.
	?/	Insert question mark where indicated.	?/	Who marked the proof
	em	Insert em dash, implying break in continuity or sentence structure.	*em*	Should we can we comply?
	n	Insert en dash, implying the word "to."	*n*	See pages 278 93.
	" / "	Enclose in quotation marks as indicated.	" / "	He marked it proof.
	spell out	Spell out all words marked with a circle.	*spell out*	He marked the 2nd proof.
	out, see copy	Used when words left out are to be set from copy and inserted as indicated.	*out, see copy*	He proof.
	stet	Let it stand. Disregard all marks above the dots.	*out*	He marked the proof.
	⌒	Draw the word together.	⌒	He ma rked the proof.
	tr	Transpose letters or words as indicated.	*tr*	He the proof marked
	⟨?⟩	Query to author. Encircled in red.	⟨? was⟩	The proof read by
POSITION	¶	Start a new paragraph as indicated.	¶	reading The boy marked
	no ¶	Should not be a separate paragraph. Run in.	*no* ¶	marked. The proof was read by
	⟍	Out of alignment. Straighten.	⟍	He marked the proof.
	⬚	Indent 1 em.	⬚	He marked the proof.
	⬚⬚	Indent 2 ems.	⬚⬚	He marked the proof.
	⬚⬚⬚	Indent 3 ems.	⬚⬚⬚	He marked the proof.
	eq. #	Equalize spacing.	*eq.* #	He marked the proof.
	⊥	Push down space which is showing up.	⊥	He marked the proof.
	[*or*]	Move over to the point indicated. [If to the left; if to the right]	[	[He marked the proof.
				He marked the proof. /
	⊔	Lower to the point indicated.	⊔	He marked the proof.
	⊓	Raise to the point indicated.	⊓	He marked the proof.
	∪	Less space.	∪	looks better

Fig. 4.4—Common proofreading marks useful to yearbook editors. Note that proofreading is done on galley or page proofs. Marks are made in the margin. A line is drawn from each mark to the spot or point of correction on the printed line.

Exercises

1. Write the first two paragraphs (50 to 75 words) of an introduction to your book, remembering and using the theme idea you have selected. Use regular prose style and justified type.

2. Follow through with the introductory copy, or at least the start of this material, for any three division spreads. Make it first blend with the theme introduction for the book. Put it into prose style with justified type.

3. Redo each of the above (exercises 1 and 2) in staccato style (incomplete sentences with dots between phrases to indicate ellipsis). Or use poetic format with ragged edges (don't attempt rhyme or, unless you have unusual talent, exact poetic rhythms like iambic pentameter).

4. In checking a story for your book, you have doubts about spelling and form of the names of a young lady listed in the student directory as "Annamarie Hotchkiss" but on a card collected at enrollment (now in typed form) as "Ann Marie Hotchkins." Staff members with varying degrees of acquaintance with the young lady (obviously none of a really meaningful nature) have varying opinions about her name, all quite strong. What is your next step? The writer has spelled it per the directory but left a question mark by it in parentheses. But the "buck stops" with you as editor-in-chief. (Note: Let each staff member assume himself to be the editor-in-chief for a moment.)

5. Comment on what is wrong with the following stories and what should be done about each. Prepare to discuss each of them in class. You might rewrite a line or so of each lead of the weak stories, using your imagination based on local observations. Here, you need not stick to the factual, since we are examining the method.

   a. Sparta City's glee club has won many honors through the years for its appearances throughout the state. Founded in 1939 while the high school was still located in the old building that was torn down in 1942, the club has held high its motto, "Music brightens the World." Its faculty adviser is Miss Francine Hartman, and this year's president was Dulcie Mae Trillman.

   b. Dogged by bad weather and injuries, and suffering from costly officiating, this year's Badgercats lost most of their games while upholding the honor of East Birdville Academy in a manner to bring great praise on the team. They took the final two games of the season by overwhelming district opposition, Hardy and Swantown, 14–12 and 7–6. The scores don't begin to tell the difference in the teams either. So wait till next year, District 9! We'll really show you something!!!

   c. This year's Mapleville debate team had as its aim winning more than half its matches, and that goal was shown to be modest when year's end came and the team had won 4 of 6 meets against clubs from all over the city and county. By far the best team Mapleville has ever had since starting debate about ten years ago, this year's team has earned the applause of all the school. We are happy to offer them this word of praise. Good work, fellows!

   d. Proving that our school has more spirit than any other school in our district, the Pompon girls have attended every game the Hallsville basketball team played this year, under the sponsorship of Hallville's most beloved teacher, Miss Susan ("Peppy") Yellman. Not even the bad play of the team, which led to the firing of Coach Bill ("the Staller") Bumble, could dampen the enthusiasm of this fine group, whose chief Pompon Girl was Mary Tassel, sister of Susan Tassel, editor of the yearbook.

   e. Probably the state's worst baseball team was humiliated by losses to all opponents this past season. Pleasant Valley High showed little punch at bat and its pitchers apparently thought they were pitching for fungo practice. Attendance at the first of the season was light, and those who went left mostly before the fifth inning. We had the worst coaching possible, and it is hoped that a new coach will be assigned next season.

6. Write six leads (first sentences only) of stories about events in your school this year or last, selecting subjects as follows: (1) a sports season; (2) a big event sponsored by a service club; (3) a project of an interesting course; (4) the year's achievements or changes made by a school publication; (5) a big project of a musical group; and (6) an all-school event. Concentrate on answering, and featuring, the five W's and the H. You may fictionalize slightly, but of course this is not permissible in the actual stories for the yearbook.

7. Refer to the list given in the text of this chapter of structural, rhetorical, or grammatical methods of writing a lead, or at least, writing the feature. Redo the above opening sentences, or write first sentences for leads for other stories about your school year, employing a variety of methods and techniques suggested here. Name the method used for each lead.

8. Now repeat this assignment, using four figures of speech and two novelty leads.

9. Rewrite the following sentences into simpler style. (Study example first.) Example: With some trepidation, he instituted exploratory action. Translation: With some fear, he began a search.

(Note: I admit to *some* exaggeration in the illustration and in these exercises.)

   a. The inevitable culmination of deviations from rectitude, or of nefarious behavior, is apprehension and retribution. (Is your dictionary handy?)

   b. "Never acquiesce to the vicissitudes of ill fortune," Mr. Puffer urged.

   c. "Improved utilization of one's domicile will ameliorate the exigencies of the fuel deficiencies," Congressman Warmwind declared.

   d. "Opulence is no excuse for ostentation or parsimony," said the prime minister.

   e. The Bureau for Agriculturalists has accumulated statistical information showing in aggregate the total of new electrical installations in rural areas. (Note: In the above not very much exaggerated examples, I have included some overly fat words that are not even needed. You might translate them into simple words, then drop them. Feel free to make complete revisions once you have simplified phrases or sentences.)

10. Correct or improve the style of the following. Be prepared to explain what you have done. I will help by italicizing problem words, punctuation, and phrases.

   a. Four interschool matches *were won by this year's tennis team.*

   b. In my *judgement,* the *acknowledgement* should speak with special *favour* of those who gave help from outside the staff.

   c. Winner of the title for the *Eastern Part* of the city was Ball High. (Note: What is the most important thing here? Should it be first?)

   d. Coach Harry Smitloff said that *Mathematics teacher,* Oscar Holmes would be timekeeper.

   e. The club's *Adviser* is Mrs. Mary Balsam. Mr. Harvey Wisdom, *Superintendent of Schools,* serves as honorary club adviser.

   f. *ROTC Commandant, Mr. Stewart Grim,* directs the ceremony.

   g. The final *Spring* assembly featured winners of scholastic awards.

   h. Suzy Clegg, *Yearbook Editor,* was class valedictorian.

   i. The English classes have been expanded to include *"creative writing,"* and *Journalism* now has a new *Junior* course, *"Editing Principles."*

   j. *Including Mary Smith, freshman president and Joshua Hobe, sophomore president.*

   k. Heavy rains fell, the ceremonies were taken inside.

   l. Originally from the *southwest,* Coach Rivers came *East* in his youth.

   m. *"Its* a long trail that has no ending," was Principal *Jone's* comment.

   n. *Silvermith's and Glover's* Grocery gave food for the occasion, and the invocation was given by senior Harry *Johnsons* grandfather, *The* Rev. R. V. Johnson. (Note: Do these two thoughts belong in *one* sentence? There is *more* than bad punctuation involved.)

11. This exercise may be based on your imagination, or on materials you have in hand. Imagine either the feature events of homecoming or of the biggest assembly program of the year.

   a. Write the lead and perhaps the first two paragraphs of the story.

   b. Dummy three to five pictures of homecoming, using either news style or mosaic for the two-page spread.

   c. Plan a headline to go immediately above the beginning of the story. Using a 30-point Roman of a style that counts 27 maximum for two columns, 31 for three columns or a full page, write a full-page single-liner, *or* a two-liner for two columns. Use a label kicker above with the name of the occasion *or* a descriptive phrase. Be sure the head does not repeat the wording of the kicker, and be sure you feature the highlight material that is given in the lead itself.

   d. Now write cutlines, bunched for two blocks located one block per page. After rereading the text, are you sure you have avoided errors I have cautioned against? Did you feature the most interesting points of the pictures (as you have sketched them in)? Have you said anything not needed or have you omitted anything the reader will wonder about?

12. Write the following headlines to the counts suggested (or substitute counts that you know to be correct for your corresponding headlines):

   a. A three-line, 24-point one-column Roman head (34-count maximum per line) to go above the report on the history club project for the year. Or substitute your own most lively, most active club in school (only you must not call it the "most lively").

   b. A two-line, 24-point, single-column Roman head (maximum: 18 count) that reports results of the football season as you anticipate optimistically they will be next season or as they were the past season (as you prefer).

c. A one-line, 44-em, 30-point Roman head (41 count) with a one-column overline (18 point, 33 count). The subject is an outstanding achievement of administration or the school for the year, one that will top a story about administration. (Suggested subjects: new construction, combination of two schools, approval by an accreditation board, school bonds.)

13. Criticize and correct the following heads:

a. **Retires after 40 years of service**
   (Center on 44 ems, 48-maximum count)

b. **Mathematics:**
   Math great discipline, says prof.
   (2 column, 32 maximum)

   (Note: Look for a repetition of a word, an improper use of an abbreviation. You need not try to discard the bromide statement, though in writing a head, one hopes you would look for something a bit fresher than that "discipline" comment.)

c. **Advance to District 5**
   before loss to Bowie
   (21 picas, 21 count)

   (Note: Does this sound like directions in one of those games in which you throw dice and move to indicated spots?)

d. *Talebearer* given
   '**All-State' rating**
   (1 column, 17 maximum)

e. **Good time had by all at All-School Carnival April 1**
   (Center full page, 49 maximum)

f. **English useful to all students**
   (2 columns, 32 count)

   (Hint: Who says it is?)

g. **Mall Display:**
   Art Club gives exhibit in mall
   (2 columns, 32 count)

h. **'Aquabugs' of phys. ed.**
   dept. perform widely
   (21 ems, 21-count maximum, and no more than 1½ unit variation on each side)

   (Note: Abbreviations need attention. Look at first line. Complete thought unit.)

i. **Usherettes club is now**
   called 'Pathfinders'
   (21 picas, 21 count)

(Note break at end of first line.)

j. **Bus. classes, Bus. Ed. Club have**
   new internship program
   (2 columns, 32 count)

14. Copyread and edit the following passage:

The year just past has been a rebuilding year for our Trojan Ba Baskitball squad. After having loost five staring members of last years' team, coach Harold Krinetowl assembled a startin line-up centerde arond Re-turninge Varsity playres Rob Hight, and James Cook, both Seniors. The Coach then filled out the teem by bringing in playerrs from last yeers Junior varisyt squad, in cluin 6-feet 5-inch Otto Blunkett, who avraged 18 pints and thirteen rebonud in for-Teen games lastyeare, Othre we Otherrs on the stqrrti gfive, were, Geo. Bilips; and don Jumper, both gardes, with these boys Coch Blunkett maneged to pu together a wining seeson, 14-12 overalls, and thrid place in city competiion. If it had not been for the officialing, si x othre games whould have been won by our valiant troyans, local fans agred.

60

(Note: I realize the above is far worse than any conceivable single piece of copy, but I have deliberately compounded the errors to provide a maximum of editorial effort in brief space. After you have corrected all spelling, punctuation, capitalization, grammar lapses, and sentence structure, recopy the whole thing. Lead with what you consider the feature, and add "facts" you consider essential to such a story—leading scorer and his average and total, leading rebounder and his average and total, perhaps some city-wide honors won, etc.)

15. Imagine the following proofs to have been returned by your printer. Mark corrections. I have again exaggerated the likelihood of error in the interest of giving maximum practice in proofreading in a short space. Since your printer has professional operators and, most likely, expert proofreaders who try to eliminate all inconsistencies between set type and the copy submitted, you are not likely ever to be confronted with anything vaguely like this in one story. See proof-marks before you begin your work. Remember to mark errors in margins here.

Wildcas wrestlres continued thier

Dominance over the rest of the East

suburban Conference teams by exten-

ding their un beaten streake to thirtyfivr

consecutiv league games, In the five

yeares that the Wild cats have been

members of the E.S.C., the hav nevr

lost a League Game.

Many of the Wildcat finissed thee sea-

sonn with excelllent recrds. outstanding

seniors were Jhon Horstman, Wilhelm (Bill)

Travis, and Ian Masterson.

Three returning letterman who contrib-

uted to the yeares records wer, James (bear")

Mussleman, Harvey ("Strong man") John-

son; and Rick ("Hapy") Beal.

Etaoin shrdlu Etaoin Etaoin Etaoin shrdlu

After you have edited this piece, comment on facts you wish the writer might have added to make the story more interesting. Remember, though, that this is not the time or place for rewriting.

5.
Photography

I. The newspaper and the magazine depend first on words for their communication. The yearbook, on the other hand, is unique among printed publications in that it relies first on photography, only secondarily on words, to tell its story.

  A. Although the major part of space in a yearbook is devoted to pictorial art, the quality of the words should not be slighted or be any less than the quality expected in yearbook photography.

  B. Many editors have used line drawings, cartooning, even color paintings for illustration of their books, with varying degrees of success, from brilliant to ugly and distracting. But let me underscore what I said earlier under the discussion of theme, and again very briefly under "Design and Layout Patterns."

    1. You will be safer to prefer average-to-good photographs above average, fair, or doubtful student art of any kind. Few schools have students who are qualified to illustrate a yearbook with their own art. If you are fortunate enough to have rarely gifted young artists in your midst who can glorify openers, dividers, or other special pages with their drawings or paintings, by all means make use of their efforts. Otherwise, refuse their work tactfully and graciously, or try to divert it to something useful but less valuable and permanent than a yearbook. You need poster art in promoting sales. And maybe what these young artists can offer will be useful and appropriate to the needs of the newspaper or the literary or humor magazine.

    2. Inside the pages devoted to academic-curricular coverage, you may feel justified in offering generous space to coverage of the creative efforts of students of art classes, clay modeling, sculpture, ceramics, drawing, commercial art, and even cartooning. But all this has nothing to do with the needs of your book for illustrating its theme or for total coverage.

II. Portraits were once proudly flaunted in seemingly endless profusion at the front of every yearbook (then called "annual" by most of those who edited or read it). Only the standard opening pages, title page, and opening scenes took priority. Now the portrait section has been universally relegated to the back of the book. Mass portraits, especially those of clubs and other groups, lose status and popularity year by year. But we must still give attention to all three general kinds of pictures.

A. Formal portraits, especially those of students, though relocated, seem to be with us as unvarying fixtures of the yearbook. Like the index, perhaps these portraits are needed as permanent references to the student, and maybe faculty, population of a given year. That has long been the conviction of planners, and most high school students at least comply with the call, "Have your pictures taken for the yearbook." (There is less reliable compliance from college students.)

   1. Portraits must be taken by professional photographers. These people are trained for this highly specialized work, have the needed equipment, have the business management and bookkeeping setup for taking pictures promptly and keeping records, and can deliver prints on or before a deadline.

   2. Quality is implicit in the term "professional." Yet you must set standards of quality that you feel are essential for your book, and having the acceptance of your contracted photographer, you should insist that these standards be met. Let me offer some suggestions:

      a. Specify the usual glossy or semi-gloss print preferred by most printers. Never accept matte-finish paper for prints. This is popular for framed or mounted portraits, but it reproduces poorly in a yearbook.

      b. Insist that the portrait stand out sharply from the background, with a range of tones that makes features of the face clear and distinct. A loss of perhaps 10 percent in clarity from portrait to finished yearbook page is to be expected and anticipated. As to backgrounds, professional photographers usually provide curtains or drapes best suited for portraits.

      c. Some authorities recommend use of a "gray scale" by the editor to determine whether portraits have suitable range of tones to reproduce properly. Eastman and likely other companies have such a scale. Ask your supplier for his suggestion, or talk to your printer. (The latter may even provide you with such a scale.)

      d. Insist that students dress in a reasonably consistent way, but unless your school requires the wearing of uniform dress or clothing for all occasions, absolute uniformity is not desirable for portraits. Jackets and ties are usually required for male students, and it is a good idea to have a supply of extras of both on hand for students who appear without them. For girls, you will likely wish to standardize requirements so there is no wide disparity of costumes, from evening dress to jeans. It is to be hoped that all appear with neat hairdos and in dresses commonly worn for semi-formal social occasions. Photographers often suggest too that girls wear dresses that contrast in color with their hair—dark for blondes, light for brunettes.

      e. Rule out senior gowns or special fraternity garbs.

      f. Set a standard head size for all portraits, or for each class.

      g. Have all students posed facing the camera, thus avoiding a scrambled look on the portrait pages. Especially rule out exotic "Hollywood" poses for yearbook use—looking over the shoulder, etc.

      h. Rule out overuse of makeup. It will be the duty of the photographer to touch out unsightly blemishes from the negatives.

      i. Put it in the contract that the photographer is expected to do this needed retouching, and also that he will promptly reshoot portraits that are of unsuitable technical quality.

   3. See suggestions (under layout) for grouping portraits into rectangular blocks.

   4. Avoid bleeding portraits off the page. This too often results in unintended "scalpings" or other unfortunate acts of pictorial mayhem.

5. Expect to pay fair prices for portraits. (Inquire around to determine the "going" rate for quality portraits.) Make arrangements for the sale of extra prints entirely separate from those for portraits used in the book, with all conditions, commissions, etc., spelled out clearly in typed words.

6. Portrait photographers are sometimes available for shooting group pictures, even action shots, in schools with few photographers and limited facilities, at a reasonable cost made possible by the fact that they have personnel and equipment already scheduled for the school. I am inclined to recommend against any portrait deal that makes the contract contingent on the taking of such extra pictures. Often, both portraiture and extra pictures suffer as the result of such an agreement.

7. Trimming and placement of portraits can complement good portrait quality and show portraits to best advantage, or the reverse.

   a. If you are required to trim, don't go so low as to scalp or deface the portrait. (I have already advised against bleeding, which can cause the same damage.)

   b. Trim no higher than the bottom of the rib cage or the waist.

   c. Keep the shape of each portrait rectangular, with slightly more depth than width. Avoid absolutely square shaping, as well as oval, circular, or star shapes. Don't trim corners, and don't airbrush or outline portraits.

B. Tradition, that mindless and impartial preserver of values and flaws, has chosen to keep the group portrait as a vestigial remnant of primitive books that reminds some observers of such useless parts as adenoids in people. Arguments for the group picture are that it enables the staff to portray a large number of students, and thus increase appeal to the readers. Those against the group portrait suggest that it is surplus, an anachronism surviving from days when photographers propped their subjects' heads to keep them still, used flash powder, and were unable to show action, having neither films nor lenses for the job. They add that in most books every student has his portrait in the class section for future reference and for the delight of parents, girl or boy friends, and doting aunts. In short, there is growing sentiment against what some call static "mug mobs," despite the fervent and nostalgic advocacy of many experts and writers of texts. I see the opposition as a recognition that times have changed and are changing, and that the "now" people are interested in the dynamic, that which represents action and life. But since traditional practices die very slowly in colleges and often as slowly in certain high schools, and since after all the complaints there is still some sound argument for retaining pictures of posed groups such as athletic teams, the band, the choral groups, and maybe honorary groups "just for the record and for future reference," let's discuss these formal group pictures.

1. Professional photographers are to be preferred for taking these pictures in most colleges as well as most high schools. They have proper equipment and trained personnel. They are able to standardize quality. They understand how to pose groups, using risers and putting faces as close together as possible. And finally, they understand how to fulfill contracts and to meet deadlines. Amateurs, even very good ones, are likely to fall short in one or more of the above requirements.

2. Set some rules for quality and posing, preferably in a written agreement or contract. Have a full and frank discussion with the photographer in advance so that there will be a clear understanding of objectives.

   a. Where there are three or more rows, risers such as gymnasium steps make good props. Keep distance at a minimum between rows.

   b. Have individual subjects pose as close together horizontally as practical, yet still allowing room for those behind to be placed looking between those in the row immediately ahead.

   c. As in other photography, insist that there be a wide range of tones and adequate contrast between faces and backgrounds.

   d. Avoid distracting backgrounds, such as lamps, busy wallpaper patterns, or clutter of any kind. And be equally sure the foreground has been cleaned of debris.

e. Try to avoid picturing vacant seats at the front, in the center, or elsewhere.

f. Don't accept a print in which there is blinking, clowning, mugging, face-making; or where someone was looking around, "making up" her face, straightening his tie, etc.

g. Don't accept "originality" (dating back at least 30 years) in which a group poses sitting in trees, crowded into a fire engine in the park, circling up the stairs, sitting on the roof of a fraternity building, climbing around on the hood and sides of a large truck or car used in an auto mechanics club, etc. This sort of doubtful humor should have departed with vaudeville and minstrel shows.

h. Don't accept poses of groups in any sort of artificial shapings like musical scales or clefs or staffs; the oval shape of a football or the round of a baseball or a basketball; a star, a moon, etc. And don't accept a substitute for a group in which cutout portrait *heads* are placed in these shapings or others like them.

i. In ruling out oddly arranged groups discussed above, rule out also numbered outline drawings with idents based on the numbers. Abandoned (with the irregularly posed group) decades ago, this strange concept has been exhumed, dusted off, and used by exuberantly proud "inventors" in college books. Only recently an author who should have known better gave it a boost in a book offering advice to editors. It is advice that I hope will be widely ignored.

j. Finally, don't pose people artificially with props in their hands or by their sides, such as a letterman's club with tennis rackets, baseball bats, basketballs, golf clubs, etc., intended to suggest graphically what sport each club member has been associated with.

3. Size, placement, and shaping deserve a few words:

a. Keep posed group shots as small as you can while retaining recognizability. (See Chapter 11.)

b. Place these groups at the lowest, least conspicuous positions, subordinating them to life-action pictures that record achievements or events. (See II-C for discussions of action pictures.) Eventually, perhaps, these groups will all be placed just before the index and advertising, as is already true in some modern yearbooks. Moreover, high schools should seriously consider revenue-raising possibilities of charging clubs for taking such group poses and for space in the book. Many colleges already do this. This seems fair enough, since the function of the yearbook staff is to provide a story in action pictures and lively words of the events and achievements of a year in the school, not necessarily to contribute to the ego inflation of groups with little or no part in the year's story. (See discussion under "Clubs," Chapter 11.)

c. Trim off extraneous backgrounds— all that do not give essential information about the locale, show an unusual setting, or help tell the story itself. Come as close to the tops of heads on the back row as possible without seeming to scalp or threaten to scalp them.

d. Trim just as closely at the sides and bottoms. Trim to the waistlines (or bottoms of the rib cage), as you do individual portraits.

e. The cutline or ident should usually be placed below this kind of picture. Set a standard distance (margin) such as a pica (em) or perhaps 3/16 inch or 1/4 inch. Once you have set your own margin, stay with it.

f. As was stated in the preceding chapter, idents may be omitted for pictures containing an unusually large number of faces. The difficulty of identifying all those whose faces appear in a picture of a 250-member marching band is overwhelming. And the bulk of gray names on a page would be visually unappealing to the reader.

C. Even traditionalists must agree today that by far the most important yearbook photography pictures the life and action in the school. Beyond merely recording the presence of individual students, teachers, officials, and others who serve, these activity shots congeal and save for all time visual evidence of life, events, accomplishments, triumphs, and day-to-day happenings, whether humdrum or dramatic. They make their own reports on what happened in classes, halls, gymnasiums and cafeteria; on school grounds, field trips, and school openings; in assemblies; and on holidays. They offer permanent records of small characteristic expressions of face and gestures of hands, feet, and bodies that made up life in a special school or college in a special year. While all other photographs are merely for reference, important as they may seem, life and action photography will, for all time to come, say, "Here is how it was in our unique school that unique year!"

1. Let's consider first the pictures that record sports and other big all-school news events:

   a. Some of these can be taken by professionals. For example, try to arrange with any local newspaper sports photographer who covers your games and other events to purchase prints of pictures suitable for the yearbook. If he can handle these for you, that is good. If he cannot, he will tell you what newspaper policy requires. (I have always had good luck dealing directly with the photographer.)

   b. The photographer who contracts to take portraits may, as I said above, be willing to take some of your spot news pictures, especially if these can be shot at the time he is already at school to take portraits.

   c. Some staffs have teacher-advisers capable of doing part of the yearbook photography, or they have access to teachers in other fields who are photo hobbyists or even professionals in the art. In such happy circumstances, admittedly rare, I see nothing wrong with taking full advantage of opportunities. But it should be remembered that even advisers with ability and equip-ment have limitations of time and energy, especially since these competent people are often given heaviest load assignments by administrators.

   d. The most reliable overall method of getting news or feature pictures or any sort of action shots is training one's own staff, having a publications darkroom (possibly shared with the newspaper staff and/or camera club), cameras, equipment, and supplies. Since this is not a photo textbook, I leave the techniques of training to others, but in later pages I will offer some suggestions of a broad nature on equipment, darkroom, and supplies.

2. Scenic pictures, taken in the various seasons and showing building exteriors and grounds, may seem to be different from any other types of picture record, but in my opinion they are logically a part of the record of life and action of the school if they are to serve the purposes of a yearbook.

   a. To begin with, be sure these pictures are of professional or near-professional quality, since they are likely to get large display in prominent places. Light streaks, improper development, excessive graininess from being overblown, or scratches or spots from poor darkroom work will show up most embarrassingly in scenic pictures.

   b. Somewhere in the opening pages, plan to include one or more shots that show at least the main or administrative building and the grounds or campus.

   c. Keep the seasons and the various times of day in mind as you plan these scenic pictures. Local professional photographers and your suppliers will be able to help you in this planning.

   d. Make the scenic pictures the settings for life and action, which they are. The photo of a dead, empty school ground or of a building with nobody in it may suggest more of a desolation and disuse than the setting for a story of life during a school year. Dramatic exceptions might include the photo of a frozen fountain; a hall scene in late afternoon after all the students have departed; a night scene with all lights blazing (get clearance from those in charge of power conservation); an unusual weather scene following a flood or after an unusual snowstorm or ice storm. Even with most of these, there is usually a way to include human life. A lone maintenance man working at the far end of the desolate hall, for instance, adds realism and a bit of drama. Some brave, adventurous students will be available for that scene after a winter storm.

   e. Trim is important, even in scenic pictures, to focus attention on points of greatest interest or beauty. Crop off whatever may take attention away from the center of interest.

3. Mood pictures are in themselves part of the drama of life. Such pictures may draw attention to facial expressions of joy, excitement, meditation, unhappiness (such as that during the losing efforts of the home team), studious concentration (during exams), etc.

   a. These are especially useful in opening pages, dividers, or the closing. They can help set a theme or help introduce the school in some special way.

   b. Even mood pictures can be given added value with cutlines or idents. While photographers, like all of us perhaps, tend to attach undue powers to their own art and may urge that such pictures require no verbal support, I believe that it is better to say too much than to leave the reader puzzled or wishing for more information. The purpose of this game is communication, first of all, and only secondarily, art. Moreover, ours is a society in which individual members sense that they are unrecognized and unappreciated, faces lost in the crowd. Identification is a deeply felt need of the human being. Give your subjects their brief moments of glory by naming them. (Obviously, a mood picture showing backs of heads or blending many faces into a crowd requires no idents,

though a general cutline may make even this picture more interesting to the reader. (But I have discussed this in Chapter 3.)

   c. Mood ideas, like words and phrases, are easily worn out. Thus thematic use of footprints, devices for time (clocks, hourglasses, watches), and hands and feet has long ago made repetition of these ideas unsuitable. Avoid them for more than spot or occasional use. (See Chapter 1.)

4. *Candid* as a word derives from the Latin *candidus*, for *white* or *sincere*. The term was adopted by the phrasemakers to designate a camera with a fast lens that took "sincere" or "natural" pictures, preferably without the knowledge of the subjects. Early editors of litho books went absolutely wild over candid pictures. These editors made much use of the word *snapshots,* because amateurs *snapped* pictures without plan or purpose, using primitive box cameras. These snapshots were trimmed in a thousand shapes and crowded with artless profusion into the book, often as many as 100 to 150 on a page. And a large section was used for these snapshots. Sometimes the young editor permitted himself the pleasure of writing, or better, hand-lettering, what he considered to be extremely clever remarks under or near these snapshots. With the air of someone who has caught his friends and acquaintances in embarrassing moments, as they grimaced toward the cameraman over great expanses of sand on a beach or across wide expanses of the school ground, the editor offered captions like "What's up, Doc?", "Lose something, Harry?", "Watch your step, Bill!", and the rare phrase of congealed genius, "Guess Who!" (That last bit was captured from newspaper columns of the early offset days.) Today's equivalent to, or modernization of, the antique candid-camera page is something carefully planned. Pictures are outlined in advance and the subjects are alerted to what is about to happen and cautioned against seeming aware of the camera.

   a. It is unreasonable to expect that random snapshots handed in by untrained student photographers will be worth using in a yearbook (or anywhere else, actually). Don't discourage such offerings, but don't promise to use them either.

b. Don't plan to use clippings of snapshots (or any other pictures) taken from newspapers. However sharp the print seems at first glance, it will contain numerous unsightly halftone dots when it is reproduced. I recently saw the results of such an effort in a magazine. If you observe something you are eager to use in your book, go to the source and try to get the original print or a negative from which a glossy print can be made. Most newspapers and magazines keep these in their libraries. India-ink sketches or line drawings are entirely different and can be picked up from any clear printing, since these have no halftone dots. But don't believe the old saw about offset lithography reproducing "anything at all, even your grandfather's mustache." Not from a once-printed halftone picture, it won't.

c. Think of "candids" the way dramatic writers, actors, or directors think of a scene they intend to present on stage or before a TV audience. They aim at a performance that, as Robert Louis Stevenson said of the good book, leaves the beholder "rapt clean out of himself," that is, convinced of absolute realism, because the author has used every art at his disposal to plan and create the illusion. Fast film and (when needed) good flash equipment will enable the photographer to shoot a number of pictures of the practice or the actual performance of a play; of students debating; of track practice or the actual meet; of rehearsals, or the real program, at a school assembly; and of the event that is hardest of all to make interesting, the presentation of a check, award, or certificate. The last-named picture is usually best taken before or after the actual program, to avoid getting in the way of spectators or disrupting the presentation with a camera and flash.

d. If you assign (or shoot) a posed or simulated action shot, don't settle for something that *looks* posed, with the actors frozen in action. An example of this is the faked shot-putting picture, with the athlete poised on one leg at the end of his spin, holding the 16-pound (or even 12-pound) shot still while someone focuses, checks flash, etc. Other artificial poses I have seen include such subjects as "frozen" basketball players, taken at the height of the act of tossing the ball, yet holding the ball; football linemen with elbows out, ready to push opposing players aside, yet standing absolutely still at the height of the rise, and reminding one of Mark Twain's famed frog which, having hunched its shoulders for a jump, discovered itself immobilized by buckshot. Insist on real action, and let the cameras stop the action.

e. For a relatively static picture in which two or three subjects are seated at a table or standing in a semicircle, the good photographer will explain what he is trying to record, relaxed informality. He will tell the group to proceed with what they are doing and to pay no attention to him or the camera. He will explain that he plans to take a number of pictures, and he may lull a self-conscious group into relaxation by pretending to snap the shutter a few times without actually exposing any film. At length, he will actually take his photo, and if wise will protect himself against error or flaw by exposing some extra film.

f. Never accept camera-gawking. (Oh, if it happens that the queen of England visits unexpectedly, and the only photo anyone got was one in which the royal party stood at attention and "watched the birdie" on cue, you will accept the picture and be glad.) Such static poses invariably remind the viewers of those old newsreels in which (a) natives of a remote South Sea island

68

gaze directly into the camera as if they thought they were looking at a magic box capable of producing witchcraft: (b) mountain goats, never before photographed, staring into the camera a moment before turning to leap to safety.

g. Don't ever pose more than four or five subjects at a time in a picture. More than this (except in what is intended as a mob scene) will make it impossible to maintain any semblance of true lifelikeness or unity in the picture.

5. Remember, for all action pictures, to insist on a center of interest that is somewhat off mathematical or geographical center, slightly to the right or left of a vertical line bisecting the picture, slightly below or above a horizontal bisector. These points are said to be *optical centers of interest*.

6. Remember, in planning and selecting pictures of all kinds, that the true test is *quality*, not *quantity*. There are limits to how many faces should appear in one activity picture. It is ridiculously impractical and undesirable to set a goal of "representing every student in school at least once" in activity shots. (I am assuming yours to be a school of average size, not one of 75, 100, or 150 students, with a small or medium-sized book.) A better goal is to try to please readers by offering them a wide variety of pictures that truthfully reflect what students and faculty did, what went on in school, in the year you are recording. The effort to strain a shy person into false or unnatural action may be more than it is worth in coverage, besides running counter to your goal of honesty.

7. Avoid favoring any person, group of persons, or inner clique. I heard of one yearbook that was said to have 42 separate pictures of the editor. (The one who reported it was a campus rival. The editor indignantly retorted that she was pictured only 21 times.) Remember that the yearbook is not a product intended to gratify the egos of the inner circle, or even the fraternity brothers of the editor.

8. Be sure the cutlines tell what the most remote reader, the most recently transferred student, the greenest freshman will need to be told to understand the picture. Cryptic statements intended to delight insiders while perplexing those outside the magic circle are inappropriate. They went out with those old "guess-who" cutlines and their counterpart newspaper columns.

9. Stress to photographers that they should always do as suggested above, take enough pictures and make enough exposures for every event, especially one that cannot be repeated, so that one bad print will not prove disastrous to coverage.

10. **One popular sort of pictorial reporting** is the photo story. It is a series of separate pictures of consecutive or concurrent action. The word story may be carried in a body block, with very brief cutlines or idents, or there may be no body block at all, only a series of, or a single block of, cutlines that relate the running story of the pictures. Let me illustrate:

a. The oldest idea is a picture story taking a typical student through a day of school life. (Or it may be a typical athlete, student actor, or student musician.) Localize it and be sure it applies to this year and is not merely a generalization that could be "any school, any year."

b. Another idea is to take the coach through the day of a big game. You may have to reconstruct this series, since the coach on the actual day may be far from relaxed enough to allow a photographer or anyone else to intrude on his schedule. But a skillful recap can be as realistic as the real thing.

c. Spring days often bring students out onto the lawn, suggesting a sort of composite story of what students do with their time between classes, at lunch period, etc., under such conditions. Here, you would likely not follow a single subject or subjects, though this is a possibility, with the cooperation of selected subjects. But the story here could easily be the variety of activities of different persons. Some sleep or drowse, some sprawl or gossip, some study, some concentrate

Photography **69**

or reflect, some play games, some pair off for romantic talk. . . .

d. Fall has its scenery, its own inspiration to action, as, in fact, does a time of snowy weather, or even a sudden shower, if your photographer and reporter are adventurous and hardy enough and the one with a camera knows how to protect his valuable equipment and keep everything reasonably dry, as Jacques Cousteau's magnificent cameramen have learned to do.

e. Favorite student haunts offer great possibilities: the cafeteria, an ice cream shop, a coffee shop, a center for bowling, or whatever your local hangout may be. (Actually, what I have suggested here is something similar to the popular page or spread of pictures that the better magazine-style student newspapers are offering their readers. I couldn't tell you which preceded which. Both publications no doubt drew inspiration from the late lamented pictorial magazines, *Look* and *Life*.)

11. Don't overlook one final type of action picture for the book, the natural crowd scene. A few such shots are essential for full, realistic coverage. Here, of course, you will disregard the general rule of keeping numbers small. The actual goal is bigness, a crowded look. Spectators at a basketball game or football game or other exciting event offer interesting studies for the alert photographer. Special days celebrated by unusual costumes offer possibilities, especially if there is an assembly program or gathering of those in unusual dress or makeup. Special dances and parties offer opportunities for the crowd scene. But there are cautions and suggestions to observe:

a. Avoid shots taken across a classroom or study hall. All of them look alike and have no special relevance to the year or the school. As they say, "When you've seen one, you've seen them all!"

b. Sometimes it is possible to focus on one or two persons or a small group in the foreground. Letting other figures blur out at least slightly may intensify the interest of the picture. Focus attention on the facial expressions or on the gestures of the key figures.

c. You need not try to identify persons in a mob scene, other than perhaps the few to whom you are calling special attention. Even here, since the idea is to portray the action and mood(s) of a crowd, specific idents may not seem appropriate. Do tell readers the *what,* the *occasion,* the *where,* the *time,* perhaps the *outcome,* if a question is raised by the picture. (Ex.: If everyone is cheering for the home team, let the readers know whether the team won or lost that day. Give a few details about the occasion.)

12. Hold fast to the philosophy that the yearbook of today and tomorrow will first concentrate on presenting a vivid pictures-and-words story of the year. Action and life will predominate, leaving static portraiture, single or group, and the other reference material, however essential, to lesser or subordinate positioning, at the back of the book and bottoms of spreads. This suggestion applies with added emphasis to sports and clubs pages. Coverage of other events will take care of itself naturally, as a rule, there being no formal group or team sponsorship, or at least none that normally intrudes.

III. **If you have a photography class, as many colleges and an increasing number of high schools do, problems of training and equipment are simple or nonexistent. But even if you have only one or two willing students, perhaps partly trained or self-educated, and a willing if dubiously educated teacher (maybe even the yearbook adviser), you are likely not far from the normal situation for most schools at one time or another. Turn for advice and help to friendly local commercial photographers, to those who are to take the portraits and perhaps formal groups and some of the action shots. This, as I said above, is not a photography text. But let me offer what some experts have told me through the years I have worked with yearbooks in one capacity or another.**

A. *Cameras:* Howard T. Harris (*Photolith,* March 1971) says that every yearbook and newspaper staff would ideally own a press camera, a twin-lens reflex and a 35mm camera. He discusses these three types of cameras.

1. The 4×5 press camera may be purchased secondhand at a considerable saving, he points out. A new one with essential equipment, such as flash, may cost several hundred dollars. Sturdy and durable, this camera offers single-sheet films that may be developed separately, as contrasted with full rolls that must be used and developed together in the other cameras. This camera permits a wide variety of adjustments, says Mr. Harris, but the slow speed of its lens makes use of the flash essential in low-light situations. Its use also requires use of the tripod for posed group shots, since holding this camera by hand results in a blur from the inevitable movement.

2. The $2\frac{1}{2} \times 3\frac{1}{4}$ twin-lens camera is Mr. Harris' first choice for high school, and the one he says is most often used. It has economical film and a faster lens, and it can generally be used in classrooms without artificial light, he says. It also has the advantage of being cheaper to purchase than the news camera and attachments. Photographer-teacher Mark Popovich (*Photolith,* December 1969) also casts a vote for this camera as most practical in taking high school yearbook photographs.

3. Mr. Harris says the 35mm camera is "a pleasure to use," but he echoes Mr. Popovich's complaints about it. The major flaw is that it shoots very small negatives, and when these are enlarged to the 8×10-inch size needed for yearbook or newspaper use, too much grain appears. Furthermore, such enlargement builds up minor flaws in the negative to major proportions. Harris votes for the 35mm as a second choice, or a second camera, but stresses the conditions: The user must take utmost care in shooting, developing, and enlargement.

4. One other camera, the Polaroid Land camera, has been tried from time to time in student publications work, but it does not seem to be recommended for this purpose by any experienced photographer. Mr. Popovich mentions it in the article cited above, but only to dismiss it as unsuitable for yearbook photography. He says that few professionals ever use it, appealing as its "instant print" seems. Of course, if that unusual event or that once-in-a-lifetime visitor passes your way leaving as a visual record only a hazy print taken by the school's Polaroid bug, you would hardly disdain it.

B. *Lenses:* Most amateur photographers, including those on the yearbook staff, will content themselves with the lenses normally used on the camera or cameras they have selected. A teacher, a photographer, or a representative from the camera supply house will offer counsel in this matter. Robert Friend, a photographer trained at Ball State University, made some suggestions in *Photolith,* March 1972, for those with an urge to experiment. He points out in the article that such lens switching has had great appeal to student photographers of the 1970s. He says that the 35mm camera is best suited for this purpose. I will list some of his observations, in full realization that other experienced photographers may have differing opinions or recommendations.

1. The normal lens for the 35mm has 50 to 55mm focal lengths. This lens sees subjects about the way the human eyeball does, without distortion, as humans recognize the word.

2. Fish-eye lenses (superwide angle lenses) are in the 6mm, 7mm, and 8mm range, and they visualize things as, presumably, a fish does, up to 180 degrees, with everything from one inch away to infinity in focus. Some very flashy pictures, usually appearing in circular shape, have been used as eye-catchers or special shots in yearbooks. Obviously, this type of picture is good mainly as a variety shot and must not be overused.

3. Wide-angle lenses are excellent for landscapes, seascapes, and large groups of people whom you wish to picture without moving the camera too far away. These lenses have 28mm to 35mm focal lengths. They distort somewhat, especially at the edges, though by no means like the fish-eye lens. Mr. Friend recommends that this lens not be used when a normal lens can be made to serve.

4. What Mr. Friend prefers to call "semi-telephoto" lenses are those from 90-

mm to 135mm focal lengths. He says they work well for candids. The 135-mm lens is especially good for basket-ball and track, permitting the photog-rapher to get close to the action.

5. Telephoto lenses are, of course, those that bring truly distant action, as in football and basketball, up close to the camera, just as the telescope brings the scene close to the naked eye. Friend speaks of 180mm or 200-mm up to 500mm focal lengths as true telephoto lenses. He suggests use of a tripod with all such lenses, since they tend to magnify the blur caused by camera movement. These lenses, says Friend, are good for the sports mentioned and also for taking pictures of construction work and for taking candids at some distance.

6. Two other kinds of lenses mentioned by this photographer are the super-telephoto (500 to 1,000mm focal lengths) and the zoom lenses that al-low instant adjustment within a whole range of lens lengths. Both are expensive and likely impractical for the average student photographer. But file the ideas away for that time when your photo staff has exhausted possibilities afforded by all the other types of lenses.

C. *Films and photo supplies:* Take the ad-vice of your professional adviser, teach-er, or perhaps the expert in your supply store. Or at least experiment until you find what films and other materials, such as developing fluids, work best for you and/or fit best your needs and bud-get.

1. Photographer Howard Harris (see above) says that in using fast films, a definite advantage in taking action, you can also avoid graininess. The secret is in *proper exposure, develop-ing, fixing,* and *washing.* On the oth-er hand, the photographer can give sharper contrast to slower films, he points out, by finding the right ex-posure time; by using right develop-ing, fixing, and washing materials; and by the use of correct techniques. It sounds reasonable.

2. After experimenting with various supplies and techniques, Harris urges the student photographer (or any other) to standardize both procedures

and supplies (see *Photolith*, Septem-ber 1971). Once you have found methods, timing, and kinds of devel-oping and washing fluids, films, etc., that give your photo staff the best re-sults, stick to them.

3. This same prolific teacher-photog-pher-author has given practical ad-vice to beginners on avoiding flaws in prints (*Photolith*, December 1971–January 1972). I can offer nothing better than a summary of these sug-gestions.

   a. Keep hands clean while working with photographic supplies. Keep hair grease, body oils, lint, dust, etc., off films and negatives.

   b. Keep all cosmetics out of the dark-room.

   c. Never touch negatives with the fin-gers. Catch them by the edges. Store all negatives in glassene en-velopes.

   d. By prewashing with a special bath, the photographer can prevent wa-ter spots from appearing on his fi-nal prints.

D. *Darkroom:* Let me repeat that this is not a text on the technical aspects of photography or of photojournalism. What the editor picks up here is a bo-nus, and I gladly pass tidbits on that have been generously passed along to me by the experts. A spare closet, with a sink and running water, has been turned into a simple and usable dark-room in some cases. Eastman, and no doubt other camera and supply houses, will provide you with booklets or at least information on how to set up and equip this important facility. Turn to your professional photographer or ex-pert in the supply store for help and sug-gestions. And even if you are well pro-vided with money to do so, don't start out with overly elaborate equipment. Wade in as cautiously as you can and establish your needs and your ability to use what you are about to acquire be-fore making any additions.

E. *Lighting:* Advisers and editors, as well as inexperienced or learning photog-phers, will benefit from knowing what trained photographers have said about lighting for informal photographs, espe-cially indoor shots.

1. Influenced by his experience with

modern film and improved cameras and lenses, Leslie Howell of Newport News, Virginia, successful teacher and adviser, has spoken out strongly in favor of "available light," lighting that comes handy in the gymnasium, on the football field, even at night and in darkish locker rooms (*Photolith*, October 1971). Most convincing arguments of all are the pictures with which his article is illustrated. He exhibits prints taken with and without flash. He gives shutter speeds, lens settings, and types of film used, and he presents a detailed chart showing his use of a special film put out by a leading company.

2. Adviser George Abbott of Redding, California, sharply contradicts Mr. Howell (*Photolith*, November 1971). He argues the need for flash equipment and mentions the costs of a Japanese-import twin-lens camera and the flash equipment that goes with it. He adds his own thumbs-down on use of the Polaroid camera ("too simple") and also the 35mm camera, which he calls "too complex" when used with all the added filters and lenses. He expresses his firm belief that "anyone can take pictures," supporting the controversial position with some pictures taken by new and relatively untrained students. "Forget all about available-light photography," he emphasizes, arguing that it is "for the 'pros,' " or for the situation where the teacher is himself an expert and has unusually talented student photographers on his staff. Undoubtedly, the truth for each staff will vary, though likely not to the extent it has between these two excellent advisers, each of whom saw and reported facts from his own experiences and point of view. Fred Price, another adviser-writer in the same yearbook magazine (September 1972) urged a moderate, commonsense approach to the matter of lighting that would neither reject natural light nor argue its universal applicability. Your own experimentation with flash and without, and your commonsense evaluation of results will lead you to your own truth about the use of lighting.

IV. Policies: At Wyandotte High, Kansas City, Kansas, Miss Niki Economy and her staff produced their own little "Publications Guide," which might serve as a model for all staffs. Let's look at some of the points on photography this guidebook should contain.

A. Start by naming the kinds of pictures you are interested in obtaining for the yearbook.
   1. Take the classifications mentioned earlier in this chapter and describe the quality and the method of posing you expect in portraits and in posed groups. For the latter, give instructions regarding risers and backgrounds.
   2. I urge you to rule out "trick" shots of people climbing trees or walls, standing on trucks, staring off rooftops, sitting in playground swings, or hanging onto or looking out of locomotive engines and railroad cars.
   3. You may wish to set desired head sizes. An old idea that sounds larger than practical in many cases was "the size of a dime."
   4. Rule out shots taken with wide-angle lenses.
   5. Rule out idents aided by numbered outlines, an archaic device.
   6. Set a style for identifying all "mug-mob shots." (See Chapter 4).
   7. Give limits of numbers of subjects desired for action shots. (Scenic pictures with action and mob-action pictures themselves are, of course, excepted from such limitations.)
   8. Discuss and locate centers of interest in action photos.
   9. Rule out obvious posing, including those horrible fake sports actions mentioned earlier.
   10. Set a cutline style for action pictures. If you have a special typographical pattern for starting cutlines, explain and illustrate it.
   11. Set rules against stating the obvious, such as saying, "Shown above . . ." or "Shaking hands above. . . ."
B. Establish clear rules for scheduling group pictures.
   1. Tell who has authority to represent staff and photographer in setting up

appointments, and who is expected to represent the club or group (president, secretary, adviser, etc.).

2. Formalize an assignment card suitable to staff needs and agreeable to the commercial photographer (or whatever photographer you use). It should have:
    a. Date and time of picture, place of meeting or of picture, name of photographer in charge (if there are two or more assigned to do such work)
    b. Blanks for signatures by staff and club representatives

3. Establish some rules regarding dress of club or group members.

4. Specify that those to be pictured shall be informed well in advance.

5. Include a reminder system that will avoid mixups and assure that a maximum number of those who should be in the picture are there and on time, and that the photographer himself will not suffer a memory lapse.

C. Devise a card to be used in assigning staff photographer(s) to take news or other action shots, to cover sports events, etc.

1. Spell out details. Give the topic of the picture(s) and the shape(s) desired. (Leave enough space for a sketch by the one making the assignment—this to contain figures and general proportions.)

2. Leave blanks for the date the assignment is made, the suggested time for taking the picture, the initials or names of the assigning editor, and the photographer assigned.

3. An office bulletin board may be considered as an alternate to or a supplement to the card system. At least you cannot mislay a bulletin board.

4. Whether a card or bulletin board is used, when the assignment is made far in advance of an event, provide a blank and set up a system for an editorial reminder near the time. (See the suggestion on group shots above.)

D. Whether or not you prepare a guidebook, make firm policies regarding contracts with commercial photographers, the time, the person(s) who should make and sign agreements, some guidelines for the requirements to be made in selecting a photographer, and the general standards to be expected. The contract form should contain the agreed costs, the kind of paper and finish to be used, the sizes of prints, the scheduling, the deadlines, quality standards, and rules governing retakes.

E. Establish procedures for handling and preserving pictures. A locked file or cabinet, with keys in the hands of selected staff members only, will prevent an experience the staff of the *Houstonian* (University of Houston) once had when all student portraits simply disappeared. The photographer was able to reprint all of them, but the time lag delayed delivery of the book two or three months, necessitating expensive mailing to all subscribers rather than direct distribution.

F. Rule that all prints are to be rectangular, not oval, octagonal, round, or any other shape, except possibly for a rare eye-catcher. Avoid squares too.

V. Planning procedures: There are two conflicting schools of thought about whether pictures are to be taken before or after page layouts are planned.

A. Photographers tend to support the former position. Photographer Lillian Junas (*Photolith,* January 1970) has argued that "form follows function," and that, until a photographer and perhaps a staff reporter or editor reach the scene of action, it is impossible to know whether horizontal or vertical shaping will serve best to record the drama of the occasion. Hard and fast preplanning stifles the artistic instincts of a photographer, say members of this school.

B. Many experienced advisers argue with logic that every layout should be planned in detail, including the photography, before a single picture is assigned. Moreover, say these people, each picture should be sketched in outline for the photographer before he goes on assignment.

C. As Betty Anderson argued in the September 1972 issue of the same yearbook magazine, the truth likely lies somewhere between. Preplanning should be moderated by an agreement, perhaps a rule, that the photographer shall be on the lookout at all times for unusual shots and that he may feel free to add these to his assignment. The policy should go further and say that photographers

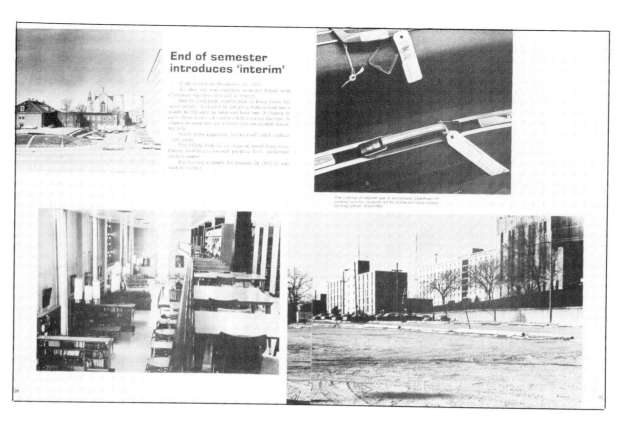

Fig. 5.5—Scenic pictures generally require many actors, but editors of the *Bluejay*, of Creighton University, took a long look at school during a holiday period and saw empty halls and grounds.

Fig. 5.6—Mood pictures can sustain the theme or close the story effectively. These thematic pages came from the opening of the 1973 *Totem*, of Chamberlain High School, Tampa, Florida. Terse mood copy supports imaginative mood pictures.

△ *Fig. 5.7*—More excellent mood-setting pictures, notably the one at upper left of the field of daisies, marked the 1974 edition of the *Totem,* Chamberlain High, Tampa. The use of four-color process in original added appeal. (Courtesy NSY/NA.)

Fig. 5.8—Double exposure added imagination to two thematic pictures shown here in a spread from the 1973 *Tahisco,* Tate High School, Gonzalez, Florida. Four-color printing (left) and tint block (right) also helped support total effect. ▽

Fig. 5.9—In today's better books, like the *Milestone* of Eastern Kentucky University, Richmond, candid pictures are as popular as ever. But, as in these fine examples, they are likely to center around an idea, like play or study.

```
            Photo Staff Assignment Card
            For News or Activity Shot(s)

Photographer:_____is assigned to take____(no.)
 of photographs of (event or activity)_____

Time:_____Date:_____Place:_____

Brief description of activity:_____
_____

Person to contact:_____

Pictures desired for book:_____

 Approximate shapings and numbers to be included:_____
_____
_____

Needed by (date):_____ Assigned by:_____
```

```
            Group Photo Assignment Card

Name of Group:_____will be photographed

for the yearbook group picture at___(time) on_____(date)

at (location)_____.

Photographer will be:_____

One in charge of arranging picture for group:_____

(Signed)_____(Signed)_____
    (for the yearbook)        (for the group)

Finished picture need by (date)_____
```

Fig. 5.10A, B—Suggested forms for assigning group and activity shots may be adapted to each school's needs. Editor will keep a copy and see that photographer and group representatives have copies.

Exercises

1. In Chapter 1, I offered some cautions about student art similar to those given in this chapter. Divide the staff/class into teams, and after taking a suitable time to jot down points, discuss the pros and cons of this statement: "Training young artists should take priority over improving yearbook quality." Write a one-paragraph policy you would suggest for your yearbook on the matter and read it for staff discussion. What about the photographic offerings of poor but earnest young photographers?

2. Since halftone dots create varying tones in portraits, speculate on what happens when matte paper is used for photo prints and these prints are then used for printing pictures in the yearbook. Would the effect be somewhat like printing glossy prints on extremes of stippled or rough paper? Draw an imagined blowup of a portion of a picture.

3. What is the case for and what is the case against taking pictures of students "as they come," in all sorts of dress? Consider parents, outsiders, and perhaps yourself ten years from now, in making your answer.

4. List five of your clubs or organizations. Plan two or three possible action pictures for each group, insofar as possible. Sketch in suggested activities for prints desired. Without writing cutlines, describe each picture briefly.

5. Instruct the photographer about backgrounds and foregrounds.

6. What professional help is available in your community in taking activity pictures for your book?

7. List five news events of the year that deserve picturing for the yearbook. In a sentence, tell how you would assign or take a lead picture for each, making a rough sketch of each.

8. Describe and make a rough sketch of one scenic picture that has never appeared, as far as you know, in your book.

9. What mood, or series of moods, strikes you as typifying your school effectively? (Alternatively, what mood pictures would fit your selected theme?) Sketch or select from magazines or newspapers and clip and mount six illustrations. Explain and comment on the intent of each picture.

10. Explain proper procedure for picking up pictures from other publications for use in the yearbook.

11. Criticize, in three or four sentences, the idea of snapping people at random, selecting pictures at random, and arranging them at random on a spread.

12. Discuss planning around a given subject, shooting pictures with the foreknowledge and cooperation of subjects.

13. Take a story or a theme idea for a series of four or five pictures and outline or sketch in the pictures for a page or spread. Write a sentence description of each picture.

14. What is the error in substituting "funny" cutlines or captions for informative ones? Are the captions likely to maintain a high standard of cleverness and wit?

15. As evidence that you can combine wit or humor or at least a mild form of cleverness, write three cutlines with humorous or eye-catching lead-in phrases. Don't forget to write the main facts, too. Base the effort on exercise 13. (Ex.: "A Witching Hour: Assembly performers compete at Halloween program for 'Best Dressed Ghost' awards.")

16. Describe and sketch a crowd scene for your book. Be sure it is one you have never observed in the book before, or at least one with unusual angles. Underscore the unusual aspects of the scene.

17. Write 150 words arguing the case for or against dummying pages before assigning pictures. (Half the group should take each side in this assignment.)

Special Assignment

For this assignment, a photographer or team of photographers should be asked to interview one or more professional photographers and bring back his or their responses to queries about camera or cameras recommended for yearbook work, costs new and secondhand; lenses needed, and costs; flash equipment suggested, with costs involved at current rates; suggested film for each camera; and suggestions on developing fluids and other supplies. The entire staff will enjoy hearing at least a brief report of results, though detailed discussion of a technical nature may be confusing to the nonphotographer.

6.
Opening Section

THERE IS no argument about where to place these pages. And there has been no vast change in basic content since the very first yearbooks, even though some major additions and both artistic and journalistic refinements have been made to the parts that have been around through the years. Let's look first at the essential and desirable parts of the opening, and then at some elements that are either dead or in the process of dying.

I. Endsheets may be plain, perhaps in a tinted matte paper, or they may be illustrated in one of these ways:

A. A school scene has been frequently used, the commonest, perhaps, being something in front of the main entrance of the main or only building. For instance, the opening endsheets have been used for a school-opening scene; the closing endsheets, at extra cost, for an end-of-year picture, such as graduation.

B. Another method of illustrating, perhaps a bit more modern, is with something related to the theme or motif idea. The 1972 *Elkonian,* Centerville, Ohio, for instance, took the Bob Dylan idea, "Those not busy being born . . . are busy dying." Birth was equated with education, the emergence of ideas, on opening endsheets. A picture of two students illustrated the idea here, and the first half of the sentence theme took a prominent spot on the sheets. The Vietnamese war, not yet ended for American soldiers at the time of the book's publication, provided the idea for the closing endsheets. The American flag and a funeral wreath dominated the pages, supporting the latter half of the theme idea, ". . . are busy dying."

II. A title page is a basic essential, it seems to me, like the title of a movie, a poem, or a book; or like the cornerstone or nameplate for a fine building.

A. First, it needs a title, obviously, and this should be in a type that stands out above all other type on the page or spread. The style of type may represent the thematic idea, but it is to be hoped it will be clear, modern, and readable, and that it blends with other headline types of the book.

B. It should also contain the name of your school or college, and at least for the high school, the name of the city or town and the state. These should all be in a type size smaller than that for the title, but matching or at least blending with that type. (Incidentally, why shouldn't college editors mention the name of the town along with the name of the college? Why not University of Missouri, Columbia? . . . Memphis State University, Memphis, Tennessee?)

C. Finally, for the title page, the volume number is as essential here as the page numbers inside the book or the volume number in the masthead of the newspaper.

III. **A table of contents, in broad outline, is a basic need for a book of any size. Readers like to be able to locate each division, by order and by page number, without being forced to thumb their way through the book looking for it. (You might wish to consider also the suggestion under "Division Pages" [Chapter 7] that a contents listing of subsections on each division spread helps the readers of larger books find what they are looking for.) Editors who have scrambled major divisions in the name of experimentation will find that composing a meaningful table of contents for the finished book is almost impossible.**

A. This table should mention only major sections. There is no need to list the title page, the sign-off or acknowledgments page, or the dedication page (if one is used). There is no need to break down divisions in this table of contents, as in giving the names of the individual classes as subdivisions of the portraits section.

B. The table of contents may be included on a page or spread used for some other important purpose, the thematic introductory spread, for instance. In a small book, the title page or spread may be shared with the contents listing.

C. A useful table of contents presupposes numbered pages for the book. As a mere list of the divisions, in their sequence, the contents page has limited value.

D. Even where the contents listing is not actually placed on the theme-intro page or spread, it may contain some thematic copy and art in forwarding the theme.

E. As a variation technique, recent editors have placed a small illustrative or thematic picture alongside each divisional title on the contents page. Don't allow these art bits and the table to take an undue amount of space. Spreading a contents listing over two pages, even for the largest book, seems extravagant.

IV. **A picture (or pictures) of the setting of your story belongs in the front of your book, whether on endsheets, on the title page, or in early pages. Possibilities (school and college) include the entrance to the main or administration building, campus or grounds scenes, old or important buildings, and major gathering places. Some or all of these ideas may be incorporated into the introductory theme-setting or mood-setting section, which is found in many modern school and college books.**

V. **The theme-setting pages, which may be developed into something more than part of the usual beginning pages of a book, should stress large and technically strong, dramatically planned pictures reviewing the life of your school for a special year in history. No leftover pictures from past years will serve, unless this is a historical review. (Note that if you do include historical matter or employ history as a theme, you should refer to it as "a historical review," not "an historical review," unless, of course, you are in Canada, England, or another British-speaking country. In the United States, the h in "history" is always an aspirate, just as it is in "house," "hill," and "home.")**

A. In the theme-setting pages, identifications and even full cutlines add much to interest. Pictures almost always leave questions unanswered.

B. Running stories, if you have enthusiasm and imagination, plus the needed energy to write them, also make these pages more valuable and more memorable. Keep them short. Staccato style, free verse, unjustified prose—all are acceptable for this section, as is standard prose.

C. Finally, headlines in narrative or magazine style can put the delicious topping on this appetizing dish, the theme-setting section or pages. Here you may exercise subtlety and employ interest-rousing phrases even at the loss of some journalistic explicitness.

A. Official messages are rarely found in leading yearbooks of these times, but in a few small and remote books, these vestiges of past years linger on. Editors perhaps saw in the superintendent's or principal's or dean's message a way to flatter an official or so. Or, perhaps without recognizing it, they were sparing themselves the time and effort required in gathering and writing meaningful copy. Let messages rest in peace, alongside the senior wills and prophesies, the snapshots pages, the "cute-lines" found on snapshots pages, and those baby pictures and cutout heads on stick bodies that were presumed to throw readers into convulsions of laughter. (See comments in Chapter 4.)

B. Formal introductions, titled "Introduction" or "Foreword" (or often, erroneously, "Forward") originated as logical and appropriate to form

C. Dedications have largely passed from the yearbook scene.

1. If you feel that you must have a dedication, because of the death or retirement of an unusual or widely beloved person long or at least closely associated with your school, stay within reasonable limits (perhaps a single page), and make your copy specific and meaningful rather than merely eulogistic and generalized.

2. Tell readers why you are dedicating to this person, mention his accomplishments and contributions, and rather than offering editorial commentary, quote someone or even a number of persons who have known the dedicatee well and are in a position that makes their statements significant.

3. Let me repeat here: Don't use a dedication unless it literally seems inevitable and inescapable for *this* book. Casual dedications to persons or ideas or institutions, used just because it is the custom to include them, generally sound contrived and unnatural.

4. As a replacement for the traditional

Pictorial Examples

△ *Fig. 6.1* — It would be difficult to improve on the clarity and simplicity of these two Florida title pages, which offer scenic pictures, essential facts.

Events — page 18

In an age when older ones
quit because of disillusion.
In a time when problems
of the world left a wake of
frustration and disinterest.
In a nation whose leaders
told youth not to become
involved.
2029 students were asked to
seek out the answers.
To start anew where their
predecessors had failed.
Some gave up when the odds
seemed insurmountable.
But for the rest lay
challenge within the
mistakes of the elders
And the potential for
something better.

Study — page 40

Sports — page 70

Clubs — page 100

Faces — page 142

2029

△ *Fig. 6.3*—Table of contents for the 1974 *Pierian,* of Richmond, Indiana, High School, spreads across two pages. Background is 100 percent screen, with type reversed, pictures superimposed. The thematic copy features "challenge." (Courtesy ………

Fig. 6.4—Opening pages of this same book from Richmond, Indiana, make thematic use of slang words such as "skimpin," "sweatin," and (here) "livin" to characterize the year in the schools.

Exercises

1. Using the theme or motif you have selected or worked in an earlier chapter, design front and back endsheets for your book. Sketch in rough details of art in the dummy.
2. On separate sheets, in at least thumbnail sizes, sketch a number of possible title pages for your book. Remembering suggestions as to type and contents given earlier, do two possible sketches. One will use art or photography that somehow typifies the school, its life, and its nature and spirit. The other page may not have a photo directly related to the school but conveys the theme idea subtly and yet clearly.
3. Design a contents page that also contains an introductory thematic passage. Write a theme passage of not more than 100 words. Use regular prose style and justified column width. Write a narrative head or an interest-rousing magazine-style heading (not a label).
4a. Rewrite theme copy in staccato style, reducing length as you cut out words (75 maximum). Dummy all this for 10-point type body, 21 ems (picas) wide, with a 24-point headline, 25–27 count. Figure about 50 counts per line when you count justified copy. It is a maximum still for staccato or free verse or unjustified style.

or

4b. Try the above theme copy in free verse style.
5–10. Sketch and dummy six spreads of thematic pictures, headlines, and cutlines, with staccato-style copy for each, no block to exceed 50 words.

7.
Division
Pages

I. Division spreads or pages (often called "dividers") have the same function as chapter beginnings or titles in a novel, that is, to give breathing room between parts of the book and to organize the book so that the reader may follow it with greater ease and pleasure.

II. Logically, a single page can be adequate for a divider. But since the two-page spread is the normal layout unit in a book, especially the pictorial book, editors who feel they can afford the space usually assign two pages to each.

III. Editors have occasionally tried to skip dividers or to compress them to the tops of the pages on which new parts of the book opened, but results have not encouraged wide imitation.

A. This is not to say that a symbolic drawing plus the division title might not be used with success in introducing a new section, even if confined to the top part of a page, with the section starting below. In fact, the idea was tried as far back as 1952, when the Medford (Oregon) *Crater* startled and pleased readers with an "outer-space" theme, or at least a theme that placed the setting of the book in relation to the outer universe and to the imagined denizens of outer space conceived as possible visitors to this school (Medford) at this spot on Earth, in the Solar System, Universe, at the time, 1951–52. Atop each starting page for a new section appeared a small drawing, noted for its taste and neatness. This sketch showed Planet Earth, emphasizing the Northern Hemisphere and the North American Continent, with a marking post protruding from the very spot where Medford would be assumed to be. A pointed sign attached to the post or stake proclaimed the book's theme phrase: "Dimension M." It served in a sense as a sectional marker, an abbreviated divider.

B. But such abbreviation brings up numerous problems, such as designing the part of the page left to make a start of the "chapter," and equally difficult, planning the page opposite so that it will blend successfully and balance the opening page.

C. Then too, when one starts abruptly like this, one seems to risk leaving a gap or hole at the end of the preceding division, or stretching chapter contents to fit, or perhaps adding filler to make things come out even.

D. Of course, using a single page as a divider creates problems similar to those mentioned in the preceding paragraph, particularly when the editor makes the effort to place the divider on the right-hand page, where it belongs. And for that matter, ending any section without undue waste of space usually requires some editorial ingenuity.

IV. **A division spread should contain certain elements: a title, perhaps the theme title, illustrative photography and/or drawings, perhaps thematic art, a copy block, cutlines or identifications for photographs, and optionally, a headline over the copy block. Let's look at the various elements:**

A. Titles: In the 1971 *Recall*, of Augusta (Georgia) Military Academy, with its theme, "There are many different ways of looking at things," these were some of the thematic titles, with actual division subjects in parentheses:
1. Vitality (Student Life)
2. Digging (Curriculum)
3. Battles (Sports)
4. Associations (Clubs)
5. Characters (Students, Faculty)
6. Yellow Pages (Advertisements)
7. Autobiographies (Index)
(Note: For the military section, not part of the usual book, there was the double label: "Formations [Military].")

B. Photographic or other art should be far above average, and it should typify the section that follows, like the picture of a marching band in a Paris (Texas) *Owl*, on the "Activities" spread, or like some representative students at academic chores of a varied nature, such as lab work, a home economics project, rehearsal on a band instrument, or whatever your own imagination, stimulated by thought and research, can produce.

C. If impressionistic drawings are used, be sure of their relevance and of their intelligibility to reasonably thoughtful readers. Also be sure they have unusu-

ally high quality, making them equal in appeal if not in technical perfection to available photography.

D. While artists and photographers argue with some logic that generalized or representative art is self-explanatory and complete in itself, practical experience and long observation suggest that at least idents of pictures of small groups add to the interest and appeal of such pictures. (See discussions of identifications and cutlines in earlier chapters.) Editors of some of the better books of the early 1970s have seen fit to include short cutline blocks on dividers. They have felt, as I do, that this gives the art more appeal by making it even more understandable. Moreover, it focuses added attention on individual students and others in a time when there is a need to avoid losing faces in the crowd and the attendant individual loss of a sense of identity.

E. There are a number of ways in which copy blocks are presented. Let me review these:
1. One is in free verse. Since this is a method requiring great skill and unusual talent, and a close relationship between art and copy and design, let me reserve my illustration for the mid-part of this chapter, at the close **of this outline text.** (Walt Whitman and Carl Sandburg were among the great practitioners of this art, incidentally.)
2. A step away from free verse is staccato style, in which omissions of unneeded words and elisions of understood phrases or sentences are indicated by ellipsis marks (three dots). Let me illustrate from the *Mahavi* of Martinsville, Virginia. Its theme was "Confrontation" (in a gentler sense than that often understood by the term). The copy block for "Curriculum" will illustrate this method, though it is not necessary to place all ellipsis marks at ends of lines, as was done here:

Confrontation . . .
With the infinite process of knowledge-gathering in 1971 . . .
Where theories were mere links in the chain of experiences . . .
Sometimes the linking was a painful experience . . .

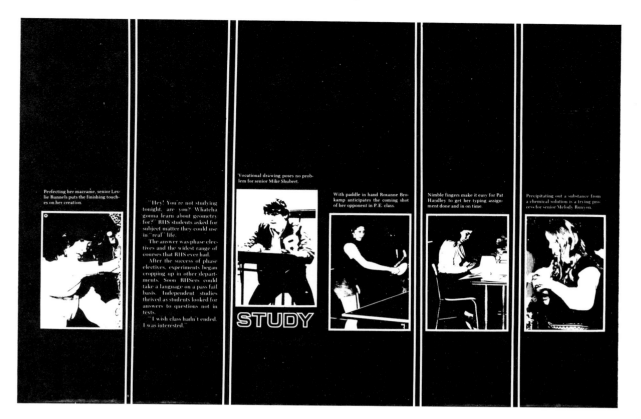

Perfecting her macramé, senior Leslie Bunnels puts the finishing touches on her creation.

"Hey! You're not studying tonight, are you? Whatcha gonna learn about geometry for?" RHS students asked for subject matter they could use in "real" life.

The answer was phase electives and the widest range of courses that RHS ever had.

After the success of phase electives, experiments began cropping up in other departments. Soon RHSers could take a language on a pass/fail basis. Independent studies thrived as students looked for answers to questions not in texts.

"I wish class hadn't ended. I was interested."

Vocational drawing poses no problem for senior Mike Shubert.

STUDY

With paddle in hand Roxanne Brokamp anticipates the coming shot of her opponent in P.E. class.

Nimble fingers make it easy for Pat Handley to get her typing assignment done and in on time.

Precipitating out a substance from a chemical solution is a trying process for senior Melody Bunyon.

△ *Fig. 7.2* — As with openers shown earlier (page 85) dividers of this 1974 *Pierian* of Richmond, Indiana, achieve drama with white on black. Design is a modified modular. Copy and art make the reader wish to go further.

Fig. 7.3 — In a large book, the *Excalibur,* of the Robinson High, Tampa, Florida, the editors broke club coverage into subdivisions and also placed subtables on each spread, as shown here. Line art is effectively combined with photography. ▽

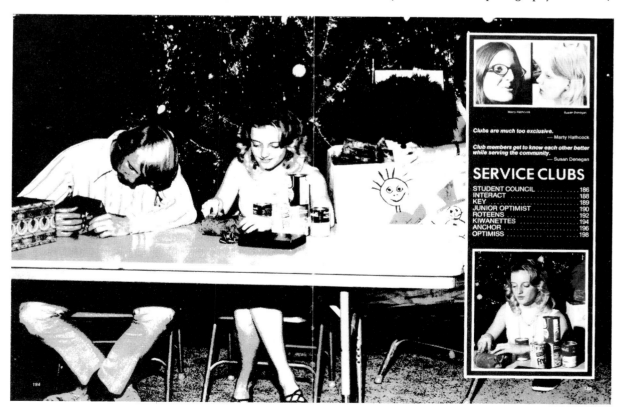

Marty Hathcock   Susan Denegan

Clubs are much too exclusive.
— Marty Hathcock

Club members get to know each other better while serving the community.
— Susan Denegan

SERVICE CLUBS

Exercises

1. Take your favorite motif idea or the theme adopted for your book and list both thematic and actual headings for the divisions you plan for your yearbook.
2. Now see whether it is possible to use the thematic idea *and* the division topic in a single heading, narrative style, for the divisions of your book. (You are allowed to use overlines or kickers if you wish.)
3. Assign the various section dividers of the book to members of the staff or class—*events and features, honorees, clubs, academics, sports, classes, and advertising,* on any basis you wish, personal choice, chance, etc. Now, let each staff member take his own assigned divider and make a full plan based on a modern design pattern (modular, Mondrian, etc.) and sketch pictures and/or art needed. Then compose the appropriate title and/or headline *and* body copy. Do the copy in staccato style first. Then rewrite it in ragged-edge prose. Then do it in a formal, summarizing prose style that clearly tells what is to come. Keep body copy to no more than 50–75 words. After a class discussion, determine what style you will follow. (If there is a poet in the group, you may wish to consider free verse style, but be sure you are not confusing *verse form* with *poetic style,* a very common error.) Agree at the start whether the theme idea is to be handled in art, a design idea or form, headline, and/or the body block. Finally, write your cutline(s), or at least the first line for each piece of pictorial art. (Later, after class discussion, if you determine that idents are enough, the cutlines may be dropped.)

8.
Feature Events and Activities

I. This section has developed as an integral part of the yearbook within the past 25 years. As in the case of the academics section, it was virtually unknown, other than in the primitive format of snapshots pages, before the advent of offset or the "photolithographic age" in yearbook production.

II. Features, or feature events, make up the content of this section. They are generally of an all-school nature, or at least they affect the total school or college life in some way. (Let me note that obviously, in the very large high school and in the so-called mega-versity or large university, there is far less likelihood than in small to average-size schools and colleges that any events other than perhaps school opening and closing, the exam schedule, holidays, and perhaps graduation activities will have an impact on all divisions and all students.)

III. Organization of this part of the book varies widely.

    A. Chronological order is commonly used in events coverage. A typical case is the 1973 Gainesville (Florida) *Hurricane*. It keeps content to general or all-school events:
        1. Spotlighting seasonal events on each spread, editors began with the summer before the opening of the school year.
        2. Each story was boxed, and editors made frequent use of seasonal quotes on these pages, such as this from Alfred Noyes: "You shall wander hand in hand/With love in Summer's wonderland."
    B. Facing the problem of coverage of spring months in a book that is in production at this time for delivery before school closing, some editors have picked up spring events of the preceding year for each yearbook. The 1972 Paris (Texas) *Owl* did this effectively:
        1. The book dipped back to the preceding March, in this case, that of 1971.
        2. Editors gave from two to four pages

per month, touching on scenes, events, and happenings.

C. Besides the plan of reviewing the late spring months of last year in the current yearbook, two other methods are used effectively for full-year coverage:
1. Inserting a "spring supplement" after the rest of the book has been printed and issued has for years permitted a staff to issue in late spring, before close of school, and yet cover the year fully up through this year's climax activities.
2. Many schools have in recent years followed a popular and common collegiate custom of summer production and fall distribution.

D. Arranging events according to general subjects, with only incidental, if any, attention to time order, is another interesting and logical method of presenting events of the year that is employed by modern editors and staff.
1. After bowing to the chronological method by inserting spreads on summer events and the first day of school, the 1971 *Mavahi*, Martinsville, Virginia, devotes spreads to such everyday topics as a typical school day, the lunch hour, school codes for new styles of dress and hair, and a topic called simply "Diversity."
2. Other books using the topical approach have been known to offer spreads on assembly programs, campus visitors or entertainers, dramatic events, musical programs, and campus gathering places like the student union, the coffee shop, etc.
3. The *Mahavi* staff was able, through the subject-arrangement plan, to give primary attention, or earlier attention, to events considered of greater importance or value. Thus the senior class play, held in March, came ahead of the presumably lesser junior play, scheduled in November.
4. Whether arranged chronologically or topically, or in a combination method, events sections in current yearbooks devote spreads to homecoming, junior-senior prom, and if the production schedule permits, graduation events.

IV. **Efforts have been made to combine general events and other materials of the yearbook. Let's look at some of these.**

A. No doubt there have been many books in recent years that combine organizations and events into one section, but one of the most interesting experiments was made as early as 1968 in the Southwestern *Moundbuilder*, of Winfield, Kansas, to achieve this combination. The staff limited pictorial coverage to activities and excluded, even from club reporting, all static group pictures. No editor has, as far as I know, solved the basic problems of integrating organizations and events, and especially not in the section dealing with events chronologically. Clubs worthy of reporting are for the most part year-round groups, with big activities throughout the year. (Groups with only single, seasonal projects for the year are the exceptions that emphasize this point.) The editor who finally solves this matter will no doubt organize everything by the topical method mentioned earlier in this chapter.

B. Combining sports with other more prosaic all-school events seems on its face to be a logical plan, and it has been tried with varying success.
1. In the 1972 *Tiger*, Holy Cross School, New Orleans (Louisiana), editors followed an order of time in covering all-school activities (events) and inserted into their proper seasons the various sports as they appeared on the schedule.
2. Dangers or weaknesses of the combination of sports and other events become obvious on closer examination:
a. Sports seasons may get lost inside the section, and readers have difficulty finding what they are looking for, whether assembly programs or the school carnival or swimming competition.
b. In addition to being harder to find, the sports seasons may seem, at least to ardent sports fans, to be downgraded by the scrambling of all events into one package.

C. Many books—the 1972 Paris (Texas) *Owl*, as a random example—have incorporated honorees like "Who's Who" in the events-features pages. (*Owl* editors placed these honorees at the end of events reporting for the year, but handled them in the style of all other events reporting for the year.)

D. Beauties and queens and other royalty, on the decline in most schools these days, once held court as the major part of what was often known as a "Features" section. Modern books, especially on the high school level, have generally dropped beauty sections, perhaps on the theory that honoring physical beauty as such is out of step with our times. "Homecoming Queen," a feature still rather generally found in schools and colleges, is commonly reported in the modern events section.

E. While determined editors with seasonal organization in mind have also tried to place academics into the pattern, this seldom comes out satisfactorily. There is no way to determine the proper season for math, history, art, English, or even journalism, though the yearbook may serve as a major journalism project that has its days of glory in the spring.

V. **Events and features in the modern book have taken on new dimensions as editors have become aware of the relation between school and community and between students and their society and world. Students, including staff members and editors, have a new sense of obligation both to examine and to seek solutions for problems of the society at large. The 1972 *Elkonian*, Centerville, Ohio, illustrates well how all the above is affecting events-features sections, and indeed the entire yearbook:**

A. One big feature in this remarkable book was coverage of a nine-day festival commemorating the 175th anniversary of the community of Centerville. Community-school linkage was emphasized: one student was pictured on her beautiful mount as she appeared in the horse show during the celebration. Other pages reported how the high school art class partici-

pated in a contest to produce a commercial seal. A junior student won first prize for his entry, which became the official seal for the historic occasion.

B. A full spread in this book commemorated a project jointly sponsored by the parent-teacher organization and the local Lions Club, which raised **funds for use by local schools.**

C. Still another spread of the Ohio book featured a school board election in which students participated, some as voters under the new law lowering the voting age to 18. An illustrated story featured results in the form of plans for a new high school building. Obviously, this community-school event belonged in the yearbook at least as much as the report on the junior-senior prom.

D. This *Elkonian* also reported on a school-sponsored recycling center where metal, paper, glass, and clothing were gathered, put into salable condition, and sold to factories or processors.

E. The same book reported on a fine workshop named RAAP (Reducing Activism and Alienation by Participation). This workshop brought students, teachers, and community leaders together for conversation about problems of mutual interest.

VI. **A few special topics unique to or at least unusual in the 1970s appear frequently in yearbooks of the decade. Let's look at some of them:**

A. Styles in dress and hair have brought a new look to schools in recent years, in some cases necessitating special codes (see reference to *Mahavi* above). At the time this text is being written, the pendulum seems to be swinging back again, at least for girls' styles. Report whatever seems important in your school.

B. Current problems and topics related to drugs, sex education, venereal diseases, youthful marriages, pregnancies outside marriage, and a host of others relatively unmentioned or taboo until recent years are being reported constructively in modern student newspapers and yearbooks. The yearbook editor has the time to do something definitive and comprehensive. Pictorial essays are especially useful for the purpose.

C. Integration, busing, and the various problems involved have been handled with great skill and to beneficial effect by student editors over the country. The books of Gainesville, Florida, and of Chicago's University High come to mind as especially effective in dealing honestly with racial problems, or rather in working toward better understanding between the races and smoother transition as schools change racial proportions.

D. The family and family relationships are nothing new to the period, but the stresses of changing times have affected the modern American family. One book of recent years devoted a spread to the family, giving special attention to the relationship of the school and the family.

E. While opinions of students (usually on quite superficial topics) have filled many newspaper feature columns of the past, in-depth interviews aimed at evoking opinions and thoughts on truly serious matters have given alert modern yearbook editors as well as newspaper editors material for interesting and significant copy. One recent book carried a spread of short interviews on such matters as school life, careers, the curriculum, etc. Small student portraits were interspersed among the featurettes. A large dominant photo at the top, a roundup story, plus many small or mini-interviews could make this a great feature for any modern book. The editor should be careful to get constructive material and to deal with significant subjects (not preferences in colors, perfumes, and ice cream), while avoiding negativism or mere pointless carping. A big order indeed!

F. A much publicized Arlington (Indianapolis) *Accolade* had a "flip-side" section of essays with pictures and copy. Topics were quite profound: "mass education: the identity crisis," "individuality versus conformity," "youth-voting" (the effects of the law permitting 18-year-olds to vote), "school

dropouts," "the cost of athletics," "the way students use their time."

G. A pioneering 1970 book, the Brookfield (Wisconsin) *Legend*, carried a full section on "The Children of Change," that is, young people, especially those of Brookfield. Topics included "Rock, Religion, and Morality," "the dress code," and a number of other aspects of student attitudes, thinking, problems, and styles. It too used large pictures and magazine format for these feature essays.

VII. The key word in this section, as in almost all other sections of the modern yearbook, is *action*. The courageous editor of that Winfield, Kansas, *Moundbuilder* of the late 1960s pointed the way. (See comments above.) Maybe Editor Carol Frost and Adviser Vernon McDaniel were too far ahead of the times, but in my personal opinion, they were giving a preview of how all or most books of the future will be. Here are two rules for the editor who wishes his book to be dynamic and appealing:

A. Stress the big, interestingly informal, story-telling, unposed picture. Limit numbers of subjects and numbers of pictures on a spread.

B. Insist on solid, specific, this-year copy that focuses on what new, different, significant things occurred this year. Avoid or subordinate less immediate historical data and general goals, except when their use will emphasize or give meaning to actual happenings or achievements of the year. Insist on lively captions—cutlines—that give the facts pictures fail to tell readers. Use only narrative-style or magazine-style headlines that summarize features or pique curiosity. (Review the chapter on copy if the details have become hazy in your mind.)

VIII. This section has had many names. Give the matter careful thought before deciding what you will call it in your book.

A. Even if you adopt a thematic title, be sure it tells the reader what the chapter or division is all about.

nesses, etc., which might, in your opinion, be incorporated into this section. (Review the discussion in the outline text if you need to do so.) Explain one of these and develop a spread on it. Sketch in pictures; write first sentences of cutlines; write a lead for the story (50–75 words); and prepare a narrative headline, one line, full page. Follow a pattern given earlier in the book for another such exercise.

6a. There seems to be quite a bit of discussion lately about the possibility that the family may be a disappearing unit, or at least that it is fading rapidly from its old, important position in society. With this fact in mind, make a case for the family in its relationship to the school—that is, how it supports and strengthens the work of the school. Develop a spread for the events section around this thesis. (Argue by evidence, not rhetoric.)

or

6b. Show how local clubs or organizations, or perhaps churches, support and supplement the work of the school and, vice versa, how the schools aid the programs of clubs and/or churches.

(Be sure in this assignment not to overlap exercise 5.)

7. Develop a spread on local styles of hair, dress, or other fads that made the year stand out in your school or that added color and variety to the year.

8a. If drugs, youthful marriage, racial problems, or other current issues and problems affect your school, develop a spread on the topic. Dummy pictures; outline; write first lines of cutlines; write the headline (two lines for single column, with count of 23–25 units); write a 50–75-word lead for your story.

or

8b. If your school is singularly free from the problems that have beset many schools in recent years, produce a spread that features this fact, portraying the spirit of wholesome and constructive effort that, as you see it, avoids such conditions as racial tensions, drug addiction, etc. Follow the same directions as above for this dummy.

9. Dummy a spread on student opinions. Start with a large, dominant picture. Leave up to 40 percent of the page for the headline and story. Focus on some issue or group of issues of special local importance this year, whether school expansion, a dress code, revision of the curriculum, a building program, or whatever is big and current. Don't overlap the topics mentioned in exercise 7, or if so, not to a degree that you bore the intended reader by repetition. Interview at least ten students representative of as wide a variety of interests as possible. Write a summarizing statement or a 75–100-word lead, and do at least first lines for cutlines for intended pictures. Sketch pictures and dummy layout in accordance with the overall book plan.

10. List the contents of your events-features section, at least in broad outline. (You need not name every event, but estimate the number and assign pages.) Offer a title for the section and be prepared to defend it in staff-class discussion.

Special assignment
for Features Editor or Assistant Editor
Get from the principal or whoever is in charge of such things a complete school calendar. (The director of student activities may be the proper one in the average college.) Check items the yearbook will cover, emphasizing big events according to some code you devise. Designate lesser events that deserve coverage, those that may or may not be covered, as space and time suggest. (You may wish to use the star system used by movie reviewers, for instance.)

9.
Honors

I. **Honorees, including beauties, queens, princesses, and the various popularity winners, have been covered along with other parts of the book ("Features-Events," "Classes," "Sports," "Academics"). They have also been assigned their own separate section.**

II. **There is a definite movement away from giving attention and space to beauties and popularity winners as such, especially on the high school level.**

    A. Some parts of the country, it is true, continue to look backward to pay what seems to most observers excessive and untimely attention to honors not based so much on achievement, merit, work, or accomplishment as on natural endowments in physical beauty or charm, or the qualities of personality that make other students vote for or offer accolades to their possessors; that is, qualities sometimes labeled *charisma* and much in demand by those going into political life or perhaps into sales work.

    B. "Who's Who" sections continue to thrive on the college level and even in many high schools. Editors of the better books using this section are asking the reasons for selection of the various honorees, and they are both picturing and reporting verbally the activities and accomplishments on which the selections are based.

    C. Homecoming queens seem firmly ensconced in the program and in the yearbook, though there have been indications of growing disenchantment with this tradition, or even the tradition of homecoming itself. In one college, students ridiculed the idea of naming a queen of the occasion by electing a male student as queen.

III. **Many editors, especially in schools where the stated emphasis is on more constructive things, and where more serious consideration is being given to the purposes of education, have begun to follow a recommendation made by many leaders in the yearbook field and one I have frequently made in articles, editorials, and critiques: Focus on solid achievement, on**

Fig. 9.3 — Scholarships are featured in this spread about senior honors in a *Quiverian,* Wyandotte High, Kansas City, Kansas. The group picture is of "Who's Who" students. Note how headline reads into story, "rocket" style. Story is detailed.

Fig. 9.4 — Sometimes honors coverage logically belongs in the clubs section, as was the case with the Junior National Honor Society featured in this spread in the 1973 *Tahisco,* Tate High, Gonzalez, Florida. Note stress on action.

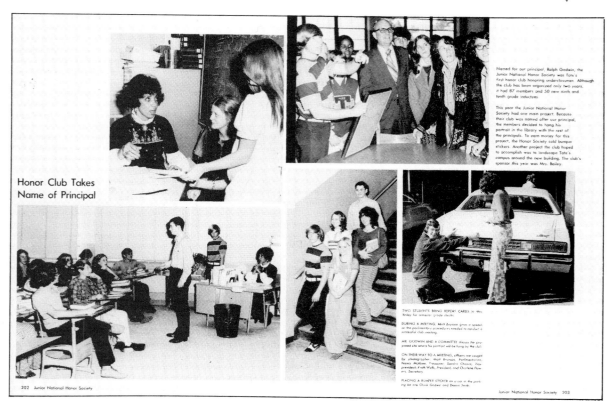

Exercises

1. Organize the staff/class into teams and debate the proposition, "Resolved: That the beauty section as it appears in traditional yearbooks is no longer relevant in our society and should be abolished." At the end of the debate, list the points on the affirmative side for abolishing this section or for not using it in your book, and opposite or immediately following, list points against, namely, those for retaining or adding this section. Immediately below, state your own conclusion, with a brief summation of your reasons.

2. List five or more reasons for encouraging popularity awards and recognition. Consider vocational or career objectives and social or avocational outcomes.

3. Argue the case against such recognition as "Best All-Around Girl," "Most Popular Senior," "Best Dressed Boy and Girl," "Wittiest Boy and Girl," and "Most Likely to Succeed." Lump them, or make a grouping for your major arguments, later adding points against any of the specific "honors."

4. How would you suggest recognizing and encouraging qualities that make people popular without actually including a "popularity" section? Take academic programs (courses), clubs, events programs, and athletics into account as you formulate your answers. (Write a 50–75-word paragraph.)

5. Outline one special sponsorship by the yearbook in your school in which you will put the focus on qualities both needed and admired in our society. Refer to the suggestions in the outline text section above, but don't feel an obligation to imitate any of them very closely. Adapt the plan to your school.

6. Dummy one honors page that you consider the most important one for your next yearbook. Feel free to sketch an informal action shot or two as well as a portrait. Write a 50–75-word story and a narrative headline. Write cutlines. You may fictionalize.

10.
Covering
Curriculum

I. **Like events-features, the section devoted to school subjects is a relative newcomer to the yearbook. Some advisers who read this will recall the days when editors of high school and college yearbooks alike were content to settle for formal portraits of the faculty, often repeats of those taken and used for earlier books. Some college editors allowed (and some still allow) group pictures of departmental or divisional teachers to do full duty for reporting on faculty and curricula.**

II. **Let's look at a few variations of content combination found in current yearbooks.**

    A. Better organized books tend to separate faculty coverage from actual pictures and stories about curriculum, a common method being to place portraits of faculty in their own section, often toward the back of the book. (See Chapter 13.)

    B. While authorities have tended to accept a fairly common combination of faculty formals, action pictures, and curricular coverage intermingled on the spreads of a single section, few editors have been able to put it all together satisfactorily as to layout, or even journalistic logic.

    C. Some editors of large college-university books have used this plan:
        1. Academic-curricular-vocational coverage is broken into schools, colleges, divisions, or departments for coverage in subsections.
        2. Portraits or group pictures of the administrators and faculty are included with action pictures (where used at all) and with covering stories, which are usually headlined.

    D. For those not ready to minimize, or place at the back, administrative coverage as part of portraits, the 1972 Paris (Texas) *Owl* offers a compromise.
        1. All administrators (school board, superintendent, principal and staff, counselors) are pictured in the academics section, along with the coverage of departments and classes.
        2. Portraits of teachers and students are assembled at the end of the book under the label, "Individuals," the faculty pictures coming first.

    E. An amalgamation or loose combination of faculty-administration personnel and curriculum was used imaginatively by the staff of the 1973 *Hurricane*, Gainesville, Florida.

1. First in the section come pictures of principals, deans, counselors, faculty, and supportive staff (staff of the library, the cafeteria, etc.). Informal poses are favored, notably in the faculty pages of the section, with widely varying sizes and shapes of pictures.
2. Next, in this section, in alphabetical order ("arts and crafts" to "vocational studies") come the departments of the high school, fully covered in words and activity pictures.
3. As in many other modern books, the Gainesville staff gave the reader an assist by using small marginal label-titles on all pages here and elsewhere in the book.
F. Occasionally, a book omits all faculty formals, reporting on faculty entirely as part of the teaching-learning program. The 1973 *Yellowjacket,* Center High, Kansas City, Kansas, made this combination under a title, "Relaying Instruction."
1. Administrators and service personnel are covered in the opening pages of this section.
2. Pictures show teachers at work, and copy on faculty-subject pages is made up largely of quotations from teachers. Headlines summarize progress for the year in each department or course.
3. Actual stories about the various courses, with narrative headlines, are placed inside the class portraits subsections. Informal action pictures serve both to report curriculum and to "relieve" portraits pages. (As a note on this format, there is an obvious coverage flaw in separating the actual departmental coverage into two sections, especially since the sections are far apart in the book.)

III. Positioning of curriculum coverage in the modern yearbook is fairly stable.

A. Since the modern editor and staff subscribe firmly to the idea of making a dynamic start, the commonest positioning is immediately after events-features, very close to the front of the book.
B. Sometimes a staff and editor are so eager to show the courses and departments of the school that they place "Studies" immediately after the opening and thematic-intro pages, dropping events to a lesser position. Such a plan was followed in the 1972 *North Star,* Roanoke, Virginia.
1. This section contains only the stories and informal pictures of the work and special projects of the various departments.
2. Although teachers appear in pictures as needed, emphasis is on students.
3. Teachers, administrators, and service personnel are saved for a portraits section at the back of the book. It is called "People." There they are pictured formally and also in attractive, sometimes very large, activity pictures. (Student portraits appear in this same section, after administrators and faculty.)

IV. In college books and in those of the larger schools, it may seem impractical to attempt to cover every course or to report any single department in depth each year. There is an acceptable solution in both college and high school yearbooks:

A. In the large college book, editors are faced with big divisions and subdivisions named "colleges" (inside large universities, on a single campus), "schools," "divisions," etc. However these may be broken down, and the editor of the book may properly select certain courses inside that division to emphasize this year, being sure they were not the ones featured last year and hoping that next year's editor may touch still different subjects or courses. (Obviously, a course or subject that is in the limelight this year because of local or national events should be reported in the book, whatever has been done in previous years. See comments below.)
B. The same policy applies to large-school yearbooks or books severely limited in space. Here, happily, divisions are not so complex and selection therefore not so fraught with the risk of slighting subjects that deserve full and regular reporting.

108

V. **Sometimes it is hard to tell a study from an extracurricular, and staffs vary in their decisions about placement.**

   A. Physical education is a prime example of this point. Usually considered a part of the athletics or sports program, "P.E." can and does logically belong in curricular coverage, and college yearbook editors, especially, have often placed it there.

   B. While musical groups (bands, orchestras, choruses) are usually represented in the organizations section, they generally carry class credit and thus technically belong to curriculum, a fact most editors tend to ignore. The *Hurricane*, cited above, incorporates not only musical organizations and courses but the majorettes as well into its section on faculty-curriculum, no doubt because this group of hard-drilling students also earns credit toward graduation for the long hours its members put into work and planning.

   C. Publications, even when parts of the journalism courses, have generally wound up inside the organizations-clubs section.

      1. There seems to be no great illogic in covering journalism as a course and then reporting the publications as parts of the extracurricular (in this case curricular-related) division.

      2. Laboratory-type activities such as newspapers and yearbooks may also be well handled in sections combining courses with subject-related organizations, as in the Gainesville book.

   D. Speech-related organizations, especially debate teams, present problems similar to those the editor and staff face in coverage of music groups and publications. The same suggestions and recommendations apply here.

VI. **As in all other sections, stories included in this section should stress what has happened this year, the year covered by the book: new courses, new texts, new facilities, new visual aids, modern equipment, and discussions and activities of the various classes that touch on current events and problems. Let's look at that last point.**

   A. Has the science department, or any of its divisions, done anything to recognize and offer help in solving environmental problems like air and water pollution, etc.?

   B. Are there any projects planned in art, history, drama, or any other subject that will have community-wide interest or will be in cooperation with or for a local club, the chamber of commerce, or any other organization?

VII. **Avoid here, as in any other section, generalizing, moralizing, or sales-promotion. This applies to stories under whatever authorship—by staff members (as all stories should be), faculty members, or officials.**

   A. Rule out the "puff" that is intended to sell a course or subject to students. And this includes your own beloved journalism, for example.

   B. This caution also excludes a story full of historical reporting, abstract goals, or claims that a subject has special virtues. Even if the math teacher is firm on the matter, don't present the argument in your report for the year in the department that this subject is a great one for teaching mental discipline.

   C. In brief, let the facts and pictures do whatever editorializing or sermonizing is to be done.

VIII. **As in clubs, events, or other coverage, the staff should work hard to get the best possible action pictures, recording the most interesting or significant happenings—unusual laboratory experiments, unusual participants (boys in what have customarily been girls' courses, or girls in study fields heretofore dominated by boys, etc.).**

IX. **Selecting a name for this section should offer no serious difficulties, but the rule still applies that a theme title is insufficient which in itself fails to tell the reader what the contents of the section will be. Let's examine some common and not-so-common names for this section.**

A. It is not unusual in these days of increased informality for editors to select rather casual titles:

1. "Know-How" is one of these half-humorous labels found in one excellent yearbook. I am not sure I can recommend it, but it is different! (See II-E above for what the title covered.)

2. Titles like "Learning" and "Studies" are soberer, and they seem reasonably definitive. (Maybe for the sake of skilled or vocational studies the practice of skills should be included in a descriptive title so that it might then appear as "Learning and the Practice of Skills.")

B. "Academics" is a sectional title seen frequently since the departmental section came into the yearbook.

1. The term has the respectability of long usage, though some dictionaries do not mention the word at all, and the one in which I found it as a noun (*Webster's New World*, College Edition) defines the plural "academics" as "purely theoretical discussions."

2. But after you accept "academics" as a proper word (as I am willing to do), you become aware of its limitations of coverage, based on the definition of the adjective "academic": "having to do with general or liberal rather than technical or vocational education" (the same source). Where does that leave vocational studies, like those mentioned above, or studies that go beyond the theoretical, general, or liberal, like journalism and fine arts?

C. "Curriculum" is the most commonly used and perhaps the most generally acceptable name for this section. Certainly no single word says it better, not even "Studies." And it has the added virtue of respectability in educational circles.

1. The greatest handicap the term has is its rather pedantic nature. A Latin term for "race course," it may seem strangely out of place in these days of informality, especially since the journalistic rule is to "prefer the simple Anglo-Saxon term to Latin words or Latin-de-

rived words." Yet a "race course" the school program of studies truly is, as no modern high school or college student will deny.

2. Since the name does generally satisfy the need for a comprehensive term, one that covers academic, vocational, fine arts, and semiacademic, semivocational studies, however stuffily formal, I suggest its use, perhaps as an overline identification followed by a thematic title or headline.

Pictorial Examples

Fig. 10.1. —Emphasis is on students in action in this spread from the *North Star*, Northside High, Roanoke, Virginia, which covers physical education and driver training. Photos are lifelike, and the copy is conversational in tone.

Exercises

1. What definitive title will you use for this part of your book—"Studies," "Academics and Vocationals," or . . . ? What thematic title or narrative line will you use? Where will you place each? Give the type style and size. Write the full title or titles at this time.

2. List subjects, courses, divisions, departments, or whatever you will cover in this section. Assign page numbers on a tentative basis.

3. List classes to which you will give special attention this year and explain or justify this decision. Select a class that has been given special significance by current events of the year. Write a sentence about it. (This may require some research.)

4–10. Each staff member–student is to select one class or course for this exercise. Singly or in groups, interview the department head or a teacher. Look for unusual angles such as projects bearing on current matters—the fuel shortage, economic conditions, ecology, or whatever; new texts or audiovisual materials; new courses or units for courses; lab plans; or proposed or scheduled speakers. In getting and writing your story and planning a picture or pictures, find out the philosophy of the teacher, the objectives of the course (but don't feature them unless they dramatize what has been done or is being done in the course). Discover the relevance of the course to the society and world we live in. What methods (field trips, speakers, projects) are being used to dramatize this relevance? Arrange to visit the class or department for observation of some especially significant or maybe typical class, lab, or field trip. If there is the promise of good pictorial matter, plan to take a photographer, being sure he is instructed and has specific plans in mind. (See chapter on photography if you need to refresh your thinking on this.) Be sure to get two or three shots of each important pose to avoid the danger of losing something that you cannot replace. Plan pictures and picture taking in advance with the teacher to avoid as much as possible the disturbance of class routine. Maybe you can set up at least some of the pictures before or after the class period. Write a 50-word lead (one or more paragraphs) and outline the remaining parts of the story. Write a one-line, 43–45-count, headline. Write the first line for each cutline. Prepare a dummy.

(Note: At least a rough dummy should precede the picture taking. In this way, you will have an idea about picture poses and shapes in advance.)

11.
Organizations, Clubs, and Groups

I. Clubs, organizations, groups, publications, fraternities, and houses have been subjects of major interest to yearbook editors since the beginning, as far as I can determine, like individual portraits (students and faculty) and sports. Sections on clubs (by whatever name); portraits of administrators, faculty, and students; building pictures; sports; and ads made up the bulk of all college and high school yearbooks through the 1930s and most of the 1940s.

II. Historically, clubs were represented in one of two or three ways, and the job of the incoming editor was simply to take pictures in exactly the same pose at the same place and fit them into the same spots on the pages, with new idents but little else. If presenting the club motto was traditional, this, plus a more expanded statement of objectives, could be picked up year after year from the book of the year before. For the editor, it was all a delight, if he (she) had no imagination and no particular urge to change things.

A. One variation on the usual group, plus title, plus idents, was addition of a picture of the club officers, apart from the others, sometimes posed around a table to give the impression (generally erroneous) that they had club business to discuss and plan.

B. Sometimes, besides the club motto, a history and perhaps a statement of purpose were added as part of the routine.

C. Years ago, some enterprising editor came up with an idea: Pose the fraternity members standing on the roof or around the gables of the fraternity house, or have members of the honor society sitting on the limbs of a tree or standing beneath the tree. (The symbolism intended by such poses was never explained satisfactorily.) Or (a real classic) have members descending a stairway in the school building or at the "house" or just about anywhere an available stairway presented itself. In all three cases, and in a host of variations, someone got a company artist at the engraving house or printing company to draw outlines of the persons shown in the pattern of the pose, always a most confused pattern. The facial outlines were numbered, and it was then possible to identify those in each wildly scrambled group picture by those numbers. Some editor of recent years rediscovered this idea, perhaps under the misapprehension he was inventing it. It had quite a resurgence of popularity in the late 1960s. My advice, already given in Chapter 5, is, "Don't do it!"

III. **This is the age of photojournalism. Modern cameras and fast film in the hands of imaginative photographers can capture lifelike expressions of facial features, can portray moods, emotions, movements of hands, feet, and bodies—in short, the drama of life as it really is.**

    A. Television and movies have spoiled the drab, the static, and the unexciting for all of us modern readers.

    B. Even the pictorial magazines *Life* and *Look*, fine as they were once considered, and hard as their editors tried to keep pace, somehow fell by the wayside. The general magazine is struggling to stay alive.

    C. Certainly all this means that even the high school-college yearbook, with what was once placidly accepted as a captive readership, may no longer depend on automatic acceptance. It must be as dynamic and vital as possible if it is to retain its readership in competition for time with the other media and with the many distractions that call for the reader's or prospective reader's attention every day.

IV. **One may only reasonably conclude therefore that the high school–college yearbook must place the emphasis on life as it is being or has been lived in the school or college. At the risk of overstressing points made in the chapter on photography, let me give some specific suggestions:**

    A. Consider, even for the most formal of clubs, putting the group picture at the bottom of the page or layout, as small as possible without losing all identifiability of the faces.

    B. After researching the key events sponsored by the club or group, arrange to have a photographer present with special instructions about subjects and about shaping and sizes of action pictures. Remember: Even honor clubs have initiation ceremonies.

    C. Display the best of these activity shots at the top of, or near the top of, the layout devoted to the group. Let the lesser pictures take positions of declining importance on the page or spread.

    D. If a club has no activities during the year worthy of recording in a yearbook, follow the lead of other thoughtful editors: Locate the posed group picture in a special section assigned near the back of the book for such groups. Let me add a suggestion made earlier:

        1. Set a reasonable charge for such pages, not necessarily as high as that charged to commercial advertisers, but certainly something more than the actual cost of the space to the staff.

        2. If an inactive group is not sufficiently interested in having the picture in the book to pay this reasonable charge, it is unlikely that anyone will be injured by the omission of its picture.

V. **In verbal coverage, as in pictorial reporting, editors are obligated to focus on the most dramatic, interesting, significant activities and achievements of clubs and organizations.**

    A. Obviously, the yearbook staff cannot plan the club's year. But those who cover clubs and organizations can and should make it clear to club officials that readers are likely to be the most intensely attracted to reports on topics of special community interest or on national events that are currently in the spotlight. As recent examples, consider such subjects as the fuel shortage, energy on the broad scale (gasoline, coal, nuclear power, solar power, etc.), pollution and ecology, voting, and the many problems of government. Each year brings new topics to the fore.

    B. A recitation of an organization's purposes has little if any appeal though unusual club goals and what members are doing to fulfill them can often give feature leads or pegs on which to hang stories.

    C. Unless it is an anniversary issue, the history of a club is little more than a space waster.

D. As is true elsewhere in the book, specific facts are preferable to general statements, and editorial comments or evaluations are undesirable. The writer may, however, add value to a story by getting and using, with full attribution, opinions of recognized authorities. (If the governor of the state commends a service group for planting trees in a state park located near the school, his remarks are assuredly a valuable and interesting part of the report on the organization and its year's activities and achievements.)

VI. Where to place and how to arrange clubs in the book are challenging questions for the staff. Let's look at some usual and unusual practices:

A. The commonest modern practice is to develop a single section that includes all clubs and organizations. These are student government; department-oriented organizations, active and honorary; service clubs; music groups such as band, choral club, and orchestra; dramatic organizations; vocational groups; hobby groups like chess; and school publications.

B. In colleges, all the above may be joined in a single section by Greek-letter organizations and housing groups; or Greek-letter and housing groups may have either a combined section or their own separate sections.

C. Some recent and not-so-recent books have placed student government along with official school-college administration in the early part of the book, thereby removing one important student organization from the section devoted to groups.

D. The previously mentioned *Hurricane* of Gainesville, Florida, put class-related clubs, special-interest groups, vocational groups, Black Students, and National Honor Society in a section the editors named "Commitments." The "Know-How" section, covering academics and academics-related activities, incorporated publications, musical groups, majorettes, and student government. (All these except perhaps student government offered credit to enrolled members.)

E. Pep clubs, cheerleaders, and other sports-related organizations have been relegated by some editors to the sports section.

F. Marching band, though closely associated with sports events, is more likely to be found inside "Organizations" as part of the music groups. In an important event like homecoming, it will also be seen giving a large supporting role, though not usually reported fully at this point.

G. Intramural and gymnasium sports have been reported under the sports section, or if part of the credited physical education program, under curriculum. As an organized group, such activities may have a proper place under clubs and organizations. In one Florida school, a course in gymnasium activities was made part of the combined curriculum-curricular clubs section.

H. The case of the Florida "gym" course brings up a logical practice seen as far back as 1969 in the *Viajero*, Coronado High, Lubbock, Texas—combining all classes and subject-related clubs in a separate section, dramatic groups under drama, language clubs under language courses, etc.

I. Following the same combination (academics plus academics-related clubs), Robinson High's 1973 *Excalibur* (Tampa, Florida) reported all other organizations in a section labeled "Service Clubs." The plan seemed to work satisfactorily for the staff.

J. Clubs, departments, and sports are all loosely interwoven into a single section called "Movement" in the 1972 *Shield*, Highland, Indiana. (Events-theme development material appears in earlier pages of this book.) Sports fall in line behind all organizations and academics-curriculum, and only these are chronologically arranged.

K. A fairly common method, but one hard to use without confusion to the reader, combines special events or all-school activities and organizations into one section which may, in fact, be named "Activities." A typical effort, though admittedly more successful than usual, appeared in the 1973 *Totem*, of Chamberlain High, Tampa, Florida, with this subdivision of parts as indicated on a sectional table of contents:

1. "Student Life"—all-school events (28 pages)
2. "Musical Groups" (8 pages)
3. "Publications" (6 pages)
4. "Honor Societies" (8 pages)
5. "Government" (6 pages)
6. "Service Groups" (18 pages)
7. "Adult Groups"—lunchroom personnel, band patrons, a parent-teachers' group, a booster club (5 pages)

L. A method rarely attempted with success is that used by the Griffith (Indiana) *Reflector* in 1973—a grouping of events, clubs, departments, and sports into one section named "Features."
   1. No effort was made to force clubs or anything else into an unnatural chronological order. Instead, clubs, like departments, were interspersed among the chronologically arranged events and sports, in the form of feature essays.
   2. The drawback here is the difficulty such an arrangement places in the way of a reader looking for specific reports on clubs, or for that matter, sports seasons themselves.

M. Steve Carlson, Arizona yearbook judge, and writer on school publications, has called attention to the yearbook of the San Carlos, California, High School, which in recent years has handled club coverage in the first section of the book, along with highlights in events, curriculum, sports, and community issues. All are covered in well-illustrated feature stories. Only those clubs whose activities seemed to the editors to be of importance to the school were included in this section.
   1. This technique requires the utmost discrimination and judgment on the part of the editors and staff, as Mr. Carlson points out. This is all the more true because staff members are very close to the events and organizations they are covering or considering for coverage.
   2. There is great danger of creating ill will by omitting or playing down an influential club or organization that has nothing to inspire a feature in its year's program, or whose members may feel that the feature used does them an injustice.
   3. In a manner suggested earlier in this chapter, the editors at San Carlos ran formal group shots of all clubs

in the "faces" sections, along with administrative, faculty, and student portraits.

Pictorial Examples

Fig. 11.1—A group that is abreast of events, like the Ecology Club, of Blackford High, Hartford City, Indiana, was easy for the editors of *Reflections* to cover. Note how action is featured on the page.

Fig. 11.2 — College books of the 1970s, like the *Milestone,* Eastern Kentucky University, Richmond, have turned to action in photography and feature the highlight events and achievements of the year in stories and headlines.

Fig. 11.3 — Displaying action first, this spread from a Gainesville, Florida, *Hurricane* gave ample room at the bottom of the group picture of the Distributive Education Club, which was in the unusual section named "Commitments" discussed on page 116. ▽

△ *Fig. 11.4*—Pages featuring vocal groups, which are part of the section "Movement" in the 1972 Highland, Indiana, *Shield,* while focusing on the posed group, have three lively action pictures, a "semiformal" around piano, a fact-filled story.

Fig. 11.5—Two pages from the subsection of "Service Groups" in the 1973 *Totem,* Chamberlain High, Tampa, Florida, illustrate a successful method of focusing on action in pictures while giving adequate attention to the posed group shot. ▽

△ *Fig. 11.6*—Newspaper and journalism share a spread in a special combination classes-organizations section of an *Edition,* yearbook of Mercy High, Omaha, Nebraska. The method has much to commend it to modern editors.

Fig. 11.7—All posed group pictures of San Carlos High School in California were placed in the index section of the book, leaving the earlier pages of the *Power* for pictures and stories reflecting the events and day-to-day happenings of the year. ▽

Exercises

1. Discuss this statement: "A large club group pictured in formal pose is a great addition to the yearbook because, whether the members ever get together again or do a single thing but pose for a picture for the yearbook, you create goodwill and readership by running their pictures." (To help you in your discussion, consider whether, if this premise is accepted, one might also agree that a book containing nothing but large groups gathered together around any sort of subject or pretext—people whose names start with the same letter, for instance—would be vastly popular, containing hundreds or even thousands of pictures of individual students. As a second point of consideration, ask yourself whether the function of a yearbook is to develop a realistic and interesting report in pictures and copy of the life in your school for a school year. If this is agreed, should the emphasis be more on "life" than on unlively and static posed groups? Does this rule out all use of group pictures? Make a case for the elimination of posed groups, even though you may lean toward the statement of the first sentence of this paragraph. What is your compromise between the two extreme views?)

2. Is an acceptable substitute for standard formal poses to be found in posing groups in simulated artificial or frozen action? List a dozen trite poses you would like to avoid in your yearbook. (As a starter mention the one in which someone is presenting a check, a certificate, or something else to someone, while a third person "looks on in approval.")

3. A club that we will call the "Uncompromising Dodos" has a membership based on a common concern for extinct or vanishing wildlife. Aside from holding an annual organizational meeting, at which officers were elected, it had no projects, or even meetings, this year. When the call was issued for yearbook pictures and this club stepped forward to have its picture taken, what would your suggestion be for handling it without wasting space in the yearbook proper and still without doing injury to sensitive feelings? (Hint: Space costs money. You sell it to advertisers at a strong markup. . . .)

4. After considering the various ways of placing clubs in the yearbook, come to a decision as to the most logical placement of organizations, clubs of all kinds, publications, honor societies, musical groups (bands, choruses, etc.), dramatic clubs, student government, even PTA and adult groups that help out (boosters' clubs, parents' clubs, etc.). Make a complete outline.

5a. Make a dummy of either the choral club or the marching band that contains pictures that stress action and puts the "record" shot in a lesser spot in smaller size than usual. Write (from imagination or facts as you know them to date and with last year's story before you) the first three paragraphs of the band or choral-club story. Be sure to follow suggestions made in the first part of this chapter. Now write a narrative headline using 24-point type and a maximum of 35 counts. Write the first line of each cutline needed.

or

5b. Assign each staff member or student one club or group (include publications, student government, music groups) and do the above assignment. On a trial basis, make it as close to facts for this year as possible. Make each dummy a two-page spread.

6. What will you use for the thematic title of this year's book? Design a title spread that blends with those of other division spreads in the book. Sketch in art and write a 50-word introduction in one of the patterns suggested earlier—ragged-edge, staccato, or regular prose style in justified type. (Note to teacher-adviser: Don't duplicate the assignment as you did it in the chapter on "Division Pages." If all division pages are already set, omit this exercise altogether.)

12. Sports

I. It may be reasonably surmised that the caveman made a sport of his pursuit of the wild game, saber-tooth tiger, or wild boar. And yet his recreational activity was, as it is for today's sportsman, a most serious business to him, sometimes a life-or-death matter. Thus, if the caveman had published a yearbook, sports would have been his major and maybe sole subject of coverage. There has never been any question about including sports in the student yearbook; it has always been an important subject, along with organizations and individual portraits.

II. The method of presentation of sports, or athletics, has always been approximately as it is today. Sportswriters have subscribed in a general way to a factual narrative style. This style, at its best, might have served as a model for the writers and editors of other sections of the book, but it is only in recent years that one has seen a trend toward such imitation. Let's examine historical and current developments in sports "reportage."

   A. In the beginning, when pictures were relatively hard to get and engraving quite expensive, copy predominated in the section. Portraits of coaches and players were sprinkled into the story, usually single-column width. There was little or no action, except in the prose itself.
   B. As stated above, the idea of narrating the year's events and even the best copy in this section offered examples for other sections; yet regrettably sports copy itself has often fallen short of the promise.
      1. For one thing, young sportswriters and editors have been prone to imitate weaknesses rather than strengths of the professionals. Words like "pay dirt," "TD" (touchdown), "thinclads" (trackmen), and other extremes of sports jargon that have made hideous many an afternoon or evening of radio listening and many an hour of sports-page reading repeatedly have found their way into the yearbook story.
      2. Wild figures of speech, particularly those based on the team mascot, have too frequently assailed the yearbook reader's eye.

a. Headlines proclaim unblushingly that the "Tornadoes blow elephants off field," or (in defeat) ". . . become gentle zephyrs."

b. The pun is often expounded to the point that results of the game or the season never quite emerge: "The rubber game [in a series] stretched out till fans feared it was about to snap in their faces." (Readers wait and wait to learn results of a game that ran 17 innings. Or was it three overtimes?)

C. Sports editors have often failed to balance coverage equitably, emphasizing big spectator sports like football and basketball; slighting or omitting intramurals or playground-gymnasium activities, physical education, and even girls' or women's sports; and sharply limiting the space and attention given to the so-called minor sports.

III. **Since a major function, perhaps the prime function, of the yearbook is to provide a repository for the record of the school year, nowhere is this purpose more important for future readers of the yearbook than in the sports section. The sports editor and sportswriters should remember these essential needs:**

A. For each sport, get and report seasonal results, the win-loss-tie record, the final standing in city, county, district, or league, and maybe state if your team had an unusually good season.

B. If new school records are made or old ones tied, the details should be recorded—the football team made the greatest number of yards or points, the defense held opponents to the lowest score or the lowest yardage, etc.

C. Individual attainments are important and interesting now and for future readers: in basketball, new records in scoring set by an individual, or even a very unusual record, unusual records, or near-records in assists or rebounds for a game, a season, or a career at the school; in football, yardage records set for running or passing in a single game or for the season, or for an entire career in the school.

D. Score boxes for the various sports have long been considered valuable to yearbook readers. Yet these elements always present layout problems. The staff of

one modern yearbook (the *Totem*, Chamberlain High, Tampa, Florida) found an unusual and an attractive solution. They placed all the sports scoreboards on a single page at the end of the section. They relieved layout dullness of the statistics with a few well-chosen action pictures.

IV. **Let's look at some special problems in the placement of sports and sports-related material:**

A. Physical education is sometimes treated as part of the curriculum. (See discussion in Chapter 10.) Sometimes editors choose to report it in sports because it serves as the coordinating force for an organized system of interclass or intramural sports.

B. When there is an organized college intramural program in baseball, basketball, touch football, etc., which is independent of curriculum, it will likely appear in the sports section. It hardly belongs in any other section.

C. Girls' (women's) sports, until integrated into the total program, should have fair space in the sports section. At least one modern book (the *Torch*, Catalina High, Tucson, Arizona) introduced a subsection for girls' sports, with its own subdivisional page. (Note: As legal decisions rapidly force integration of men's and women's sports, this rule for proper coverage will become increasingly outdated.)

D. Cheerleaders and pep squad are either in sports or the organizations section. There is some logic to each placement. I have seen the coverage of cheerleaders leading off a sports section, but more often it will appear after the sports season, or perhaps after the football or basketball season.

E. Sports and related activities normally have a separate division in the book, but sometimes editors have included them with other materials. Two examples already mentioned:

1. Sports and all other big events of the year are in chronological order in the *Tiger*, Holy Cross, New Orleans, Louisiana. (See Chapter 8.)

2. Clubs, departments, and sports are combined in a section called "Movement" in the Highland (Indiana) *Shield*. In this case, sports are actu-

ally grouped together, not scattered, and they are arranged in sequence of time. (See Chapter 11.)

F. The big homecoming game always appears in the sports section, but it may also get at least casual handling inside all-school events coverage as one of the big features of "Homecoming."

V. **Sportswriting requires a most careful attention to style. (See discussions in Chapter 4, under II-C and II-G, and under IV.) Let the sports editor and his staff follow, and the editor insist on application of, these points of style that are too easily forgotten:**

A. Simple, direct reporting marks the true professional. Sports events are by nature colorful, dramatic, and action filled. Reports on them need little style embellishment, just as pepperoni pizza needs little or no added condiments.

B. This is not to deny in any sense the inherent drama of the simple, direct report of emotion-filled or significant events. Although not of course to be considered a "sporting event," the Creation, as reported in the first lines of *Genesis*, illustrates my point here as well as any fine sports story I might offer. Young sportswriters could also do worse than examine the style of Geoffrey Chaucer (particularly in his "Prologue" to the *Canterbury Tales*), of the French writer Maupassant, of Ernest Hemingway (and not only his stories about bullfights), and of that great "amateur," Samuel Butler. There have been and remain a few professional sportswriters who are worthy of imitation. These artists have held to the purpose of telling what has happened and doing it so clearly that readers are able to see and experience the action through the narration.

C. It is proper to use the language of the sport. Thus a "home run" is and will always be a "home run," and in the eyes of the fan so glorious an achievement, even in Little League, that it need not be adorned with tinseled clichés. And what is so wrong with a "touchdown" that many a sportscaster can never bring himself to acknowledge it by its real name? Tennis has its unique scoring system, and it would be improper to report

it in any other way. Golf has its language. So do all sports.

D. Perhaps more than any other writer, the sports reporter needs to exercise restraint in his use of adjectives. To speak of a player as the "best hitter" in school history (without attributing the evaluation to an expert) is less desirable than stating that he has a better average over a three-year period than any other baseball player in the school's history, according to official records. Even then, someone may cite a player with a great two-year record or one with an unmatched home-run record. To speak of an official's decision as the "worst ever seen," to label a game or a season "the most disastrous ever," or to use any other superlatives or comparatives (*-est* or *-er*) is to invite the charge of bias and to bring into question one's journalistic abilities. The reporter, whether for the school or college or city newspaper, or for the yearbook, serves as a sort of animated camera and recording machine. While he must select the "negatives" and the "tapes" or portions of "tapes," what he finally presents to the reader's eyes must both resemble fact and create in the reader's mind an impression of factuality and truth.

E. What has been called the "crying-towel method" of sports reporting has been with us in student publications for at least 25 years. In it, the staff writer apologizes extravagantly for home-team failures, and laments loudly, placing the blame on outside persons or forces. As Steve Carlson has observed about some of the modern practitioners of this unsportsmanlike art, these writers seem to suggest that "the rain falls only on the home team's side of the field," that officials harass our boys and favor the outsiders, etc. Just as the sportsmanlike coach or player accepts his losses and congratulates the winners, the good yearbook sportswriter tells it "like it is," and lets the record speak for itself.

F. Three common journalistic style rules mentioned in the chapter on editorial content have special applicability to sportswriting:

1. Use the third person, never the first. ("They," "the team," "it" sound better and more professional than "our team," "our boys," "we," and "us.")

2. Use past tense, not the present, in copy. A few editors have managed to maintain readability with the historical present, which some have assumed to be more dramatic than past tense. But like excessive use of italics and bold face, such writing becomes tiresome. Prefer this: "The Cougars *recorded* a creditable 50–50 record in track, winning three of six dual meets during the season. They also finished third—in the middle—in the county meet. . . ."

3. Prefer news style in headlines. In this style, the present tense implies past, whereas future may be indicated either by the future auxiliary or by the infinitive.

> Lions *take* 3rd in county meet   (past)
>
> School *will enter* new league (future)
>
>   or
>
> Board *to ask* bids on new gym

VI. Although yearbook readers are accustomed to seeing the formal group pictures of the various athletic teams, these are for reference only and should never be allowed to dominate a spread or the sports section itself.

A. Let the action of each sport provide the subject for dominant photographs and most other pictures in this (as in every other) section. If you get a variety of poses and have planned each season's coverage well, you will likely include pictures of a high percentage of players and certainly all the most active and best-known ones at least once per player. Then if your cutlines, stories, and headlines follow the rules already set forth in the chapter on editorial content, no one will have reason to feel slighted.

B. One value of the group shot is that it will include, for the permanent record, the faces of players who may have been of great value in practice sessions or have been leaders in building team morale, but who for one reason or another compiled little actual playing time and received correspondingly small credit during their careers as team members. Trainers, managers, bat boys, and water carriers also get into these record shots and receive attention they richly deserve.

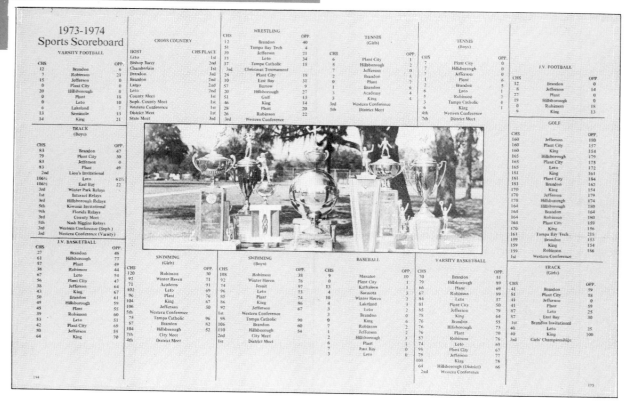

△ *Fig. 12.1*—"Scoreboard" in the 1974 *Totem,* of Chamberlain High School, Tampa, Florida, puts all seasonal records for the year in one spread. Relief is provided by the picture of the school's sports trophies. Action shots have also been used here.

Fig. 12.2—Intramurals are attractively represented in this spread from a *Bluejay,* Creighton University, Omaha, Nebraska. The story is brief but factual. Pictures were carefully planned and are displayed with equal care. (See comments on page 123.) ▽

Fig. 12.3—Girls' sports, actually organized into classes in Prairie Bible Institute, Alberta, Canada, were given this excellent pictures-and-words coverage in the 1973 *Prairian*. Note the truly ''striking'' bowling shot in the dominant position.

Fig. 12.4—Cheerleaders are shown in practice or at games, and posed groups, if used at all, are played down, as on this sports spread from an *Ambassador*, Stevenson High School, Sterling Heights, Michigan. The story details new developments of the year. ▽

Gridders capture
4th straight title

Fig. 12.5—Action dominates in this opening football spread of the 1974 *Pierian*, Richmond High, Indiana. Team shot and scorebox, both frequently placed later in today's books, are modestly integrated into the layout. (Courtesy NSY/NA.)

Exercises

1. Each staff member will take a yearbook sports story and a story on an all-school event other than sports. Write a lead paragraph for your sports story, then one for your selected event. Discuss how the sports story lead has contributed to the vigor and readability of the second lead.

2. Using the following facts, write a 150–200-word story: Your basketball team won 11 and lost 15 games this season. The record included 5 wins, 9 losses in your Class A division in Metropolis. Your school is East High, and your Bears lost two games each to the major rivals, West and Central, but beat third-place winner, Highlands, in both contests for the year. The Bears finished fourth out of eight teams in the division, and the top guard and top forward placed on the second team and honorable-mention list, respectively. The team had a glorious moment when it led Central by ten points at the half while Central was still favored to win the division. The victory over Highlands at home was decisive, though Highlands was threatening at the close and came within three points of tieing. The Bears also beat Garfield, considered a power in AA competition, in an early-season game. Joe Brown, guard, had a 14-point average for the season, or 364 points. Bill Owen was the forward who got honorable mention. He averaged 9 rebounds.

3. Criticize or rewrite each of these leads. Feel free to add facts needed for completeness:
   a. The Mountain Goats butted their way to three first-half touchdowns, but at last the East High Bears (our team) began acting like bears instead of Cub Scouts, getting two TDs in the 3rd quarter and hitting pay dirt early in the fourth, hanging on to earn a tie with the perennial champs of the district.
   b. The visiting Mountain View Explorers tallied what seemed a safe lead, 13–0, in the first quarter, but then our boys, East

High's Bears, chased the Explorers up a tree by making three TDs and all PATs in the second quarter. Our fine boys clawed and scratched their way to two more TDs in the second half while keeping the Explorers from a single trip to the store. When the final buzzer sounded, our heroes had sent the visitors back home licking their wounds, 32–13. All of this was done despite some very bad officiating throughout that cost our brave guys 90 yards in all.

c. Poor courts with unkept gravel and high winds that disturbed our Bears combined to enable an inferior Midtown tennis team to sweep six matches on their home courts, four girls' and boys' singles and two doubles matches. Our team was able to take a doubles match between runner-up teams, and a mixed doubles match after the winds had settled late in the afternoon. It would have been a far different story if Ronnie Smidt and Larry Howard, our Nos. 1 and 2 players, hadn't both had colds. Ronnie, in addition, said his right ankle had been bothering him because of a fall last year while playing touch football. Mary Josephs has chronic sinus which was irritated by the windy and dusty court. Susan Ballard, member of our best girls' doubles team, complained that officiating hurt her more than anything else.

(Note: this needs discussing *more than anything else*. It would be difficult to rewrite on the basis of the materials here.)

d. Although our football boys did not win many games this year, dropping all but three, one of them a tie game, which they should easily have won against crosstown rivals, the Lakeside Cranes, as Coach "Happy" Fellows said, their spirits never flagged. "I'll always remember them as the team that never quit trying," said Coach Fellows. "Illness with flu cost them one game, bad officiating at least two more. And bad weather, combined with injuries to key reserves, took their toll. But you'd never have guessed our Bears had had any troubles. They just kept plugging along. . . ." (You might first comment on this; then, largely from imagination, write a lead that carries the needed elements. Use such hints as are available in the above emotion-packed report obviously made by a gentle but noncommital sports editor.)

4. Give brief critiques. Then do a rough revision of each of these. (You are allowed to invent needed facts.)

   a. **Bears roar, as Hyenas quit laughing, in traditional Homecoming meeting**

   b. **Thinclads, Racqueteers, Horsehide Artists Promise Homeville's Greatest Spring**

   c. **'Tornadoes' sing 'Gone with the Wind' To Traditional Hopeville Opponents**

   d. **Grunt-Groaners pin most opponents, taking 2nd place in our conference**
   (Note: Observe slang sports name. Also observe pronoun use.)

   e. **Mets compete in better league next year**
   (Note: While this style in the verb is not unheard of, improve it in one of two ways. Be specific about the "better league" also. Improvise.)

5. List all parts of your own yearbook sports section for this year. Tell where each will be located. If you believe any usual sports material should go elsewhere, explain why (a sentence each). Tell where you plan to put it (or advise putting it).

6. Dummy one spread for a major sport of your choice (or as assigned). Follow the design pattern you have selected or would select for the book. Sketch picture(s) in outline. Write the first line(s) of the cutline(s). Write the lead paragraph (about 50–75 words) Write a two-line headline, 28–30 counts wide.

7a. Repeat the assignment above for a "minor" sport or a girls' sport.

or

7b. Dummy the cheerleaders' spread.

13.
Portraits

I. **Like clubs, organizations, and sports, individual portraits have been part of the yearbook since the very beginning.**

   A. In early yearbooks, all faculty-administration portraits were formal, but many high school and college editors have for the past 20 years or so accepted the use of informal portraits as supplements to the formals. For administrators, at least, these lifelike action shots have served as complete picture coverage in some books.

   B. Student portraits, mostly formal, have traditionally had their separate section. Senior portraits generally have occupied greater space and more prominent positioning than have other class pictures.

   C. A few editors have tried to save space, as well as to focus more on seniors, by picturing underclassmen in large posed groups, either as full classes or as homerooms. This plan has never aroused great enthusiasm, and it certainly lacks layout charm. Large posed groups of any kind, especially in quantities of three to a dozen that all look alike, always present problems of display.

II. **Earlier custom placed faculty-administration portraits very near the front, immediately followed by student portraits sections. Such was true in my high school and college days, and such was certainly the case in the first yearbook whose production I supervised as faculty adviser at Fort Stockton, Texas, High School. But even the most rigid traditions fade and pass.**

   A. The 1958 edition of the National School Yearbook Association's (NSYA) *Judging Standards,* and all its successors as the "little bible" of thousands of yearbook staffs through the years, suggested placement of at least the student portraits at the back of the yearbook, thus "clearing the decks for action" in the early part of the book.

   B. By the 1964 and 1965 editions, I made the wording even plainer in *Standards:* "We like to see the student portraits placed at the back of the book." It was equally acceptable by that time to place faculty portraits at the back, though NSYA was inclined, like the other critical groups, to give more leeway in this matter.

III. **For many years, portraits pages contained nothing, or almost nothing, but portraits and identifications. Adding elements of informality would have seemed strange indeed to early-day editors.**

A. One exception is worth noting. Although the 1940 West Texas book to which I have referred was, as I recall it, free of adornment, an earlier one of the late 1930s followed a fad that apparently had a relatively short life —the use of borders on all pages, including portraits pages. In some books, such borders were of various geometrical designs and patterns, or even standard "doodads" available in most printing shops. In the Fort Stockton book, however, our staff artist followed the book's theme, the movie reel, and drew rather untidy strips of what the reader was expected to consider the stills that make up movie reels. In retrospect, I believe almost any design taken from the printer's stock would have been more appealing. On the whole, however, the concept of borders (at Waco High School about a decade before, the yearbook border had been a daisy chain) seems to have deserved an early demise.

B. By 1950 a Maryland book reviewed in *Photolith* showed a current trend, adorning some of the portraits pages with action pictures. In this book, these activity shots were used on the class officers' pages. Spot or cartoon art appeared on other class portraits pages.

C. By 1951 a reviewer in the same magazine comments with enthusiasm on the fact that the Maryville (Missouri) *Maryvillian* carried on each portraits page one or more group action pictures. Each portraits spread also contained a narrative headline. Incidentally, the staff and adviser of this book were remarkably advanced for their time. They placed all the portraits sections or subsections at the back of

the book—administration, faculty, and students.

D. In the very first *Standards* booklet for NSYA, in the early 1950s, I urged, "Relieve portraits pages with informal activity pictures," advice that apparently all of today's critical services and yearbook authorities find highly acceptable.

E. In quoting a source very close to me for more than 20 years, I do not mean to suggest that NSYA was alone in urging relief of drab portraits pages with informalizing elements. Certainly, many fine advisers, services, and critics must have been speaking in harmony in this as in many of the other advances we have seen through the years. A yearbook company text of 1960 suggested, for example, that headlines, spot art, and informal portraits can help the layout of the seniors pages. Spot art may now be in some disrepute, but the other recommendations were and are quite sound.

IV. **Layout of the portraits themselves is better served if the designer will place elements in the largest practical rectangular blocks, rather than scattering them around on the spread.**

A. Retain room for adequate use of informal relief, usually action pictures.
B. Blocks or panels of portraits, as units, can be used in layout patterns just like action pictures of varying sizes.
C. Don't use the square shape in panels. It lacks dynamic appeal, whereas rectangular shaping with marked contrast between height and width gives a sense of action.
D. I have already cautioned against scattering portraits about. Don't be misled into an organized pattern of single portraits such as the checkerboard design. It is unappealing and tiresome, and it is also a space waster.

V. **Listing seniors' honors and memberships on portraits pages is an old custom that is dying because it usually destroys layout and orderliness of the portraits pages of seniors and because it offers unfair or misleading comparisons between types of** students, those who jump into all sorts of organizations, for instance, frequently giving little attention to any of them, and those studious and serious ones who may concentrate entirely on study, or on study plus one or two special outside activities. In college, the student who must work to support himself is obviously at a disadvantage when such reports of achievements and honors are put together.

A. One suggestion is to include an index of the seniors, listing the honors and memberships at the back of the book, along with other indexes. This has been very popular, and it solves many problems, especially of layout.

B. Another is to put portraits above, reserving an area perhaps one-third page deep at bottoms of seniors pages on which to compile memberships and honors.

VI. Class histories are at best archaic, and in most schools they departed years ago along with class wills, senior prophecies, and baby pictures. Imaginative editors have in recent years, however, shown that brief class reports and those containing only significant highlights and worthwhile achievements can fit appropriately into the story of the year. Perhaps all this proves is that editors and staffs with great ingenuity and skill can transform a relatively bad idea into something appealing and useful.

VII. In using informal action pictures to vitalize portraits pages, consider that one strong, interesting, relatively large picture per layout normally serves better than two, three, or more.

A. Place this picture prominently on the spread, preferably at the top left or top right of the spread.

B. Don't apologize for it by making it only slightly larger than individual portraits, and don't bury it inside portrait blocks.

C. Don't use pictures here that have been rejected from other sections. Make sure every picture you use has the quality and interest to deserve its space and position.

D. Unifying activity pictures via a central idea or theme has taken a number of forms:

1. If class histories are to be given, stories, pictures, and headlines may be interwoven into their respective subsections.

2. Honorees for the various classes have sometimes been used as subjects for the relief pictures in class portraits pages.

3. Informals of students involved in or discussing current problems relieved portraits pages of a Kansas book. Headlines and brief copy were also used.

4. Try supplementary action pictures showing how students of the various classes (junior, senior, etc.) spend off periods or casual moments during the day.

E. Remember that cutlines, full and well written, are as essential for action pictures on portraits pages as anywhere else. Perhaps, because of their prominent display, these need clear cutlines even more than most action shots do.

VIII. Naming of portraits sections and the positioning and arrangement of portraits have shown some interesting variations in recent years. Let's look at some of these:

A. The 1972 *Hack* of Centenary College for Women, Hackettstown, New Jersey, omits the portraits section as such, and instead carries all portraits, faculty and students, on the lower one-fifth of the pages throughout the book. Upper and lower portions of the pages show no correlation; the portraits simply fall in sequence with no reference to the material above them.

B. "Faces" is the name editors of the 1972 *Reflector*, Griffith, Indiana, gave the section of faculty and student portraits. Following its theme, "The Name Game," division spread copy contemplates the matter of how superficials, a beard or long hair, or a crew cut and a close shave, affect a person's "image," or earn him a name.

C. "People" is the name of the faculty-students portraits section of the 1973 *Parkerscope*, Parker High, Greenville, South Carolina. Editors used thematic

132

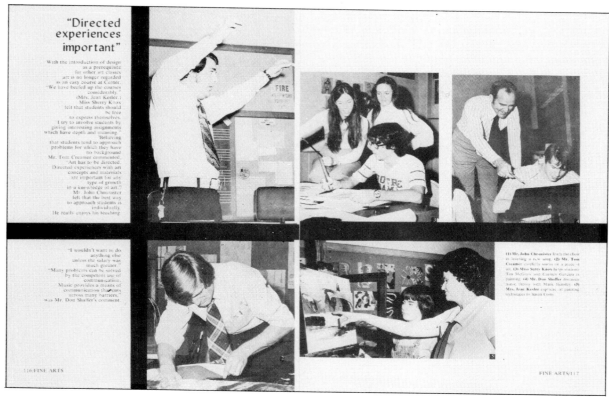

△ *Fig. 13.3A* — In an unusual plan discussed in Chapter 19 (see page 108) the Center High *Yellowjacket,* of Kansas City, Missouri, has a full section devoted to faculty informals, and to equally informal faculty comments.

Fig. 13B — In the portraits section of the same 1973 book (the *Yellowjacket*) student formals are accompanied and relieved by action pictures that feature students. Copy speaks of curriculum from the student viewpoint. ▽

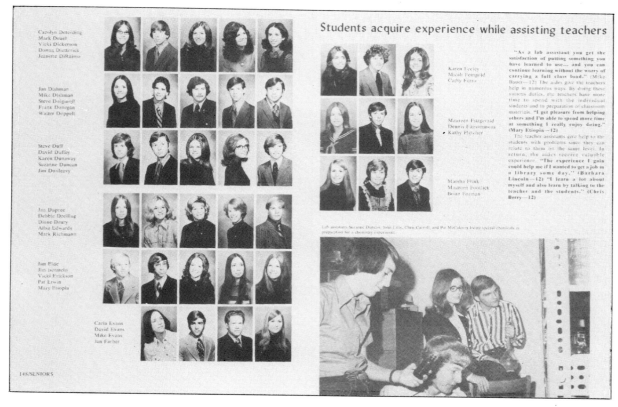

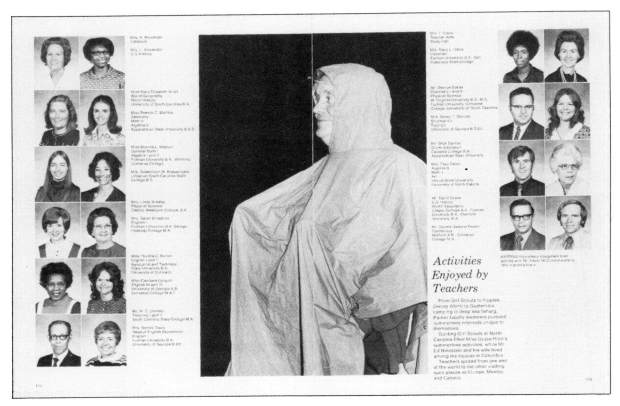

△ *Fig. 13.4*—Informal copy about teachers, and large, dramatic informals like the one here, made the faculty pages of the "People" section stand out in the 1973 *Parkerscope,* Parker High School, Greenville, South Carolina.

Fig. 13.5—Editors of the Creighton *Bluejay* (Omaha, Nebraska) alternated full pages of student portraits with facing pages of activity shots. The added vitality of the practice may not always justify the added use of space. ▽

Exercises

1. Make as long a list as you can of names that might be given to the portraits section or sections. Which of the suggestions would be better omitted because of their vagueness or unintelligibility to the outside reader? Write a paragraph (50 words or so) arguing the case for the name of your choice.

2. Argue the advantages or the disadvantages of placing faculty and student portraits together at the end of the book. Do it in list or paragraph form.

3. Argue the advantages or the disadvantages of combining faculty-administration portraits with curricular coverage. List points, or write a paragraph.

4a. Assuming that you will use the plan followed in the *Hack* (see the text section), devise a method for making a logical connection between portraits and the divisions with which they lie. (A ladder outline offers a good format here.)

4b. Using the plan of the *Oaken Bucket* alternately (also in the text), tell what action pictures you would plan for pages opposite portraits pages of seniors (limit to three pages maximum).

5. Following your favorite plan for giving interest to portraits layouts, dummy two spreads, one from each of your choices of (a) faculty and service personnel, and (b) underclassmen. Outline action pictures and sketch in portrait blocks. Write the first sentence or the first line of each cutline. Write narrative headlines that include names of spreads or have names in overlines. (You need not identify the portraits.)

6. Do a model seniors portraits spread for your book. Follow the instructions above.

14. Advertising

(**Note:** If your staff sells ads in the fall, you will wish to move this chapter to an earlier spot in the course. I have placed it here for the benefit of those who plan a campaign in late spring for a sales effort in summer or early fall.)

I. **Advertising is a well-established part of the student yearbook, having been used since very early times as a major—often, next to book sales, *the* major—source of income, as it has been for the student newspaper and magazine. The place of advertising is even more firmly assured now that the yearbook seems well established as part of the activity program and, via journalism, the curriculum.**

A. Not everyone agrees that yearbook advertising is good, however, and as a matter of fact, some school officials still will not allow students to sell space. Even a few advisers and publications directors have had serious objections to ads in student publications. An article in the March 1966 *Photolith* by Robert Steffes, a publications adviser at California State College, Long Beach, made a case against such advertising. He asserted that ads "cheapen the book," that they constitute little more than a "nuisance to the reader," and that they are "of no benefit to the merchant-advertiser." Besides all that, he said, ad copy is often "typographically weak and monotonous." He pointed that much of it was still "complimentary," or at best, institutional, that is, goodwill building.

B. In a *Photolith* article of April 1966, Mrs. Peg Westmoreland responded to Mr. Steffes, echoing points in favor of advertising that I have often made in articles and talks for conferences. Let me detail some of these arguments:

1. The preparation and sale of advertising is a valuable educational activity. It teaches students skills in copywriting, design, art, business practices, and sales techniques. In fact, it offers an overview, a sampling of the so-called free enterprise system itself. On a higher level, it has all the virtues so ably attributed by newspapers to serving as "little merchants" by distributing daily newspapers. It reminds one of the best projects of

the national Junior Achievement organization.

2. But the major reason for selling advertising is that it is an established and respected method by which almost all magazines, newspapers, and other printed media, the yearbook included, support themselves. It is a legitimate and useful method by which merchants and those who sell services may reach prospective buyers. And, in the case of the yearbook no less than the other media mentioned, revenues derived from the sale of ad space are crucial to the operation of the project, the production of a book that will be worthy of the school. Without this income, the staff would be forced either to engage in endless money-raising chores, perhaps to the detriment of essential production work, or to set a high price on the book, perhaps a prohibitive one.

3. Ad sales can be a valuable link in the public relations program of a school with its community, Mrs. Westmoreland argued effectively. Students who are properly trained can serve as excellent representatives of the school to the business community. I will not belabor the importance of stressing the positive qualities of high school or college youth or of exhibiting these qualities in a time not fully recovered from the "bad press" young people got in the late 1960s and during the early part of the 1970s.

4. As stated above, the advertisers can benefit by good advertising, properly planned and given the right display in the book. And this benefit does not stop with immediate sales, but in the yearbook more than any other medium, lingers in the form of accrued and renewed goodwill, since the yearbook will be around for reference in the months and years ahead.

II. Let's examine types of advertising—bad, weak, and good:

A. A form that often borders on the unethical, or may even be considered unethical by merchants and sensitive journalists, is one that "salutes" or "congratulates" graduates, seniors, the band, the team, or whatever is in the limelight at the moment.

1. This kind of advertising is more frequently sold with the assurance (at least implied) that those saluted will (a) be flattered and delighted with the recognition and will convert this delight into trade with the merchants or service people whose names appear in the ad; (b) be unhappy with those niggardly people who refuse to pay the price to have their names thus inscribed. (I exaggerate, perhaps, but only slightly. Readers may have suspected already that I consider this sort of promotional advertising inexcusable, in student publications or professional publications.)

2. Whether sold by implicit promise or threat, or in the most tactful possible way, such high-pressure advertising is the kind most likely to lead merchants and school officials alike to agree that yearbook advertising (or that in high school and college newspapers) is worthless and should be abolished.

3. The lowest possible kind of "compliments" advertising is that which carries the identification, "A Friend." This anonymous label suggests that the victim knows he is being "taken," but does not wish his name to appear so that it can be used by others seeking donations to causes of various merit. Certainly school people should not participate in this sort of near-racketeering activity.

B. The "sponsored page" is a form that has been tried here and there but has never actually caught on.

1. The name of the advertiser appears like this, usually at the bottom of the page, above the margin: "This page sponsored by Muriel's Beauty Salon"

2. Logical association of the company with a department or an organization may offer some limited possibilities: Home economics may appeal to an appliance dealer; sports pages for sporting goods firms, etc.

3. My feeling is that this sort of advertising clutters up the layouts, interferes with readability, and perhaps irritates the reader. The practices of TV and radio notwithstanding, I consider annoying our "audience" objectionable.

C. A plan not too much unlike the one above is to scatter advertising through the book, perhaps closing each section with some pages of advertisements.
   1. In this form the advertiser is allowed to present his sales message, not merely his name and address or business card.
   2. The argument is that the advertiser gets a better return for his money by having his ad placed right in with editorial matter and the pictorial story of the year, as is the case with newspaper advertising.
   3. There is even the possibility of placing an advertisement near a subject or activity in which the advertiser is especially interested. See comments above about sponsored pages.
   4. On the debit side, in intermingling the ads with the story of the year you risk interrupting the flow of copy, forcing the reader to read around commercial material, as in some women's magazines. You also invariably and inevitably disturb layout patterns and injure the unity of your book, critics point out. Television looker-listeners go to the refrigerator during commercials, but if your readers drop the book to go to the kitchen, will they ever get back?

D. The page or section of "patrons" is relatively common, especially in books published by private schools or colleges located in a relatively small area. While the community may be able to afford only limited advertising, professional people, people in government, parents, members of the sponsoring church, and individual churches have such intense interest in the well-being of the school they may be counted on to make contributions to the school and its activities willingly, even cheerfully. At least, this is the assumption.
   1. The page or section contains lists of those who have been asked to make contributions to the yearbook as a worthy project of the school and, frankly, "because we can't finance a book here without help of all our friends."
   2. For reasons already stated, this form of advertising or goodwill donation has aroused far less antipathy than the "compliments" ad, though there is little to choose between the two forms. Maybe "patrons" are usually closer to the school geographically or psychologically, and maybe they are asked to contribute in smaller amounts.
   3. Even though this kind of financing is handled discreetly, among the members of a church or from parents of staff members and other students, I suspect that many of those who are asked for a charitable donation are at least secretly annoyed, whether or not they contribute. The project may even result in loss of goodwill to the yearbook and its school.
   4. There is one positive thing about the patron's list other than that it helps finance your project. It enables the staff to involve persons besides business people who have obligations to the community, such as politicians, officeholders, lawyers, dentists, and doctors. Professional taboos actually forbid all but those in politics from regular advertising, and even politicians rarely have the opportunity to put their names forward in a strictly favorable way except immediately before election.
   5. Negatively, aside from the risk of bad public relations cited earlier, there is little training value for students in soliciting donations for the book, as though it were a kind of charity like the Muscular Dystrophy Foundation, the Red Cross, or Disaster Relief. (Students get plenty of practice the year-round in helping charitable drives in most schools.)
   6. Before you decide finally on this sort of program of fund raising, consider very carefully whether you might not get similar or even better results from a legitimate adver-

tising campaign, selling space and sales messages to service people and merchants and others who have something to offer your students and faculty.

E. Then there is the "business card" ad. Set page after page in similar type and style, this sort of ad made decades of old letterpress books close on a drab and dismal note and gave salespersons ever-increasing problems as they tried each year to get advertisers to repeat last year's space. These people realized they were not really getting their money's worth.

    1. The unvarying content was the name of the company or person advertising, the kind of business (if not incorporated into the name), the address, and the telephone number. Some of the better ones carried a slogan: "We aim to please," or "50 Years at the Same Corner," or . . .

    2. The business card is what it seems, not an exercise in hypocrisy like some forms already mentioned, but it has serious flaws. It is dull. As already suggested, it has no actual sales value. Its claims, or those of salespersons, to "goodwill" value, immediate and long term, are highly debatable. And, perhaps worst of all, it exhibits either staff laziness or a complete absence of creativity and imagination.

    3. As a postscript, let me add that this sort of format in advertising had at least one good effect. It drove business managers and ad salespersons to the necessity of devising something better. The end result has been today's yearbook ads aimed at attracting students to the ad section, making them read it as if it were part of the book, and persuading many of them to spend their allowances or income on products and services advertised there.

F. Today's ad, the one most often found in successful yearbooks, is a pictorial ad and one that so combines art and copy as to perform a sales function for the advertiser.

    1. The best subjects for pictures are students. These volunteer "models" should be selected for photo-genic qualities, for personality, and for ability to represent the school and the merchants properly.

    2. Copy, as suggested above, is written with the purpose in mind of selling readers on whatever is being presented. It is an unabashed commercial message, but the more natural and believable it is, the more effective the ad will be.

    3. The pictorial ad is not at all new. I tried it or persuaded my staff to try it in my West Texas yearbook (Fort Stockton) in the late 1930s. The 1940 book of that school, the *Panther*, made good use of student models. In one ad for a style shop, a pretty girl student is shown as she tries on an Easter bonnet under the attentive eyes of the proprietress. Copy ties students, alumni, and the business together in a happy relationship involving clothing and jewelry. A cutline refers to the student's pleasure in seeing herself in the "perky little Easter hat." (Some teachers who read this phrase will remember what that 1940 student was talking about.)

    4. Modern books abound with clever, selling ads. One example at random is found in a recent Whitehall, Pennsylvania, book. Two students are pictured vertically as they sit at a window table examining a dinner menu. A cutline tells us the names of the boy and girl students, gives a few details on the place (City Vu Diner) and the time and occasion, informing us that City Vu serves meals on a 24-hour basis. A block of ragged-edge type lists foods offered and describes facilities and services, using descriptive words that make the school reader eager to repeat Richard and Rita's experience as diners.

III. Who sells advertising? Ideally, it is the assigned members of the business staff of the yearbook. Not even the members of the editorial staff, unless some of them are endowed with unusual versatility, should really be expected to sell advertising. But since not all schools are large enough to provide a separate sales staff, the ideal cannot always be the actual.

A. In smaller schools the entire staff is quite often conscripted to sell space.

1. Because, in the compact community, everyone is well known to everyone else, this is not an overwhelming handicap, except for those few introverts who can write fine copy, take good pictures, or do superior layouts, but who have negative sales ability.

2. Recognizing the handicaps (and strengths) of these staff members and assigning them to chores that fit their abilities is the responsibility of the adviser or business manager.

3. It is essential, in a school where all the staff must participate in sales, to conduct an especially thoroughgoing sales-training program in which the most basic skills are taught and rehearsed. (For instance, the art and skill of making and keeping an appointment and the persistence to see it through with a hard-to-reach prospect are techniques that can be taught.)

B. In an occasional private school, especially, all members of the student body may participate in subscription or ad sales. Or at least the force may be drawn from among many groups not connected with the yearbook.

1. In one recent book from such a school, homerooms competed in ad sales, and the room that sold the most ads was honored with a large group picture inside the ad section. A caption below the picture gave the group credit for its work.

2. Obviously, a presales campaign training program is especially important in such cases. And the first part of the "course" will be information about the product itself.

3. Salespersons should be armed with standard sales talks, with prepared dummies, and with suggested ad copy and pictures. (All this will be more fully discussed a little later.)

IV. When should ads be sold? The answer to this is largely dependent on the experience of the adviser and of preceding staffs.

A. If merchants have been accustomed to a fall or winter campaign, or a summer sales drive, and if sales at this period have been satisfactory, there is no big reason to change and thus risk unforeseen difficulties.

B. It is desirable that such a schedule allow the staff time for listing of prospects, going over sales techniques, and preparing suggested ad copy and dummies to show prospects.

C. A summer sales program proved highly successful to me when I served as adviser of the staff in a small school. The full staff had time after we had sent the final copy to the printer to turn their attention to an ad sales program for the next book. Summer business doldrums may have cost us a few sales, but we felt free in fall and early winter to make second efforts to round up strays.

D. Obviously, fall is the period in which most ad sales must be completed if there is to be adequate time for gathering copy, securing and checking proofs, etc.

V. The "how" of sales is the subject for a separate book. But here are the elements, the bare bones of a successful sales campaign:

A. Administrative support for the sales program must either be assumed or secured. If this support is in any way lacking in strength, your first step is to reinforce it by a sales program to the administration.

B. Should any lurking disapproval of the project exist among members of the community, arm yourselves with a strong letter of explanation and authorization from the principal, superintendent, dean, or whoever is appropriate in your situation. It should outline the value of the yearbook to the school and community and the place of advertising in such a medium.

C. A survey of student spending is a valuable tool to carry on an ad sales campaign. Ron Phillips and his students at Black Hills State College, Spearfish, South Dakota, made such a survey, which they summarized in a 16-page report. Results—great success in convincing merchants of the value of student publications as sales media—are reported in an article of April 1967 in *Photolith* magazine. Less elaborate surveys, which nevertheless sample enough students to be convincing, can be conducted in small schools no less successfully than in large ones or in colleges like Black Hills State.

D. Prepare your arguments for yearbook advertising.

   1. Northwest Classen's *Round Table*, 1970, of Oklahoma City, argued as follows, using figures that are subject to adjustments for inflation and, in the final point, for locally verified statistics.

      a. "Today's teens, having been exposed since infancy to Madison Avenue techniques, know more about products than perhaps any other age group."

      b. This group accounts for "more than $15 billion of the nation's purchasing power."

      c. In the Oklahoma City area, "students make up 50 percent of the community's consumers."

   2. Develop a case for the value of your own local yearbook as a medium of advertising, not only by general statistics and survey information, as suggested above, but in ways like these:

      a. Know and cite high ratings or scores your book has earned in competition or critiques on the local, state, regional, and national levels.

      b. List virtues of the book as the staff sees them and may have seen and stated them in previous subscription and advertising campaigns. Excellence and number of fine action pictures might be worth citing. So might inclusion (in the forthcoming issue) of a special community-school section.

      c. Know and tell, if at all possible, what the theme of the book will be. If it has special community-wide appeal, it will have added sales value.

      d. You can always support your argument with letters or quotations from business people who have advertised and who liked the results they obtained, and from student leaders or prominent alumni or other boosters willing either to be quoted or to write letters of commendation. (You may not consider this kind of support necessary, but if sales have been dragging, the idea is to get all the help you can.)

E. A copy of last year's book, especially if it was a winner, is good ammunition for a salesperson to carry.

F. Develop and print a rate card, and be sure each sales "rep" has a copy of his or her own and enough extras to pass out to prospects who may wish to consider a number of possibilities. Include key points of your "sales pitch" on one side of the card, in brief form.

G. Develop a policy relative to the use of pictures and copy in advertisements.

   1. Will seniors, popular students from all classes, or others serve as models for ad pictures, if pictures are to be used?

   2. Rule out "Compliments of . . ." and similar wording suggestive that a real sales message has little or no value in your yearbook.

   3. Decide on general style and format of ads and prepare some model or sample copy and layouts. A sample division spread would be helpful.

H. Editor, business manager, adviser, and staff should develop a policy about the sale of the yearbook to advertisers. For those who purchase full pages, perhaps a copy of the book might be given as a bonus. There could be a discount to others, dependent on the size of the ad. This offer could be part of the sales approach, or at least might properly be handled at the time of ad sales.

I. Put everything together in a sales kit of materials each salesperson will carry on calls—a letter from the administrator; statements or compilations of data about teenage purchasing power in the area covered by the yearbook; a copy of last year's book, or even an earlier one; a copy of the merchant's last year's ad; perhaps letters from merchants, alumni, students, the editor (citing policies and plans for the current book); and rate cards.

J. Plan a sales-training course, from a few days' to perhaps a week's length, as seems needed to cover the subject and to give salespersons opportunity to practice before the "class." Among other things, the course should include the following points. Learn them, and plan to put them to use in sales.

1. Establish a method of setting up appointments with prospects or at least of going to see them. (Some merchants will not make appointments but will talk to you "anytime I'm not busy with customers.")

2. Take with you the sales kit mentioned above but have your facts, figures, and arguments well in mind. These are matters to be learned and practiced in the sales course.

3. A plain-speaking old dean once gave this advice to the assembled teaching staff at the first of the school year: "Keep clean. Be neat in your dress at all times." His words offended many of his hearers, who were insulted that he would doubt their attention to personal neatness. But it is good advice for the sales staff, especially since, as Mrs. Westmoreland stated (see above), these salespersons are public relations representatives of the school to the members of the business community.

4. Be on time for your appointment. If you find on the first call that it is inconvenient for the merchant to see and talk to you then, arrange for another, more convenient time.

5. Learn and practice proper methods of opening the so-called sales talk. There is an art here on which the whole business of selling hinges.

6. Each salesperson should emerge from the course with some notion of the general order in which he will bring up points and arguments. Each prospect requires an individual technique. The merchant who has been buying a full page for the past 20 years would be bored to have a salesperson give him the arguments prepared for a new merchant in town who has never seen the book and has had little time to consider advertising in it.

7. Here is a rule you might ponder in the sales-training course, from an adviser-author of 1950: "Take *no* for an answer!"

   a. Whether the rule would work for those selling resort acreage or insurance, I really do not know, but for students dealing with businesspersons of the community, or patrons of the college or school, I am inclined to think it an appropriate suggestion. I doubt that high-pressure tactics ever won friends or earned much money for a student publication of any kind.

   b. Perhaps this point belongs somewhere else, but the whole selling process depends on it, including the ability to present your sales talk with enough confidence that you are not disturbed or discouraged by the occasional turndown. Simply put, it is this: If the staff will make sure the yearbook is complete and attractive, advertisers will follow the lead of your general readers, as they did a few years ago in one fine Michigan school. There, they literally "stood in line" for available advertising space in the yearbook, according to the adviser at that time, Miss Vida B. McGiffin, widely known author and authority on yearbooks.

8. Be sure to practice the actual preparation of advertising—the art, copy, layout, cutlines, and headings. Planning alternative sizes and shapes for the same prospect may have value in many cases, especially for those who have not previously purchased advertising space in the book.

VI. There are things to be considered after the book comes out:

A. Adviser Laurence D. Christman, writing in the November 1970 *Photolith,* told of the value of a letter thanking advertisers for their support.

B. Mr. Christman, like my own yearbook

business manager and sales director at the University of Houston 20 years earlier, included with his thank-you letter a proposed renewal contract, suggesting that the merchant might wish to assure himself favorable space in the next issue by signing the contract and returning it. Jack Wilson and Ralph Poling at Houston actually waited until the time for the new ad sales campaign before they sent the letter and contract. But the principle is the same. Incidentally, these two Houstonians enclosed *two* tearsheets of the ad with each letter, one to be kept by the advertiser, the other, it was hoped, to be returned with instructions. Results of both mailings exceeded expectations. Christman reported a 60 percent affirmative return, and we at Houston had a 75 percent response from old customers authorizing a repeat of the space order. All this before a salesperson made a call!

C. If you decide to send out such a mailing, you may wish to enclose your new rate card, as the business manager and sales director at Houston did.

D. Wilson and Poling also enclosed a reply card with the letter. This gave the merchant a number of choices for a reply, leaving blanks for simple check marks. The first two options were these: "___Contract enclosed. This authorizes repeat of the same space," and "___Have salesman call."

E. At one school, the business staff asked for the returned dummies of full-page ads. To each of those they attached a note stating, "This advertisement appeared in the *(name)* yearbook." Then they gave the ad dummy to the advertiser. Many pleased advertisers displayed these ad layouts in their show windows for a period of time after the yearbooks had been received and distributed in the school.

F. An alternate idea to the above would be to get tearsheets from the printer. (These must be ordered well in advance of printing, of course, likely at the time you submit your advertising section layout and material to the printer.) Individual ads. of whatever minimum size you determine, may then be mounted and submitted to the advertisers. A note telling where the advertisement appeared should be attached to the mounting board or to the ad itself.

G. Don't forget to deliver copies of yearbooks ordered by advertisers, or the books their purchases made them eligible to receive. A member of the sales staff is the logical one to make each delivery. You may decide that this is the occasion on which to suggest renewing the order for next year, and if so, be sure the salesperson has the sales talk well rehearsed and a contract ready to be signed. In some or even most cases, this may seem the time to enjoy the current ad and yearbook and not the psychological moment to do any additional selling job.

H. This may be the time to consider future prospects. Wilson and Poling used the period of thank-yous to write a brief letter to a select list of what they considered good prospective advertisers, telling them about the yearbook, current and next year's issues, and the advantages of joining other merchants as advertisers. Rate and reply cards were enclosed. One order via the mail more than paid for the whole mailing. A substantial number of those receiving the letter replied, asking a salesperson to call. (To the good salesperson, such a reply is tantamount to a sale.) As one who for 23 years supported a scholastic magazine, at least in part, through advertising secured largely by mail, I can heartily recommend the technique of advertising solicitation by letter, particularly if your prospects are very widely scattered. In a small or compact community, the method has less value.

VII. Experiments in format and handling have been varied and imaginative in recent years:

A. The Boone High *Legend,* of Orlando, Florida, came up with an arrangement that offers exciting possibilities: ads fitted into the holiday seasons. Each group, such as the ones representing the Christmas season, shares a story that mentions each store. Pictures and captions relate to the holiday. Each spread has a well-written narrative headline.

B. A slight variation of the above plan omits the holiday motif but associates a number of ads on a single spread. Three-column layout leaves part of a vertical column open for a combined story about advertisers, each of whom is given a separate paragraph. A headline ties the often diverse advertisers together quite ingeniously. This plan was used in the *Warrenite,* Warren Township High School, Indianapolis. As in other modern books, student models are used, along with merchants or their employees.

C. A "Booster Section" replaced the standard ad section in a small college book (Baker College, Baldwin, Kansas) back in 1966. Essays in words and pictures replaced usual ads (subjects: the local banker, the newspaper editor and his wife, the local museum, etc.) and business leaders and others were asked to finance the section. I suggest use of such a section to introduce or lead the reader into pages of lively advertisements.

VIII. **Division spreads and other introductory pages offer an opportunity to bridge the gap between school and community and to minimize or remove the equally large gap between the story of the school year and the advertising section. Methods vary in subtlety. Here are a few selected examples:**

A. Opening copy on the division spread of the 1973 *Reflector,* Highland, Indiana, imaginatively tells the disadvantages that would befall society if all ads were suddenly banned.

B. Boat scenes representative of the Tampa area, and student interviews about the community, with pictures of the students, make unusual dividers in the 1973 *Excalibur,* Robinson High, Tampa, Florida. The idea of bringing students into the section and relating them to the community and business can hardly be overdone.

C. The Gainesville (Florida) *Hurricane* almost follows the plan of the Kansas college I cited above, combining an attractive division spread that is illustrated by pictures of downtown business scenes, with an added spread of six appealing community pictures, mosaically arranged.

1. The modular strip of pictures that lies horizontally across the first of these spreads is tied across the gutter with a cut portion of a five-dollar bill. (Be careful of government regulations about how much of a bill you can legally show.)

2. Flora and fauna (azaleas, birds, an alligator, a squirrel) and a small fishing boat are pictured on the "community" spread.

3. A boxed copy block, serving as an element in the mosaic, offers a brief chamber-of-commerce description of Gainesville, its industry, its beautiful surroundings, and its varieties of flowers, shrubs, and other natural attributes. And the story is much more convincing than most copy of this kind found in promotional brochures.

D. Students gathered in front of a local business, whose name is obscured by the art, set the theme of student-community friendship on division pages of the 1973 *Cavalier,* Houston Academy, Dothan, Alabama.

1. Headlines, pictures, and copy here and on the inside advertising pages repeat and emphasize the mutual dependence and friendship between business people and students and between those in the community and Houston Academy itself.

2. One spread goes so far as to emphasize how parents of academy students support the book and the school as they buy ads for their businesses. These may sound like high-pressure tactics, but if a national insurance company can urge people to buy its insurance because it is "a good neighbor," and if a gasoline company can suggest that it is worthy of your trade because its attendants and managers are "very friendly," then why not make frank assertions in the yearbook that "students spark community growth" and that "merchants become better friends" as they advertise in the yearbook?

3. At least this staff did it and, apparently, with success. Why not apply the idea, with your own wording? As a starter, I suggest the clause, "We need each other." It hardly

146

overstates the proper community-school relationship.

IX. Let me sum up some points about content and form of your ads:

A. In line with the idea of bringing the ad section into the book, be sure your headlines, cutlines, and inside copy come up to standards set elsewhere in your book; that they are specific and meaningful; that they establish a relationship between the school and its students on the one side and the merchant on the other; and that they help sell a service or merchandise. Don't settle for just "building goodwill," attractive as that goal may seem.

B. Pictures should be realistic and as nearly as possible dramatic, and must never seem artificial, posed, or canned. Rule out camera staring. Keep the number of subjects small, except in some special mass scene like the one described earlier for the advertising dividers. Put the center of interest in the right place. (Reread Chapter 5 on photography if this or any other point is vague in your mind.)

C. Layouts, too, should seem reasonably consistent with the rest of the book. They should satisfy the eye by observing layout rules, just like other pages.

X. Finally, let's consider the sectional title.

A. "Advertising" or "Advertisements" is honorable and honest, certainly, and perhaps one of these words should appear on the division page, even if only as a small overline or label.

B. "Community" is understandable, though not all books go as far as the Dothan, Alabama, book in developing the story of school-community relationships, and fewer still go as far as the Kansas book cited earlier in its so-called "Booster Section."

C. "Yellow Pages" is the equally understandable title given by editors of the Augusta (Georgia) Military Academy *Recall* a few years back. (They ran yellow pages, like the ones in the telephone book, but you might get by with a touch of yellow on the dividers.)

D. "Finance" and "Enterprises" are titles used by the Highland (Indiana) *Reflector* and the Gainesville (Florida) *Hurricane*, which may require a little explanation and justification.

E. Your own title, at least the thematic one, may well be the as yet undiscovered and unused divisional name that is unbeatable for your book. If it is clear and imaginative, it may even set an example for many other editors to follow in the years ahead.

△ *Fig. 14.1*—Student models are used in credible action shots in "Community" pages of the 1974 *Totem* of Chamberlain High, Tampa, Florida. Ads are broken up with posed club-group pictures. Best modern books have readable ad sections.

Fig. 14.2—An unusual plan used in the *Wildcat,* Hillcrest High, Dalzell, South Carolina, relies on strong pictures, an open modern layout, a combined block of copy about all advertisers on the spread, and feature-style cutlines. ▽

Fig. 14.3—Floridians are proud of their state and their communities. This community spread on a "picturesque paradise . . ." opened the advertising ("Enterprises") section of the Gainesville (Florida) *Hurricane*. (See page 146, VIII-C.)

Exercises

1. Evaluate and rank from 1 (best) to 6 (worst) the following arguments for buying a clothing store ad in your yearbook:
   a. Our students will appreciate your patronage and remember you when they buy merchandise.
   b. All, or almost all, students read the yearbook, cover to cover, and a recent survey shows that the average student buys $400 [or whatever the amount is, as determined by actual survey] worth of clothing per year.
   c. If you don't buy an ad from us, you can't expect students to patronize you!
   d. A yearbook ad costs less per reader than corresponding space in the community newspaper.
      (Hint: In considering this argument, think of the kind of medium each is and the different kinds of readers the two media have.)
   e. Would you like to buy an ad in the school yearbook? It's only $100 per page!
   f. Yearbook ads will be read 20 years from now, and they will still be helping you sell merchandise, if you're in business.
   Discuss each of the above statements in a sentence, or at most two.

2a. Make an outline response to the statement and the closing query: "Yearbook ads aren't read by anyone, because yearbooks are generally pretty dull, and the ads are always the dullest, least readable part of the book. So why should I spend my money that way?"

   or

2b. A local chain store has asked your school board to discontinue sale of ads by student publications, including the yearbook. Your principal must be prepared to discuss the request at a forthcoming meeting. Write a page argument (150–250 words) for continuing advertising sales for the yearbook and newspaper, emphasizing the yearbook.

3. Prepare a sales letter intended for merchants who do not now advertise in the yearbook. Localize it. Keep it to a page, or about 250–300 words maximum.

4. For your rate card, plan five or six statements about the yearbook and school and students and the yearbook that "sum it all up" as to the value of yearbook ads.

5. Write the first 200 words of a sales talk to a local bank about the yearbook as a good ad medium for a bank. (Feel free to assume a survey and to use imagined figures.)
(Note: The teacher or ad manager may wish to divide the class or staff and assign the bank talk to one or two members and sales talks for other types of business to others.)

6. Write a thank-you letter to advertisers, keeping it to one page, double-spaced.

7. Discuss the desirability—or undesirability—of "patrons" pages in your book. Be sure that the case for "legitimate" advertising is fully explored along with the positive case for seeking contributions from patrons.

8. Develop a division spread or a spread inside the advertising division on "Community" or whatever your special theme suggests. Dummy and sketch pictures in outline; and also dummy copy, cutlines, and a headline. Write copy, not to exceed 125 words; the first line of each cutline; and the headline, which may be one or two lines and one to three columns wide. If this is to be your main division spread, be sure that it is clear from the heading that it is an ad section.

9a. Let everyone prepare a dummy for a half-page or full-page ad, with art sketched in, a cutline, and 25–35 words of copy.

or

9b. If anyone would like to make a case for mingling ads with the rest of the book, let him argue the case in outline.

10. Produce an idea or motif around which to arrange ads in the section. I will not rule out "holidays," the special idea given in the text, but try for some others like it. List advertisers who would fit in the categories mentioned. You need not go too far with this unless and until the staff settles on one for the book. Then let your fancy run free!

15.
Circulation

A. The activity fee is mainly, though not exclusively, found in colleges.
   1. While this provides a guaranteed distribution, the amount allowed for each book rarely or never covers the cost of production. The difference must be made up by advertising or some kinds of money-raising projects.
   2. This form of subsidy is at best precarious. Opposition to the yearbook can develop overnight from administrators, from students, or from groups who for one reason or another, often political, have developed an antagonism to the book or the staff. One university yearbook that I am intimately acquainted with found itself suddenly and almost without warning removed from the list of favored organizations. Its share of the activity fee was totally withdrawn, and the adviser and staff were informed by the administration that they must henceforth sell their subscriptions directly and individually to students without any help from the administration. (Note: The adviser informs me they sold 4,500 copies individually in 1975!)
B. Some private schools and colleges have subsidized the yearbook, assuring free distribution to all students. I have no statistics, but I suspect that the number of such schools is diminishing to the near-vanishing point. Private schools are having their financial problems, and costs of paper, printing, etc., are growing with alarming speed.
   1. If you happen to be enjoying this rare situation, begin at once, quietly, to plan a substitute program of direct sales.
   2. File the plan away in confidence that, like the cradle Mark Twain described as standard furniture in every rural home in his day, it will eventually be in great and urgent demand.
C. And finally there are direct sales of subscriptions to the book. This is the commonest method of circulation in most

high schools and in many if not most colleges, and with changes that are occurring in student publications, a method that becomes more and more important as time goes on.

II. Who sells subscriptions? Ideally, as in the case of advertising sales, assigned members of the business staff, that is, a circulation manager and staff salesperson do the job best. I see nothing wrong with there being some overlap between circulation and editorial staffs. A good salesperson may also be a good or excellent writer, artist, photographer, or even the editor. For the period of the circulation drive, the circulation sales staff should be mainly if not exclusively assigned to selling yearbooks.

A. Alternately, in smaller schools and colleges, the entire staff pitches in to sell subscriptions during this drive, just as, during the ad campaign, all or nearly all the staff members become salespersons. Unhappily, this involves staff members who have no aptitude in sales, and, now and then, less interest than aptitude.

B. Sometimes, classes or homerooms agree to serve in sales campaigns. Prizes or special recognition are given as incentives. (See example of this plan from Indianapolis, below.) The disadvantage cited above to using the full staff is doubled and redoubled here. Inertia and flat disinterest are added to the list of problems. Since the yearbook is not actually of deep concern to most of those assigned under this plan, it is hard to motivate any substantial number of the participants for any sustained period. The only counter to all this is very careful supervision by interested staff leaders, the prompt switching of assigned jobs from those indicating disinterest or lack of ability to others with more promise of getting results.

III. When should you sell subscriptions? As with ad sales, the answer depends on local experience and past practice. Here is one plan, recommended especially for a spring-delivery book:

A. Start with a one- to two-week advance sales drive as early in the fall as practi-

cal, that is, as soon as things have settled down into a routine, and yet before students have become too deeply involved in other matters, such as homecoming or the week of a crucial football game.

1. Be sure that you have the campaign worked out in minute detail before you start, that all promotional material is ready, and that the publicity—public relations program is on schedule.

2. Have your sales techniques honed to a fine point. (See discussion on the program later in this outline-text.)

3. Keep to the set schedule. Don't drag things on and on, like the dreary community welfare drives that miss the goals they have set and extend their closing dates again and again. Announce in advance what the dates for starting and closing will be. Set an exact hour on which advance sales will stop.

4. Generally, staffs establish a lower charge for advanced sales. Thus, for instance, the price might be $9 during the early drive, $10 thereafter.

B. A fairly general and apparently successful technique of collections is to ask one-third the price as a down payment with the order, perhaps another one-third by a second date, and the final payment on a date well in advance of your sending the final order to the printer. Some staffs combine the second and third deadlines, collecting the total balance in this second payment,

C. Conduct a cleanup drive in late winter or in early spring, depending on your printing deadline.

1. This may be held to a week or ten days, according to the size of the school, the complexity of the drive, and the size of the sales force (whether composed of members of homerooms or classes, or a half-dozen or so eager, competent staff members). Success of the earlier drive might even make this sales effort relatively unimportant.

2. Obviously, this campaign must be closed before the time when you are required to give the final order to the printer for the total number of books or (if you have a different program) after you have sold the absolute maximum number of books you can

deliver, based on sectional runs already completed by the printer.

A. Outline the arguments you can honestly present for buying, owning, and reading the yearbook. Prepare counter arguments against complaints made about last year's book. (*That* book was an all-picture book? Tell them *this one* will have pictures and an ample story in words. This assumes that the staff has already met, conferred about past flaws, and determined on a course of action in planning and producing the current book.)

B. Consider how the theme or motif idea will work into your sales talk and effort. (Remember how a community-school idea was worked into the sale of advertising, as discussed in Chapter 14 on ad sales.)

C. Get your posters ready. It is possible that posters provided by your yearbook printer may be your best bet. But if you have a good artist and one, maybe even two or three, apt sloganeers or ad copywriters, original and localized material is best. The cartoonist whose work you were tempted to use for the yearbook itself, but did not, may be able to give you just what you need for a winning poster campaign.

D. Prepare a publicity schedule or campaign for the school newspaper, a less ambitious one for the community press. (It is important to let parents and patrons know your plans. In many if not most cases, the money you are seeking will come out of parents' pockets.)

1. The motif or theme, unless it is to be a big surprise at book-delivery time, makes a good subject for a news release, especially if it is fresh and has an exciting sound to it. If it touches the community, give a little story to the local newspaper(s) too.

2. Staff assignments—naming of the new editor and business manager in the spring, assignment of other editors or top assistants, perhaps in early fall —are newsworthy items that keep the public talking about the year-

book. (All this has a direct bearing on sales, please remember.)

3. Plans for improvement, enlargement, addition of color, and greater focus on action pictures stimulate interest in the book and conversation about it. Such conversation creates a desire to own the book.

4. Naturally, you will announce the schedules for advance subscription sales and for second and final sales. Do this well before the start of the drive or drives.

E. As news develops or is created, keep the announcements flowing over the school loudspeaker system. This is especially vital just before and during the sales campaign itself. Skill in writing spot announcements, radio news, and even jingles will pay off here.

F. Assembly skits are good for kicking off or climaxing a sales campaign. Cleverness and skill in writing and in acting are useful for these. You are trying to elicit the response of sympathy and support, not pity for ineptness or silliness. Drama students and teachers can help here. If there is a good working relationship between the newspaper staff and adviser and the yearbook, as is likely and usual, you may wish to seek cooperation from these good journalistic colleagues. (I realize there is great overlap here, too.)

G. Display of good photographs on the bulletin board, with appropriate captioning, can supplement posters. Be sure you have negatives and prints on file before risking these prints to public exposure and handling.

A. Prepare and formalize the sales approach for individual salespersons.

B. Prepare a speech, or at least an outline for a speech, for presentation in homerooms or classes where orders are to be taken during the drive.

C. Let salespersons practice their sales techniques, including talks, on each other.

D. Issue receipt books. Set and be sure everyone understands the exact routine for listing orders, keeping records of orders, collecting down payments, issuing receipts, and keeping file copies of receipts.

E. Consider techniques and special points for approaching community patrons and such merchants and service people as operators of beauty salons, barbers or stylists, doctors and dentists, and any others who have waiting rooms or places where clients, patients, or customers assemble. There may be an unexplored gold mine of orders in your community.

VI. Experienced advisers have offered suggestions through the years to supplement ideas I have picked up and used in my own work.

A. The late John S. Enwright, a longtime successful adviser of the *East Detroiter* yearbook of East Detroit, Michigan, has made these relevant suggestions:
   1. "The best salesman is last year's book," said this fine adviser. Of course, this point depends for validity on whether you are really proud of your last year's book. If so, take it with you as you sell.
   2. "Avoid duplicating sales approaches," Enwright warned. In East Detroit, one salesperson was assigned from each social studies class. (*Every* student there was enrolled in such a class, one assumes.) Social science teachers agreed to serve as special "assistant advisers" during the drive. Yearbook staffers presumably coordinated the various class representatives.
   3. "Avoid begging or pressuring students." Do give every prospective buyer the facts and a full opportunity to make a decision and to buy. (Remember what was said about selling ads: Be willing to take "no" for an answer.)
   4. "Transfer names of all subscribers to record cards that have assigned spaces for their names, classes, amounts of payment [leave enough blanks to allow for the various payment deadlines], and for a specific identification number by which each buyer will receive his book."
   5. At East Detroit, receipt cards were assembled under the names of the salespersons, who were then assigned to distribute books at the assembly.
   6. One idea of Mr. Enwright avoided overage. After all sales were in, the staff or sales manager and adviser figured out the number of file copies needed for staff room, library, etc., computed the total, and ordered *that number*. There was no speculation based on possible "impulse" purchasing at the date of yearbook distribution. (By contrast, one experienced adviser says, "We always order 25 extra copies!")

B. As a sales gimmick and possible added element, a record of the events and sounds of the school has sometimes been sold with the book, usually enclosed in a pocket or envelope attached to the cover of the book.
   1. As far back as 1955, Nancy Sweeton, yearbook editor at the University of of Houston, recorded excerpts from programs, songs, and musical events at familiar spots on the campus. She used facilities of the radio-television department, with the cooperation of department personnel and officials.
   2. School songs and cheers heard at rallies and games make up the major content of some school records.
   3. The idea may have been outdated as students have become more sophisticated. Yet one never can predict customs. The idea may become a fad any year.
   4. The value of the idea in sales and in finished results depends on the planning of contents and the technique and art of recording and combining the sounds. The writing and the reading of needed intro, linking, and closing narration require great skills too.

C. The late John Schrodt of Indiana offered three interesting ideas:
   1. At the assembly in which promotional skits are offered, place a salesperson at the ends of all rows, or at least as many rows as practical. Salespersons can work their rows during a planned intermission in the program.
   2. For the occasional all-grades yearbook, in which elementary students are also included, send a letter home with each elementary student. See that an order form is enclosed with or attached to the letter.
   3. Be sure, Mr. Schrodt advised, to tell students what the yearbook actually costs, as well as what the sales price is. Since it is one of the few commodities in this inflation-ridden world that

often or even usually sells below cost, this is a persuasive sales point. We all like to get a bargain.

D. A staff at Washington High, Bethel, Kansas, had great success with two ideas:

1. Skits in the form of radio programs in old melodramatic style were given over the address system. They featured a heroine, a villain, *and* the yearbook, known there as the *Hatchet*. A Brooklyn dialect added flavor to the lugubrious accounts of the near-loss of the book, nick-of-time rescues, etc.

2. Humorous ditties, caricaturing or paraphrasing well-known commercial jingles and featuring the yearbook (had you guessed this by now?), caught on so well that students sang them on buses as they rode to ball games.

E. At Brebeauf Prep School, Indianapolis, Indiana, when it became essential to raise the yearbook price, this unpleasantness was offset by vigorous sales tactics:

1. The staff took the campaign into the cafeteria, decorating the room with banners and posters.

2. Each class sold yearbook subscriptions, and the class with the highest percentage of sales got a free page to use in publicizing its activities. (This was above any regular reporting of classes in the yearbook.)

F. As a final note, suggested by the experience at Brebeauf, which is common to all of us these days, let me suggest:

1. Take careful stock of likely costs and income this year, and determine on the basis of facts whether you need to raise the price to subscribers.

2. Don't be caught with an embarrassing deficit because you wait too long to face up to the realities of inflation. Skyrocketing paper costs and rising prices of other supplies of recent years make this precaution doubly important, or is it *triply* since I wrote the above?

Exercises

1. Write a 250-word story for the school newspaper about the approaching circulation drive.

2. Plan a promotional poster. Sketch in the art, or paste up a picture from a magazine that approximates what you have in mind. Do a narrative or punch-phrase title or heading. Write a staccato-style copy block of 50–75 words.

3. Write five spot announcements for the school sound system or for radio. Keep each to no more than 50 words. Time your own delivery of each.

4. Write a 250-word presentation to be given before a homeroom or class at the start of a drive. Begin by making a point-by-point outline.

5. Plan a skit for an assembly program during a subscription-sale campaign. Outline it (about a page).

6. Select a commercial that might be changed enough to be useful in your sales drive. This is a kind of mild plagiarism, but I am sure such companies as McDonald's will not object to your adapting a jingle for school use.

7. In consultation with whoever makes out your budget and with last year's business adviser and/or business manager, consider prospective income and likely expenses. Consider whether this is the time to raise the price of the book, and if so, how much. Discuss your decision (if it is to raise the price) with school officials and student leaders. Outline steps you will take in publicity and sales talk to justify the raise. List points you need to make in defending any increase. Alternately, if you can avoid an increase, write a list of comments, or write a paragraph telling your public how you are holding the line against the increase.

8. List various groups to whom you might sell copies of the yearbook. In a group session, make a master list of prospects. Don't hesitate to use a directory for this. If subscriptions and ad sales are to be tied together for selected merchants, leave these companies out or star them. There are many others who cannot advertise (doctors, for instance, and small companies) but who may wish to buy the yearbook for clients, customers, or patients.

16.
Index and Closing Pages

I. Although common and expected in most books, the index was rather slow to develop in the yearbook, making its start with college and larger high school books. Today, it is considered almost essential to readability even in smaller books.

II. Acknowledgments, credits, and other closing remarks of the editor appear in most modern books, before or after the index.

III. The thematic close, rounding off the thematic or linkage elements, appears in the final part of the book, usually just after the editor's acknowlegments page or spread. This new closing often replaces the material once found on the endsheets.

IV. Common elements of the index itself, whether in a single index or as separate indexes, include:

   A. Advertisers' directory
   B. Club index or directory
   C. Index of faculty, administrators, and other school personnel (custodians, maintenance personnel, cafeteria workers, etc.)
   D. Student index
   E. Index or directory of senior memberships and honors

V. Some elements that have been found in final yearbook pages in addition to the above include these:

   A. Pictures of senior honors, which are more often located in the honors pages or in the senior portraits section
   B. Listing of honor students, those with grade averages in the upper 5 percent for the year, as found in the 1973 *Excalibur,* Robinson High, Tampa, Florida
   C. A page of photo credits, as found in the 1972 Paris (Texas) *Owl*
   D. As part of the club index, a listing, under each club name, of all club members

VI. Seeking to make the index especially useful, the staff of the *Owl* (mentioned above) not only referred to the picture of each person as it appeared in the book, but if a student had been omitted from the picture of a club to which he belonged, gave a parenthetical reference to the page number on which that club appeared. (Thus a Key Clubber who somehow missed being photographed would still have a reference in parentheses to the page on which the Key Club appears—a rather nice touch, typifying the thoughtfulness of the adviser and editors of this superior publication.)

VII. An index can and likely should be started as soon as work for the year starts. Of course, it can be done at any time of the year, as long as full records of all pages and their contents are at hand, and assuming that there is adequate time before the deadline for the section(s).

A. Begin by getting from the proper offices the official lists of administrators, faculty, other personnel, and students.

B. You may work from the lists themselves, or far better, make up permanent file cards. These may then be sorted into their various divisions for easier handling and use—faculty-administrators, seniors, juniors, sophomores, etc.

C. Each time a spread or a section (usually called a *signature*) has been completed, someone should be assigned to put page references on the proper cards before the pages go into a package ready for the printer. If you wait until deadline time, or the short period before it, you put an undue strain on those doing the checking and secretarial work and multiply the danger of error. Or it could make you strain or miss a deadline.

D. Decide early on the typography you will use for index material. Then as soon as the final page of material has been dummied, typed, and made ready for shipment, and after the last entry has been made on an index card, typists can begin without delay the job of typing up the material you have collected on the cards.

1. For one thing, you will likely be setting the index in a size of type smaller than body type, perhaps 8 point, if regular body is in 10 point.

2. You will also be typing for relatively narrow columns, perhaps as narrow as 10 picas for a 4-column index or 14 picas for the usual 3-column index.

3. You may choose, as many staffs have done, to set names of clubs and names of advertisers in all-capital style ("all-cap"), or perhaps better, in boldface. This is especially likely if you incorporate all parts of the index into a common index.

4. You will not space out after the comma between numbers as is usually done in body type. (Ex.: *Woolf, Virginia: 13,107,256.*)

5. You may choose to type two columns to a page horizontally, to keep count of space more effectively.

6. Since indexes are at best composed of rather drab expanses of gray type, plan to allow for generous margins of white space around headings and to establish a style for both top headings and letter headings that make good use of "all-cap" or boldface. Some editors have used exaggerated sizes of alphabet breaks or even fancy letters to help adorn or relieve pages.

E. This section can use ample illustrations. These may be of a variety of kinds.

1. The *Excalibur*, Tampa, Florida, mentioned earlier, used pictures of "Senior Notables" in this section. Perhaps if you feel, as most modern editors do, that such dubious honors are outdated altogether, you might wish to consider academic, citizenship, or other achievement honors for this section.

2. This might be a good place for those old group formals that you have decided not to use inside the story-telling part of your book. There may still be enough interest in them to justify their space here, especially if you can sell space to the clubs pictured.

3. Imaginative action pictures are ideal for prominent use in the in-

dex section, as elsewhere in the book. Let them supplement and not duplicate what you have used in other sections.

    a. One strong picture per spread may be adequate, and two per page would seem generally the maximum, though every book is an individual case. You may be able to prove yours a striking exception by using pictures lavishly here.

    b. A large dominant picture on the right-hand page could feature individual accomplishment or activity. One or two smaller ones on the opposite page could then balance this dominant photo.

    c. Perhaps the smaller pictures mentioned above could focus on faces and facial expressions.

    d. Consider faculty hobbies as subjects for action pictures displayed in the faculty index. (This assumes you have not touched on them in the regular faculty coverage earlier.)

    e. For the student index, vocational or avocational interests of individual students, which failed to "make it" in the major sections, could provide subjects for some appealing "relief" shots in the index. A senior works on weekends in a bicycle shop, a musical combo of students plays widely in spare-time "gigs," and a junior models in a local clothing store in her spare time. All these would make subjects for great index pictures.

VIII. Here are some suggested variations gathered from modern books. (I will present some pictorial illustrations later in this chapter.)

A. Headlines have been used to enliven the index. For example, a Roanoke (Virginia) *North Star* had heads like this: "Pupils use time between classes to see friends."

    1. Illustrations may then tie in with heads. (In the *North Star,* for instance, the picture showed crowded halls between classes.)

2. One should expect a full explanatory cutline for each illustration, just as inside the regular sections of the book.

B. The content and order of the 1971 *Quiverian,* Wyandotte High, Kansas City, Kansas, are worth noting:

    1. Immediately after the senior portraits section near the end of the book, editors place a section of "Senior Summaries."

    2. This is followed by a "Faculty Index." Each spread here has two illustrations (teachers in action). The index carries information about the faculty, degrees, and special assignments in addition to subjects taught.

    3. The "General Index" carries page references to faculty members, sports, clubs, organizations, departments, and courses all in capital letters, with student names in capital-and-lower-case form.

    4. Immediately after the "General Index," there is a staff page that features the picture of the editor.

    5. On the facing page, completing the spread, the editor has explained the purposes of the staff in planning and producing the book and their hopes about the final product. She gives credits to the adviser, the publisher's "rep," and the professional photographer; and she acknowledges the source of the theme poetry used in the book.

    6. The very last page, just before the endsheets, is devoted to theme ending. It repeats the statement, "You are you and I am I," which was featured in the opening and which has been used to link sections. A most effective picture shows a student walking away from the camera up a railroad track toward the horizon.

C. Editors of the 1971 *Whitehall,* of Whitehall, Pennsylvania, set business pages and index and closing pages apart from the rest of the book by using a 4-column format throughout all these pages and boxing each column at top, sides, and bottom. Let's look at elements of the index and closing pages:

    1. The faculty directory comes first. Information includes teaching and extra assignments, memberships,

special honors, invitations to speak before outside groups, medals and citations received from national, regional, and other organizations, and finally, pages on which pictures or mentions occur.

2. The student directory gives individual class membership (9, 10, 11, 12), club and group memberships and honors, and pages on which their names or pictures appear.

3. The editor's note mentions outstanding features, such as the fact that this was the largest book produced at Whitehall up to that time.

4. The final spread of this big closing section gives specifications—paper stock, typography, book format—in the extreme left-hand column and the listing of credits in the extreme right-hand column. *(Remember that all columns are boxed.)* In between, there is a mosaic of activity pictures.

5. Layout on all pages at the end of the book—indexes, editor's note, and sign-off—stands out because of the boxed effect. But pictorial relief has been carefully planned, has high technical quality, and is adequate in quantity to do its job. Finally, white space is generously used at the corners for artistic effect.

D. Five thematic closing pages of the 1973 *Hurricane* of Gainesville, Florida, reflected:

1. A kaleidoscope of recent world events, here the deaths of two U.S. Presidents ("Kaleidoscope" was the theme, and world-community awareness was a goal of the editors)

2. Student life in the school and community, with imaginative art largely picturing the Gainesville area

3. A final sign-off page, including a staff box, a large picture of a birthday cake commemorating the 25th anniversary of the book, a box containing the editor's "last word," and a box of credits to photographers, printer, and cover manufacturer

E. Closing pages of the often-cited Robin-

son *Excalibur* of Tampa, Florida, offer some ideas I would like to share:

1. Two spreads about graduation and graduates are placed *after the index*. One, titled "Escapes," presents interviews with graduating seniors about their plans ("just loafing," "college," "study abroad," etc.) and about ways in which they enjoy relaxation ("chess," "being alone," and a variety of recreational activities). There is an idea that can be adapted to any book.

2. The sign-off page, following these spreads, rounds out the book on a note of thematic inspiration. Jonathan Seagull wheels above, and in a more ordinary picture, a student confers with a school official. Near-poetic copy, set unjustified at the right like free verse, considers topics related to the idea that runs through the book, *the business of looking for truth, of examining ideas, and of voicing opinions.*

F. Index and advertising are fused into a single unit in an *El Burro*, Burroughs High, Ridgeway, California, giving life and variety to both parts.

G. In the closing pages of an imaginative *U-Highlights*, University High, Chicago, there is a special salute and valedictory to seniors of the year.

1. A full page is given to the picture of a gowned senior, diploma in hand. On the facing page of this spread, two pictures of seniors at graduation divide space with a substantial block of copy, summing up, in stream-of-consciousness style, a senior's recollections of his years in high school and his thoughts about the graduation time and the future.

2. Because U-High is a small school, one page serves for the entire combined index. Tinted gray, the page is overprinted in black type.

3. A large picture of the editor and a smaller group shot of seven staff workers and subeditors illustrate the sign-off page. There is also a full staff box set 8 point, and there is a chatty report of problems and triumphs of the year.

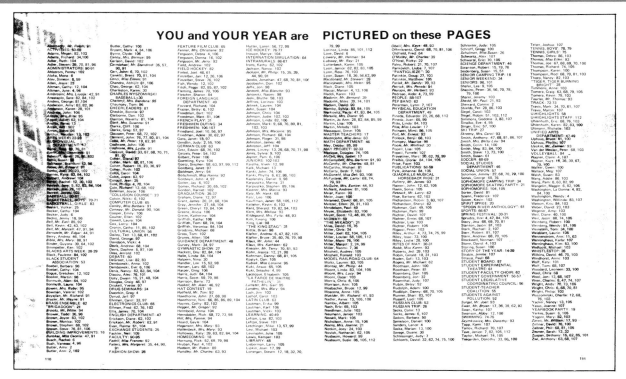

Fig. 16.1—For a small book like that of the University of Chicago High School, a two-page index is enough. Students' names are in regular style; teachers' names are in italics; and names of clubs, sports, and events are in all-cap style.

Fig. 16.2—By use of pictures and narrative heads all through the general index, editors of the North Star, Northside High, Roanoke, Virginia, tried to give life to the gray pages. They also reversed type on a solid color.

advertising index

Fig. 16.3—Seniors index in the *Torch* yearbook, Catalina High School, Tucson, Arizona, lists senior memberships and honors, with page references. General Index follows.

Fig. 16.4—An advertisers' index follows student and faculty indexes in a Whitehall, Pennsylvania, yearbook. Pictures brighten all the index pages, and ruled columns give them distinction.

Fig. 16.5—Closing "Reflections" page of the Gainesville (Florida) *Hurricane* echoes the pattern of opening and division pages. Pictures are imaginatively thematic, and copy reminisces on a student's school life.

Fig. 16.6—Emphasis was on the free-flying gull, symbolic of the thematic "search for truth" in this attractive close of the *Excalibur,* Robinson High School, Tampa, Florida. In the small picture, a student talks to a school official.

Exercises

1. Make a list of things you wish to cover in the closing pages of your book.
2. Write a paragraph for, or against, breaking the index into parts. What parts would you include, whether separately or as a unit? Explain briefly.
3. What lists will you need? Where are they found in your school? (Assign members of the group to get and bring these to a meeting.)
4. Determine size and style (Roman, cursive, italic, script) of type you would recommend for the index and special closing pages. What family or families (Garamond, Bodoni, etc.)? What width(s) of column(s) will you use in the index, and how many per page? (Note: You will need to confer with your printer or see his type book or chart, or both, before coming to any decisions. A conference with a type expert would also be of help. Not all printers' representatives are type experts, of course.)

5. Suggest a topic or motif for action or other pictures you might use in the index. Suggest and sketch five pictures following this idea. (On the basis of numerous ideas, the editor and staff can determine what to use in your book.)
6. Produce a spread for a suggested thematic closing to your book. (It need not be, but may be, the full closing for the book.) After dummying the spread in the rough, sketch picture or pictures and write thematic copy and headline. (Keep to 50–75 words, even if you feel that much more needs to be said.) Write first line(s) of needed cutlines(s).
7. List those to whom you (as editor, or if you were editor) would make acknowledgments at the end of the book. Suggest and sketch an illustrative photo and dummy the acknowledgments page.
8. Argue the case (75–100 words) for, or against, placing the posed "mug-mobs" or relatively inactive clubs and organizations in the closing section, after portraits sections. Are you prepared to make any compromises about your position? (Remember that following a plan either because it has been done that way before or because it is something new is not very rational.)

162

Index

Themes: linking ideas, or motifs, 2-12; patterns or designs, 2; worn-out ideas, 2; combined art and words or phrases, 3; illustrations drawn from modern yearbooks, 3-6, *10, 11;* words or phrases as ideas, 3; abstract or poetic ideas, 5; selection of a theme, 6-7; where to apply the theme in the book, 7-8; special thematic art, *9, 10;* thematic introductions, 13, 82-83, *84, 85;* thematic closing, 14, 156, *162;* applications to the divider, *18, 89, 90;* use of a mood photo to develop the theme, 78; the anniversary motif, *100*

Title page, 81-82, *84*

Training courses. *See* Sales

Trimming photos, 21. *See also* Bleeds in layout; Photography, posed groups

Typography, 21, 22, *30;* column widths for the book, 21; counting for cutlines, 21-22; kinds to use for cutlines, 21; classifications and groups, 22, *30;*

fitting body type, 29; hand-lettered type, 29; ragged-edge type, 45, 89, *90;* sizes of type for title page, 89

Unity as a layout principle, 25-26. *See also* Layout and design

Up-downstyle, 51

Upstyle, 23, 51

Voice, active versus passive in copy and heads, 43, 49

White space as a layout element, 20, 24, *33*

''Who's Who,'' 102, *105*

''Widows,'' 21

Women's or girls' sports, 14, 123, *127. See also* Sports

Yearbook course, x-xi

''Yellow pages,'' 147. *See also* Advertising